GEORGE BEVERLY SHEA

tell me the story

from Fernie & Mike
Christmas 2012

GEORGE BEVERLY SHEA
tell me the story

Paul Davis

AMBASSADOR INTERNATIONAL
GREENVILLE, SOUTH CAROLINA & BELFAST, NORTHERN IRELAND

www.ambassador-international.com

George Beverly Shea

tell me the story

Printed in the United States of America

ISBN 978-1-932307-29-0

Cover Design & Page Layout by David Siglin of A&E Media

Photographs courtesy of Russ Busby - BGEA

AMBASSADOR INTERNATIONAL
Emerald House
427 Wade Hampton Blvd.
Greenville, SC 29609, USA
www.ambassador-international.com

AMBASSADOR PUBLICATIONS
Providence House
Ardenlee Street
Belfast, BT6 8QJ, Northern Ireland, UK
www.ambassador-productions.com

The colophon is a trademark of Ambassador

DEDICATED TO MY DEAR WIFE HAZEL, OUR WONDERFUL CHILDREN AND GRANDCHILDREN, OUR FAITHFUL PARENTS AND OUR LOVING CHURCH.

Tell Me the Story of Jesus

Tell me the story of Jesus, Write on my heart every word;
Tell me the story most precious, Sweetest that ever was heard.
Tell how the angels, in chorus, Sang as they welcomed His birth,
"Glory to God in the highest! Peace and good tidings to earth."

Fasting alone in the desert, Tell of the days that are past.
How for our sins He was tempted, Yet was triumphant at last.
Tell of the years of His labor, Tell of the sorrow He bore,
He was despised and afflicted, Homeless, rejected and poor.

Tell of the cross where they nailed Him, Writhing in anguish and pain;
Tell of the grave where they laid Him, Tell how he liveth again.
Love in that story so tender, Clearer than ever I see;
Stay, let me weep while you whisper, Love paid the ransom for me.

—Fanny J. Crosby 1820-1915

Table of Contents

Acknowledgments

Special thanks to George Beverly and Karlene Shea, Franklin Graham, Cliff and Anne Barrows, Kerri Bruce, Russ Busby, George Hamilton IV, Bob and Terry Carrise, Maury Scobee, Donna Lee Toney, Pat Boone, Jerry Arhelger, Wes and Sue Davis, Sir Cliff Richard, Bud Tutmarc, Connie Smith, Chet Atkins, Danny Davis, Richard Bewes, Wanda Jackson, Paul and Jill Wheater, Judy Leighand, and Stewart Hamilton.

The people at Ambassador International have been most helpful, with special thanks to Samuel Lowry, who worked with me to make the book a reality and also to Timothy Lowry and Alison Storm for their invaluable assistance in the production.

Appreciation

For a lifetime I have loved to sing "the story of Jesus and His love."

Paul Davis has been so kind in bringing together some of his thoughts concerning those who have served the Lord Jesus in the ministry of song. What a privilege I have had for all these years, here in the homeland and in far-off places, just another voice lifting up praises to the Lord our precious Saviour.

Paul has known great success for almost a lifetime in the production of sacred recordings of gospel singers in the UK and the USA. Knowing many of the fine vocal artists of the Nashville scene he has presented an interesting time line of composers and performers of music over the years. For all of us there are still songs to sing, and God's promises to rely upon.

—George Beverly Shea

Foreword

My father, Billy Graham, is known for a phrase, "The Bible says." And the Bible says that "a threefold cord is not quickly broken" (Ecclesiastes 4:12b NKJV).

In the early beginnings of my father's global ministry, the Lord gave him a rare gift—a team of godly men who travelled with him and ministered by his side. George Beverly Shea and Cliff Barrows were especially equipped to strengthen my father's vision to win lost souls for Jesus Christ. Along with others, this band of brothers travelled together across the nation and around the world with a singular focus—to fulfill their calling to "go into all the world and preach the gospel" (Mark 16:15b NKJV).

One of the great testimonies for Jesus Christ has been the longevity of this trio of men who have prayed together, preached together, and praised the Lord for bringing them together to serve the Lord longer than any other evangelistic team.

In this book, *George Beverly Shea: Tell Me the Story*, its author Paul Davis shines a rare spotlight on George Beverly Shea, a common man in his own eyes, but endowed with an uncommon gift of seeing his life as a vessel for the Lord's use. There are not many people today who reach their 100th birthday with the vigor manifested in this unique Christian gentleman I have always addressed as "Uncle Bev."

Paul Davis has captured Bev Shea's talent, humor, commitment and outlook on life that describes one of God's true servants. In these pages you will get more than a glimpse into the depth of a man who believed God's Word would open the hearts to searching souls and provide comfort and bring peace through the wonderful gift of music.

In over sixty years of ministry together my father often said that the Lord used Bev's message in song to prepare the hearts of those in the audience and set the tone for the gospel message. There is no doubt that God orchestrated the paths of these two servants of the Lord to intersect. I thank the Lord for the remarkable witness and impact that George Beverly Shea has had for a century. May God continue to bless him and use his music to draw others to Christ as long as time lasts.

—Franklin Graham
President & CEO
Billy Graham Evangelistic Association

Introductions

I've esteemed it to be one of the greatest privileges of my life to have worked with a man whom I loved and respected from afar as a boy. My mother got one of the early copies of his song, "I'd Rather Have Jesus," and she told me, "Son, I want you to memorize this song. These are wonderful words, and I covet them for you." Well, I did memorize them and they moved me greatly, and they have all these years. Bev is not a performer, but one who ministers. Many soloists try to let you know how great their voice is through some dramatic fashion, but Bev would never do that. He did not want to draw any attention to himself. Bev Shea had been the anchor in all of our Crusade programming through the years. We've had many varied and talented artists who have stirred and moved the people, but we always knew that when Bev sang before Mr. Graham preached, the Spirit of God would overrule anything that had been said, sung or done, and would prepare the people for the preaching of the Word. No one knew this better than Mr. Shea. That certainly goes for me, too. My greatest privilege through the years was to say, "and now before Mr. Graham speaks, here's George Beverly Shea to sing for you." I thank God for my brother, for the friendship we've enjoyed together around the world. God has been so gracious to us, to allow Bev to live so long,

and I cannot imagine the world of Christian music without the voice of my beloved friend, America's—and the world's—singer of sacred song, George Beverly Shea.
—Cliff Barrows, Charlotte, North Carolina

A 100th birthday is always a fantastic achievement, even more so when the centenarian is still commanding a public stage. The first time that I ever heard George Beverly Shea sing was in the sixties at a Billy Graham crusade. I was really amazed and, if I'm really honest, slightly envious. He stood there and this voice came out that sounded so confident, rich and resonant. What also really amazed me was it didn't matter whether he sang something ancient or modern. With the passage of time, things haven't changed. He still sounds confident, rich, and resonant today, a century since his birth."
—Sir Cliff Richard, Surrey, England

It was my great pleasure and thrill to work with Dr. Billy Graham and George Beverly Shea and observe first hand their dedication to the extension of God's Kingdom. Without hesitation, I say that the experience is one of the highlights of my career. As a truly historic singer throughout almost all the twentieth century, George Beverly Shea is an icon in gospel music who has no equal in his interpretation of whatever gospel song he performs. I speak for all gospel singers past-and-present when I say that it is to your advantage to read Paul Davis' great book—*George Beverly Shea: Tell Me the Story.* You will certainly be blessed!
—Dr. Jessy Dixon, Chicago, Illinois

I think it's quite likely that George Beverly Shea has sung the gospel to more millions of people than anyone else who has ever lived. That deep, warm soulful voice has stirred the hearts and spirits of millions. I believe angels are longing to have him join their chorus.
—Pat Boone, Los Angeles, California

Words cannot express the influence George Beverly Shea has had on my life, music, and faith, both as a local church pastor and as a Christian singer. Bev's decision to turn his back on the world and the world's music had a great influence on me. I praise God I finally had the honor of meeting this godly gentleman. All I can say is he is one of a kind!"
—Clint Miller, San Diego, California

In March of 1984, Cliff Barrows invited me to be a guest singer at my first Billy Graham service in Anchorage, Alaska. No sooner did I check in at my hotel and get to my room than the telephone rang and it was Bev Shea welcoming me to Alaska! He asked if we could meet in the coffee shop for a chat and, during that, invited me to ride with him to the arena that evening for the sound check and preparations for the service. I didn't realize it at the time, but Bev was taking me under his wing and helping me through my first Billy Graham Crusade experience. It was the same later that year, during Mission England when, night after night, Bev would always give me a wink and a nod before my singing assignment. Bev became my mentor and encourager during those days and some of my warmest memories are singing "Rock of Ages" with Bev and Cliff Barrows at the site where Rev. Augustus Toplady was inspired to write it (Cheddar Gorge, near Bristol). I remember also, with Bev and Cliff, standing by John Newton's grave in a little churchyard in Olney, England and singing his hymn—"Amazing Grace." Getting to know Bev Shea and having the privilege and blessing of his friendship has been a pivotal moment in my life—I always tell folks that if I had been a non-believer, just being around Bev Shea would have convinced me of the everlasting truth of the good news of the gospel! I'm forever grateful to Bev Shea for his inspiration and friendship night after night. In my concerts, when I sing his wonderful song "The Wonder Of It All" I always mention that it was written by 'the greatest gospel singer since David, the shepherd boy—George Beverly Shea!' Amen! and may he stay: 'Forever Young!'"

—George Hamilton IV, Nashville, Tennessee

Chapter 1

I'd Rather Have Jesus

"Of all the gospel singers in the world today, the one that I would rather hear than any other would be George Beverly Shea."
—Billy Graham, Montreat, North Carolina

THE FIRST WORD

Through hundreds of events, thousands of miles and decades of ministry, the trio of Billy Graham, Cliff Barrows and George Beverly Shea have never had an argument. It's hard to imagine that despite the stress of live events and the inevitable nerves of standing on stages in front of millions of people that tensions never flared. It's hard to believe until you meet the three men.

But once you meet them you are struck by their humbleness, their humor and their patience. Their teamwork, faith and single-minded purpose are what gave this trio the longevity of relevance that transferred from one generation to the next.

Each member of this trio brings special talents and abilities to their mission. Billy Graham brings the gift of communication. He has the rare ability to speak to an audience of thousands and touch each individual in a personal way. He simultaneously served as a leader of a huge ministry as well as a humble servant to those around him and, most importantly, to the Lord.

Music and Program Director Cliff Barrows shares the gift of music combined with a humor, humbleness and honest concern for all people. His expansive responsibilities have ranged from hosting the radio broadcast *Hour of Decision* since it began in 1950 to organizing varied crusade choirs for events around the world.

And then there's George Beverly Shea. Often labeled as the "soloist" for the Billy Graham Evangelistic Team, Bev's busy schedule included radio and television appearances, concert performances, and dozens of visits to studios to record more than seventy albums.

The preacher gets the first word on his lifetime friend, Bev Shea. Dr. Graham said, "During the past years of Crusade evangelism, the singing of the large choirs and George Beverly Shea under the direction of Cliff Barrows have been a vital part of the services. The gospel message-in-song has leaped over international barriers and truly proved that in Christ there is no east or west, or north or south, but one great fellowship of God's people throughout the world. In whatever language or accent, these songs express the same message—the message of redemption of the Lord Jesus Christ. God has blessed the thousands of miles of travel in order to bring this music and songs of global evangelism.

I believe music speaks to hearts frequently where sermons fail. The value of a gospel song sung in the power of the Holy Spirit cannot be estimated. I feel that a well-chosen hymn is the greatest preparation I know for the message of the Word of God. Over the years, Bev's voice has ministered to people everywhere and will continue to do so until our Lord returns. His humility is genuine—he really means what he sings."

Bev's friend Cliff Barrows remarked in jest to Bill Gaither on the Shea tribute DVD, "Someone has said that preaching will be no longer needed in heaven but music and singing will be enjoyed throughout eternity!" With a grin on his face, Billy would add jokingly, "In heaven, I'm going to be out of a job but Bev will be working harder than ever!"

A competent, trained musician of intelligence and accomplishment, Bev is accurately described as the most influential and most popular gospel singer of the twentieth century. His rich, bass-baritone voice are known worldwide as a result of his nearly three quarters of a century association with Billy Graham. Their evangelistic work took them to every continent on earth. Together with song leader Cliff Barrows they forged a uniquely powerfully effective partnership in evangelism. Convincingly, Bev told me, "Working with Mr. Graham all those years? I've had no regrets! It has been a great privilege!"

Only Prominent Survivor

By the beginning of the twenty-first century, Bev had survived longer than any other gospel singer of his generation. He first sang at a Methodist camp tent meeting in the mid-1920s and he has never showed any immediate intention of retiring. Instead, he remained dedicated to the cause of evangelism whether preaching or singing.

Throughout the troubled twentieth century, the name of George Beverly Shea was synonymous with quality, true blue Christian music. During his long lasting, illustrious career, he genuinely never coveted awards yet he achieved an unprecedented reputation and utmost respect. When he sang the words, "I'd rather have Jesus than men's applause," he really meant them.

Fame never turned his head. He remained highly focused from starting block to finishing post. To say that he never succumbed to the underhanded attitudes of show business is praise indeed. Long after the blazing lights of stardom burnt out in others, Mr. Shea continued humbly crusading with Rev. Graham. Others conveniently made their reluctant excuses to slip out the back door of world attention as their lights waned.

As the new millennium dawned, among the well-known specialists of music in any field, no one enjoyed a more enviable reputation. Throughout his ninetieth decade of life, he remained universally popular. His easy listening, traditional style was still enjoyed by millions of music lovers all over the world.

In his Canadian boyhood days, there was no big showbiz dream of stardom. He was no wide-eyed youngster seeking fame and fortune. Playing contentedly in his family's comfortable living room, he would listen attentively with curiosity to the old fashioned get-togethers around the parlor piano. It was the golden age of late Victorian and Edwardian inspirational singing. Sentimental songs of personal faith such as "The Holy City," "Rocked In the Cradle of the Deep," and "Smiling Through" prospered. Bev would later successfully record and popularize these childhood favorites again. Slowly, even as a boy, he exhibited a growth of profound sophistication and professionalism in his singing. Deservedly, he reached the dazzling heights of his chosen profession without selling out to the world and the flesh and the devil.

TRAILBLAZER

Modestly motivated yet paradoxically a trailblazer, he set high standards for himself. With Christ-like humility using his musical gift he devotedly strived, as he said, "to be faithful and true to the truths of the unchanging message of the gospel of Jesus Christ. It still has the power to turn any man from a sinner into a saint when he comes back to God in repentance and faith."

Literally and proverbially able to stand tall (six feet, two inches) with the best of them, he never craved the limelight of a star performer. Had he wished, he could often have selfishly coveted and seized the stage as a world-renowned performer. He had what it took for fame and fortune: big talent and a great personality. He was a commanding gentleman, but in show business terms, he was too low on ego and too high in integrity. Yet amazingly, he arose from an inconspicuous office worker in an insignificant insurance office to become the world's most prominent gospel singer. This phenomenal change of career direction, was nothing less than a divine call.

Record company giant of his day, RCA Victor astutely recognized Bev's commercial potential, signing him up in 1951 and keeping him on contract for a quarter of a century. His plentiful RCA Victor recordings became immensely popular earning him numerous industry awards and nominations. Such recognition was a strong affirmation of the high esteem in which he was held by the music industry and gospel music enthusiasts alike. His recording artistry is evident even in his early recordings, being the first and only evangelistic soloist to secure a long-term recording contract with a major record company.

He may have played down his fame and popularity but truly, he achieved the kind of reputation, following, and fame from which legends arise. His warm, classy vocals displayed a distinctive quality that stood out from among the best artists of his genre. Even now, listening to his exciting, original recordings in the crystal clear remastered digital CD sound, one cannot help but marvel at the quality. No wonder there is a continuing longevity with his music. One appreciates just why Bev Shea is still renowned and revered.

VARIETY OF REPERTOIRE

Every Christian music enthusiast knew the evergreen, musical evangelist's special, deep-brown bass-baritone sound. For eighty years, the Canadian-born, American citizen graced songs embracing almost every conceivable spiritual sentiment and orthodox theological theme. Without theatrics and immensely conservative and reverent, whatever the musically inclined mood, the beloved Psalm singer always hit the bullseye every time.

Worshipers thrilled to the mighty anthem of "How Great Thou Art!"
Converts shared the emotion of "Just As I Am!"
Witnesses testified to the experience of "He Touched Me!"
Disciples empathized with the feelings of "I'd Rather Have Jesus!"
Patriots were stirred by the call of "The Battle Hymn Of The Republic!"
Missionaries witnessed to the truth of "Great Is Thy Faithfulness!"
Hope-seekers cheered to the expectancy of "The King Is Coming!"
Dispirited souls awoke to the fervent high spirits of "Roll, Jordan, Roll!"
Art lovers esteemed the sheer simple beauty of "Amazing Grace!"

All these classic recordings and many more became high-scoring hits when his deep, rich, heavily sweet vocals caressed them. His prized recording achievements were all the more outstanding considering his unlikely, diverse mixture of majestic church anthems, evergreen hymnal favorites, spirited Southern gospel toe-tappers, sentimental country gospel ballads, charged charismatic praise choruses, and well beloved pop inspirational standards more associated with crooners.

Such artistic variation was unique in Christian music and richly kept his popularity flying consistently high for three-fourths of a century. Amid the shortages of the Great Depression, the violence of World War II, the fearful Cold War shadow of atomic warfare, and the outrages of worldwide terrorism following 9/11, plaintive songs such as "In Times Like These" and "Tenderly He Watches Over Us" began notching up a steady popularity in many parts of the globe. Bev's heartwarming repertoire became the standard choice of hundreds of Christian radio shows worldwide. In those dizzy, busy days of Billy Graham Missions, his hit records barely kept pace with demand as his multiple admirers flocked to see him in person or on the silver screen in his movie musical shorts or cameo spots in Christian feature films.

APPLAUSE, AWARDS AND HONORS

Despite his reluctance to pursue applause, awards and honors, they accumulated anyway. In 1956, he earned a Doctorate of Fine Arts at Houghton College in New York. A Doctorate in Sacred Music from Trinity College in Deerfield, Illinois followed in 1972. In 1965, he won a prestigious Grammy Award in the sacred category from the National Academy of Recording

Arts and Sciences for his RCA Victor album entitled *Southland Favorites* with the Anita Kerr Singers. Indeed through the years, he had ten nominations for Grammy Awards from the National Academy of Recording Arts and Sciences.

In 1978, he was elected to the Gospel Music Association Hall of Fame in Nashville. In February of 1996 he was elected into the Religious Broadcasting Hall of Fame. In 1998 at the age of ninety, Bev was surprised when he was honored by the University of North Carolina Public Television station with a TV production of his life story entitled *The Wonder of It All* which aired for several years.

A living testimony of life long service to the Lord, Bev says, "I surrendered to the claims of Christ in my early boyhood years as I carefully observed the simple sincere faith of my dear Christian parents. Their godly prayers for me, their son, played their part, too. It's confirmation once again for those who have faith in the Lord and pray, all things are possible!" Indeed, his parents wholeheartedly dedicated Bev to Christ and Bev says as the decades rolled on he came to love the Lord even more. Bev lived out the words of the Bill and Gloria Gaither song: "The longer I serve Him, the sweeter He grows. The more that I love Him, more love He bestows!"

Before World War II, Bev progressed into radio work turning down lucrative secular offers knowing that his voice was dedicated to the divine cause alone. Finally, the opportunity came in 1944 to cooperate in a popular live hymn program called *Songs In The Night* featuring an unknown pastor from Western Springs, Illinois named Billy Graham. Bev would choose songs for the hour, Ruth Graham would write lines, and Billy used this as the basis for his comments. A hundred or so young people came to see and hear the WCFL broadcast on Sunday nights from 10:45 to 11:00 p.m. in Chicago. To make the broadcast more interesting Bev installed colored lights surrounding the audience of mostly young people in semi-darkness. So began the lifetime association of fruitful service. Later the duo became a trio of dedicated co-workers as song leader Cliff Barrows joined them.

Cliff recalled, with great affection, "God has given Bev a wonderful gift. My memory overflows with the numerous occasions that his rich and vibrant singing has brought inspiration and strength. It is as though Bev offers a personal plea in song to the Holy Spirit to visit every soul with His saving grace. No wonder Mr. Graham always wanted Bev to sing before he spoke. Few singers make ready the hearts of an audience like Bev! People were moved to veneration and praise to our Lord when he sang!"

Bev gave his entire being to the task of singing the gospel. Like his preaching and song-leading partners, he successfully contributed to the fulfilment of Christ's Great Commission in the last century. As the musical mainstay in Graham crusades, Bev initially was called "America's Beloved Gospel Singer" but nowadays the title should read more appropriately read "Earth's Beloved Gospel Singer." A most effective gospel song stylist and a loyal friend of thousands, he is not just a greatly successful singing evangelist, he is also a sharp, unassuming and favorable human being both on and off the platform and in and out of the limelight.

OLD WORLD CHARM AND CHRISTIAN COURTESY

Fully dedicated for a lifetime to believers and to his Lord, Bev stands out as a worthy example, suitable for any young person to follow. Above and beyond his evident singing abilities, he also employed skills in narrative speech, an uncommon talent but important for effective communication. His rich communication skills were diverse ranging from storytelling to poetry. Enthusiastically, he delighted to relate unadorned truths wherever a congregation, big or small, was convenient.

Universally known for his strongly held spiritual beliefs, he remained a lifelong impassioned champion of Christianity. Today his reputation is global and legendary for always maintaining a cheery sense of humor. With gentle speech, he is known for his engaging charm and Christian courtesy.

In a lifetime of service to the church, he promoted evangelical interests around the world with great class and dignity. No matter where he was, he demonstrated his testimony through generosity and kindness. He promoted the wider cause of Christ's Kingdom virtuously and sacrificially. His life of service and spiritual influence was a productive yield that promises much more harvest to come. Even as Bev approached a century of life, he was still a reasonably physically fit, well-built gentleman. When he spoke or sang, he had a richly distinctive, deeply melodic tone and endearing accent. His velvet Canadian brogue immediately identified him on all his prized audio recordings.

Despite the advancing years, the hardworking Bev still conducted himself with sophistication and considerable distinction. He was always fashionably groomed, often wearing a shirt and tie. As a seasoned celebrity, his charismatic presence could not be confused with aloofness or ego. His unblemished reputation was one of insight, morality and faith. Many of his associates gladly testified that Bev always donated quality time and effort to regular people and unselfish tasks.

The worldwide exposure Bev gave to Christian music should not be ignored. He tremendously advanced the founding of a flourishing Christian music industry. After three-quarters of a century of uninterrupted appearances, the arduous rigours of the road never blunted his eagerness. Nearing the middle of his ninth decade, he continued an active schedule in support of his lifelong friends, Billy Graham and Cliff Barrows. He performed, although somewhat more infrequently, in live concerts and church services nationwide and abroad.

An eternal optimist and an evergreen enthusiast, he hailed every new dawning with childlike vitality and excited contemplation. He lives with his beloved wife, Karlene near Billy Graham in historic Montreat, North Carolina in a spacious southern home that he laughingly calls his "Readers Digest home." He was able to purchase it in later life from his Readers Digest CD sales. Friends enjoy seeing the Grammy award and numerous nominations, but they especially liked the pipe organ and hearing Bev play the Steinway grand piano. Friends consider Karlene and Bev to be twice blessed as a married couple. Firstly, they were well suited for each other. Secondly, they enjoy a closely cherished circle of family and friends.

Somewhat younger than Bev, he felt his charming spouse Karlene was often—in the words of the Lee Greenwood song—the "wind beneath his wings." Self-effacing and shy of the limelight, she was genuinely gratified that her charming spouse vigorously persisted in using his unique, God-given vocals to attest his faith to so many people around the planet. Karlene sees Bev as a disseminator of light in a darkening world.

GREATER RICHES THAN EGYPT

Bev would modestly understate his achievements documented in this book. Although as a singer, his vocation at times clearly overlapped with show business, he resolutely refused to be classified as a performer. He prefers to be like the Old Testament hero, Moses—another man of faith and sanctification.

> "By faith, Moses, when he was come to years, refused to be called the son of Pharaoh's daughter; Choosing rather to suffer affliction with the people of God, than to enjoy the pleasures of sin for a season; esteeming the reproach of Christ greater riches than the treasures in Egypt: for he had respect unto the recompense of the reward" (Hebrews 11:24-26).

Bev understood the stance and stand that Moses took in ancient days. Many people do not realize that Moses was a psalmist too. He declared, "The Lord is my strength and song, and He is become my salvation: He is my God, and I will prepare Him an habitation; my father's God, and I will exalt Him" (Exodus 15:2).

The New Testament book of Hebrews tells us that Moses made his stand with God's people for the sake of Christ. Although Moses' understanding of the Messianic Hope (Christ Jesus) was perhaps extremely limited, he chose to be associated with God's people through whom that hope was to be realized. He resisted the lures of the priceless treasures of Egypt. (For example, it is told that when excavated, King Tutankhamun's tomb alone included several million pounds worth of pure gold.) Instead, Moses' divine reward was infinitely greater than the luxury and prestige of Egypt's royal palace. Bev's heavenly reward for rejecting the pleasures of sin for a season in return for a lifetime of Christian service will only be measured in eternity.

From the beginning, he held very deep Christian convictions. Modestly, he said that he is a sinner saved by grace. He was not happy to be called a saint as the term is used of someone who is seemingly perfect. Bev said that, just like all humans, he made mistakes, all types of them. The significant thing for him was in realizing that he personally had to make individual peace with God!

As a Christian singer, he constantly feared the menacing pitfall of making a pretentious spectacle of religion. He knew that when he declared his Christianity so straightforwardly that a searchlight would be always on him. That meant he had to walk his talk!

"I always say that my Christian life started with God's grace, His unmerited favor to humankind. Down through the years of my life, there was a growing light on this revelation. The words of the gospel song 'Amazing Grace' always one of my favorites still hauntingly speaks to me of God's grace. Christ truly died for the sins of the world but I, as an individual, had to personally come to terms with such grace. In my soul, I concluded that salvation was a personal gift to me."

So George Beverly Shea personally came in repentance and faith to the Saviour of the world, pleading His grace rather than any personal good works! This beautiful thought was a truth that he experienced in his deepest being. Like a magnet, Christ drew him to Himself!

Looking back over his lengthy career, Bev was appreciative of the times when, as he explained, "Christ's keeping power was essential to me! He has stood by me faithfully and helped me to stand, as He promised. I'm indebted to Him. He was truly with me at all times, and especially a very present help in time of trouble. As the old English hymn "Come Thou Fount of Every Blessing" declares:

O to grace how great a debtor daily I'm constrained to be!

Let that grace Lord, like a fetter, bind my wandering soul to Thee.

Prone to wander, Lord I feel it, prone to leave the God I love,

Take my heart, O take and seal it, seal it for Thy courts above!

—Robert Robinson (1726-1790)

Chapter 2

Faith of Our Fathers Living Still

PRE-1908

"It doesn't matter who is in the audience- youth or adult, friendly or unfriendly- they can tell that Bev Shea is the genuine article! His focus is of such intensity that you just have to listen. Bev's interpretation of gospel music is so moving that it seems as if each song is his last opportunity to sing to you! Without a doubt, Bev Shea has blessed more people by his singing than any other gospel singer, past or present."
—Ralph Carmichael, Los Angeles, California

SINGING AND MAKING MELODY

Orchestral arranger of class and distinction, Ralph Carmichael felt he knew the basic reason for the ongoing popularity of George Beverly Shea. He called Bev "the genuine article," personified as the Shea musical chronicle spanned the twentieth century.

Bev Shea observed with firsthand involvement that, more than any centuries before in history, his one hundred years of life were abundant in opportunities for Christian music. In the words of his hymn "Faith of Our Fathers Living Still" faith was undoubtedly still alive and well in sacred musical expression throughout the century. Bev recognized that history's story of sacred music really began at the dawn of the creation. It continued throughout the Old Testament and New Testament generations and into his lifetime. Singing performed a large role in the worship and daily life of God's people throughout history.

The earliest song in the Bible was articulated by Lamech, a son of Methushael and a descendant of Cain. Later Lamech's enterprising sons founded the nomadic life, invented metal crafts, instruments of war and, in contrast, the musical arts. Scholars state that Lamech's song in the book of Genesis expressed every feature of Hebrew poetry (alliteration, parallelism, poetic diction, etc.). Later it was not uncommon for the Jewish people to write sacred songs honoring distinguished conquests or godly experiences such as the escape from Egypt and the Red Sea crossing of Exodus 15. The book of Psalms, designated "The Song Book of Israel," embodies many classifications of songs covering diverse experiences. Later, in his New Testament epistles, the Apostle Paul enthusiastically stimulated Christians everywhere "to sing." He declared:

> "Be filled with the Spirit; speaking to yourselves in psalms and hymns and spiritual songs, singing and making melody in your heart to the Lord; giving thanks always for all things unto God and the Father in the name of our Lord Jesus Christ; submitting yourselves one to another in the fear of God"
> (Ephesians 5:19).

Later still, in the book of Revelation, the Apostle John looks into eternity and repeatedly describes pictures of celestial singing.

Historically, Bev strongly believed with other Christians that it was important that their testimony-in-song should spontaneously bubble from lives truly regenerated by God's grace. Committed to His cause, they should sing about the great unknowable God who was now personally knowable in the person of their Lord Jesus Christ.

From the early church to the middle ages, the godly use of sacred music continued. For instance, the German reformationist Martin Luther delighted in the use of sacred music. As a monk and theologian, he pioneered the Protestant Reformation, translating the Bible into the common language of Germany. He declared that, "next to the Word of God, music deserves the highest praise! The gift of language combined with the gift of song was given to man that he should proclaim the Word of God through music." No one better understood those powerful words than George Beverly Shea. His unquestioned love of gospel music displayed a genuine sincerity that inspired many millions in the twentieth century.

MY GREAT REDEEMER'S PRAISE

Three hundred years ago, the wide circulation and specifically the publication of contemporary gospel songs and hymns had their real beginnings in colonial North America. In 1737, English preacher and prime mover of Methodism, John Wesley published his first songbook in Charleston, South Carolina. Wesley's first hymnal was distributed throughout America. Astonishingly, it also served as the first volume of hymns and gospel songs published for the use of the Church of England in the United Kingdom. It was the musical support of evangelical Christianity for nearly a century. Denominations on both sides of the Atlantic then issued numerous collections of hymns and gospel songs suited to their particular needs.

General policy was to incorporate all deserving offerings into their books, no matter what the denomination. Every possible source of suitable material was explored but initially the hymns of English dissenter Isaac Watts and Charles Wesley generally dominated, outnumbering those of any other single writer.

In Bev's first church hymnal, he could see that Isaac Watts conformed to familiar rhythmic schemes for tunes already known. Such hymns as "O God Our Help In Ages Past" were typical of Bev's Methodist home-church culture and were songs that he later recorded.

> *Our God, our help in ages past,*
> *Our hope for years to come,*
> *Our shelter from the stormy blast,*
> *And our eternal home.*
>
> *Under the shadow of Thy throne*
> *Thy saints have dwelt secure;*
> *Sufficient is Thine arm alone,*
> *And our defense is sure.*
> —Isaac Watts (1674-1748)

After Isaac Watts came writers like the eighteenth century's brilliant Charles Wesley, brother of John Wesley. In their century, the two Wesley brothers spread the gospel throughout the United Kingdom with an irrepressible enthusiasm and determination. Against all the odds—John, the preacher, and Charles, the songwriter, traversed a quarter of a million miles on horseback to hold their indoor and outdoor services. It was common for them to work a fifteen or eighteen hour day. When Charles died in 1788 at the age of eighty-one he had composed no less than

6,500 hymns! Many, such as "Christ The Lord Is Risen Today," "And Can It Be," "Jesus Lover Of My Soul," "Hark The Herald Angels Sing," "Love Divine all Loves Excelling," and "O For a Thousand Tongues" are now all well established favorites, and all famously recorded by Bev.

O for a thousand tongues to sing my great Redeemer's praise,
The glories of my God and King! The triumphs of His grace!
Jesus! The name that charms our fears, that bids our sorrows cease,
'Tis music in the sinner's ears, 'tis life, and health, and peace.
My gracious Master and my God, assist me to proclaim,
To spread through all the earth abroad—The honors of Thy name.
—Charles Wesley (1707-1788)

Charles wrote regardless of any known tunes or conventions. Timeless gems from his pen became regular repertoire in missions, worship and recordings of the twentieth century. John Wesley established the practice of using gospel song translations from other languages, especially German. John and Charles sowed the musical seeds that grew into an enormous crop by the time George Beverly Shea was born in 1909.

History records that the Methodist church was the seedbed of the Salvation Army and the evangelistic campaigns of Dwight L. Moody and Ira Sankey. By Bev's time, sacred music-poetry was an energetic array of contemporary writers, singers and musicians. Even the great popular composers of the secular field were contributing to the blossoming field of popular hymnody. For instance, Arthur Sullivan of Gilbert & Sullivan gave the church "Onward Christian Soldiers," a song that is still popular and which Bev recorded for RCA in the 1960s.

VICTORIAN TRAILBLAZERS

At the turn of the twentieth century, in Bev's native Canada, a new church culture evolved. Invariably, all local calls to worship meant congregations assembling to not only hear the Word but also to sing the gospel. Basically, attendant music was simple and conservative. What counted in local churches, like Bev's, was down to earth earnestness and heartfelt identification with the emotion and truth of the songs. Singing in harmony flourished where church worship was an enjoyment rather than an obligation. It was usually backed by piano, harmonium or organ. Sometimes traditional stringed instruments, such as autoharp and guitar, were used. From era to era, gospel songs and hymns were devotedly handed down generation lines and kept alive in church communities.

The hardworking Victorian trailblazers of the Industrial and Agricultural Revolutions persistently hammered out this new religious culture amid adversity. They daringly sought economic and social progression via philanthropic commitment regardless of the impediments. To disburden the suffering of their deep struggles they would often take to singing songs of inspiration. Like most families, the Shea's front parlor's piano became the family gathering place. To the music of his mother, the Sheas loved to take pleasure in testimony and songs about their faith.

Throughout the previous century, ever-expanding evangelistic campaigns and revivals spawned new spiritual life. New churches and tabernacles sprouted up everywhere, each church community evolving its own particular brand of music ministry. Choirs, quartets and soloists sprang up, blossomed and flourished. Where buildings were not available, traveling ministers and musicians carried the gospel into the wild countryside and urban environs particularly in the new frontiers of North America.

Even as a youth, Bev was aware that the spiritual revivals of the nineteenth century seeded new forms of Christian musical expression that blossomed in his lifetime. In Bev's home church in Canada enthusiastic, new Christian converts from Victorian and Edwardian days were common working class people zealous for familiar, singable melodies to use in their worship. Previously, composers writing for the church were typically educated musicians. Homegrown writers and singers were springing up as a result of the Victorian revivals. Their emphasis became the creation of more folksy, singable types of Christian verse. Evangelicals, Pentecostals and most Puritan enclaves being democratic and of the people in outlook, embraced these radical changes with some enthusiasm. Later as Evangelical and Pentecostal denominations became more and more accepted by the establishment, the further use of popular tunes was expanded. The generation of newly converted common people that George Beverly Shea was born into, within a generation prevailed in inaugurating spirituality into their every day poetry and music.

Very significant in the ongoing growth of singable Christian music was the 1873 publication of *Sacred Songs and Solos*, a songbook by Ira Sankey. Decade after decade, millions of copies sold as he personally popularized hymns and gospel songs on both sides of the Atlantic. By the early twentieth century, history documents that this musical movement helped Christianity to move nearer to the artistic soul of the common people. Thus back just before Bev was born, Christian music impacted society as never before. Individuals, and even western civilization as a whole, were emotionally being touched. Folk-styled music blended itself into the music of almost all denominations.

Distinguished sacred music celebrities appeared. Two of the greatest bridged the end of the nineteenth century and the start of the twentieth century. Fanny Crosby epitomized the best of the newly evolving gospel songwriters and Ira Sankey was called the best of the gospel music performers. Both were still alive when George Beverly Shea was born in 1909.

SILVER THREADS

Beyond any other sacred songwriter, Fanny Crosby captivated millions with her uncomplicated, yet eloquent gospel songs. Miss Francis Jane Crosby was born on March 24, 1820. She died on February 12, 1915, just forty days before her 95th birthday. Bev was six years of age and World War I had just begun. She followed two main personal pursuits. First, she served the dropouts and drunks of New York's inner city missions. Secondly, she devoted herself to the ministry of transposing the great spiritual Bible truths into singable rhyme and melody. Fully persuaded of these truths, her life radiated the gospel. Her songs outsold secular hits of the day such as "In the Good Old Summertime," "When You and I Were Young Maggie," and "Silver Threads Among the Gold." If there had been a pop chart in those days, she would be a regular at the top. Through the years, Bev Shea recorded enough Fanny Crosby songs—such as "To God Be the Glory" and "Safe In the Arms Of Jesus"—to fill close to two albums.

A hero of the faith when Bev was a boy, the Fanny Crosby story was often retold in his church and Sunday school circles.

Notwithstanding her blind affliction, never self-pitying, she lived out a remarkably normal life demonstrating confidence in Christ. A highly competent poet of worldwide influence with a stunning memory, her poems were composed and edited in her mind, then dictated. She rose to be a social guest of six US presidents, yet she humbly accepted a mere two dollars for each of her compositions, deliberately choosing to live simply and soberly.

Her many distinguished associates included such people as mass evangelist, Dwight L. Moody and his song leader, Ira Sankey. Her emotional songs were translated into many languages and attracted world attention. Countless recording artists throughout Bev's years performed her songs. Some devoted entire concept albums to her compositions including Bev's friends, Pat Boone, Eddy Arnold and George Hamilton IV. Her legacy was approximately 9,000 hymns and poems, over sixty of which are still used commonly at churches throughout the world in the third millennium. In spite of being physically blind, almost all of her songs refer to *seeing, watching* and *looking*.

Fanny Crosby turned her tragedy to triumph. Her visual disability drew her more closely to the Saviour she loved. Casting aside any thought of handicap, Fanny simply got on with her life. Using her talents for the Lord in the way she knew best, her first song appeared in print in 1828 when she was only eight-years-old. Even in youth, she evidently enjoyed a closeness to her Saviour. This divine fellowship became the anchor of her life and her songwriting inspiration. She penned the song "Rescue the Perishing" that speaks of the underprivileged and disadvantaged of society. She became a champion of second class citizens knowing that a personal life-changing encounter with the Lord Jesus Christ could bring new life and a new start. The Bible story of blind man Bartimaeus whom Jesus healed, was the basis of her beautiful song "Pass Me Not O Gentle Saviour" that Bev recorded for RCA Victor.

Fanny Crosby's grave is located in Bridgeport, Connecticut. While making the movie *Songs Of Fanny Crosby*, Bev was filmed at her 18-inch high tombstone. What impressed him was the simplicity and smallness of her stone that bore the inscription: *Aunt Fanny—She hath done what she could.*

Ironically, Bev observed that not far from the outstanding songwriter's modest gravestone were very much larger and ostentatious monuments to show business legends Little Tom Thumb and James Bailey of the Barnum and Baily Circus.

Printed below, is Wes Davis' biographical ballad of Fanny Crosby. Entitled "Her Story, His Song," it was featured on the Word Records tribute album, *The Best of Fanny Crosby—Blessed Assurance* that also featured several tracks by Bev.

In Putnum, New York State Francis Jane was born
In the year of 1820 in the coldness of the dawn.
And the doctor saw the child in the sixth week of her life
And in trying to prevent it, he took away her sight!
And life was very hard and many said unkind
For it gave her, in her innocence, a mountain hard to climb!
But she never was alone and she never climbed unheard
For her loving Heavenly Father held His hand in hers!
One Broadway, New York night, aged 30 years was she
In the year of 1850 Francis Jane believed!
And a vision caught the eyes that had never seen the light
For the echoings of mercy had come into her life!

And this is her story this is her song....

Inspired, she went forth and she rose above the storm.

Soon Francis Jane was teaching at the local city school

Where she loved her poetry and the Bible by her side

Now daily she'd be writing about a different kind of sight!

For her eyes were eyes of faith and the Cross her only sight

Soon God gave her a ministry as a minister of light!

And she'd sing for the President for her music touched his soul.

From the White House to the farm-yard, to the high and to the low

And the writer wrote the songs that caused the crowds to see

The blessed assurance of a God who meets her needs!

And the songs became the prayers of the many who believed

That there upon the pages, Francis Jane could see!

And this is her story this is her song....

On February 11 she wrote her final song,

For on the very next day Francis Jane was gone!

In the final words she wrote when the silver cord would break

And she would she His face and tell the story, "saved by grace"!

For the ninety years she gave, nine thousand were her songs,

But countless is the blessing as her ministry lives on!

And to God went all the glory for she always looked above

To a life full of assurance, for the whisperings of love!

And this is her story this is her song....

Yes the writer of songs that still many sing tonight,

You can still hear God speaking through the music of her life!

From her trouble and despair her story speaks to me,

That trusting in her Saviour, Francis Jane could see!

Yes there upon the pages, blinded eyes could see!

—Wes Davis (1969-)

POWERFUL REVIVAL SONGS

Fanny's special friend was gospel singer Ira Sankey. An enthusiastic admirer of her work and a prototype for the young Bev Shea, Ira David Sankey was born on August 28, 1840 in Western Pennsylvania. Fifty years before Bev's birth, serving in the American Civil War, Ira's regiment was deployed to Maryland. He was called upon to lead singing at Christian church services held in tents of the camp. Soon he found several young soldiers with fine voices and a sense of harmony. A military choir led by Ira was formed that gained neighborhood renown.

Ira said he owed his life to divine protection and to his popular singing voice. His closest call was while on sentry duty. He came into the rifle sights of a Confederate sniper who would have fired if he had not been moved by Ira's beautiful, baritone singing. Instead, the gunman lowered his rifle and the vulnerable Union soldier's life was spared; spared for a lifetime of gospel song.

Leaving the army, Ira chose to return to Pennsylvania as a tax collector for the Internal Revenue Service. In the Methodist Episcopal Church, he was elected as superintendent of the Sunday school and leader of the choir. Soon his rich baritone voice began to attract attention. People would come from miles around just to hear his singing. Unknown to him during these years, he was unconsciously making preparation for his life's work.

Jovial and elegant, he was well known for his immaculate dress sense. In 1870, at the age of 21, he made a powerful connection at the International YMCA Convention in Indianapolis. Up-and-coming preacher, Dwight L. Moody recognized Ira Sankey's God-given musical gift. The powerful partnership was forged that took Ira and Dwight all over the world. In the generation before

Bev's birth, Ira sang to hundreds of thousands in preparation for the stocky, no-nonsense DL Moody to preach. Their audiences ranged from the very poor, to the Royal Family of England's Queen Victoria and America's President Ulysses S. Grant. Several decades later, Bev would fulfil a similar role with Dr. Billy Graham.

Ira Sankey's 68 years were packed full of dedicated work. He popularized a new style of gospel song designed, as Sankey said, to "awaken the apathetic, melt the cold heart, and guide the honest seeker in repentance and faith to the Saviour of the world." As a performer of powerful revival songs, he became as effective a gospel communicator as his preaching associate, Mr. Moody. In his heyday, untold multitudes heard Sankey's richly inspired voice sing "The Ninety and Nine," "Under His Wings," "Hiding In Thee," "A Shelter In the Time Of Storm," and "God Be With You 'Til We Meet Again." Since then such songs became well-loved, evergreen classics, recorded by Bev Shea. Ira gave birth to many vocalizing successors. Subsequent decades saw many performers successfully fulfil their gospel singing or song leading ministries usually in the evangelistic arena. This relatively new phenomenon of white gospel music professionals prospered essentially through the pious efforts of highly motivated, evangelistic singers after Sankey. Ira's followers included Charles Alexander, Homer Rodeheaver, Gypsy Smith and finally Cliff Barrows and George Beverly Shea. The duo expanded the sacred music genre via exposure offered by more than seventy years of working with Billy Graham.

Through the years, Bev recorded at least two albums worth of Sankey's songs. Bev recognized Ira as the greatest Victorian pioneer of inspirational sacred music, perhaps the greatest of all time. Much of the sacred music of Bev's early era was inherited from his dedicated labor. As Bev grew, Sankey's story illustrated to him how useful gospel music could be. Ira believed ardently that in periods of sunshine or tempest, gospel music acted as salt and light.

In history's rich vein of sacred singers came a soloist, faithful and true.
He sang of God's deliverance and mercy, and of a land beyond the blue!
Born in 1840 was Ira, early he learned to sing of God's love,
And many a cold heart was melted, strangely warmed by the Heavenly Dove!
Raised on his parents' homestead, he saw God's creation close around.
There were cows to milk, barns to clean, Crops of vegetables in the ground.
When Unionists and Confederates divided, they fought a violent civil war.
Soldier, Ira marched for the North, and sentry duty was his chore.
A Southern sniper aimed his rifle to put the singing sentry down.
But was captured by Ira's psalm and surrendered to the sound!
Ira's life was spared that starry night to sing to noble and low,
Destined to influence England's Queen and presidents we know!
Always looking smart and groomed, in a tax office Ira earned his pay,
And after leaving the army, became a delegate for the YMCA.
At a prayer meeting God brought to Ira, preacher Moody, a partner so true.
Together, they sailed the oceans telling lost souls of life anew.
Many hymns co-penned by this tunesmith spanned the pages of history.
'There Were Ninety and Nine' safely 'Under His Wings' plus 'Faith Is The Victory!'
At the dawn of the twentieth century, still singing, the half has ne're been told!
Then 'Til We Meet Again!' filled chapel rafters, God's balladeer was finally called home.

—(Roger Hill © New Music Enterprises 1999/ Used with permission)

SOLOIST AND SONGLEADER

Another Victorian, Philip Paul Bliss also produced timeless songs focusing on two key themes—evangelism and worship. A contemporary of Crosby and Sankey, he was born in a rough, frontier log cabin in Clearfield County, Pennsylvania on July 9, 1838. Life was tough. Young Philip left home at the age of eleven to seek paying work on the farms, sawmills and lumber camps. Disadvantaged, he obtained his education wherever he could.

A year later, he became a Christian and joined the Baptist Church near Elk Run. Rural work lasted five years as he developed a study of music. His instructor was JG Towner, the father of DB Towner, writer of "At Calvary," "Trust and Obey," and "Marvelous Grace," all songs that Bev later recorded for RCA Victor and Word. That same year, Philip attended his first musical convention conducted by WB Bradbury, writer of "Saviour Like a Shepherd Lead Us," "Jesus Loves Me!," and "Sweet Hour of Prayer," all recorded by Bev. Clearly the eager-to-learn Bliss rubbed shoulders with some quality role models.

In Bliss's days, popular music training in America was centered in so called singing schools—an important part of the social fabric of small towns and rural communities. Characterized by strong spiritual and musical emphasis, each was strictly a one man operation usually run by an itinerant musician who organized classes. In poor farming communities, fees were often paid with farm produce instead of cash. Classes, often held in the evening, consisted mainly of learning how to sight-read and conduct a choir. In country schoolhouses, churches, or town halls, the students sat in rows on planks of wood hung between chairs. Pupils' sight-reading used the tonic sol-fa, each beating time for himself while singing and moving hands and arms in a prescribed pattern. Many musicians of this period started musical careers as singing school teachers. Revived and regenerated by the hugely successful *Homecoming* videos of Bill and Gloria Gaither, their tradition has lasted more than 150 years.

As a boy Bev may have read how Philip Paul Bliss was strongly attracted to a singing-school way of life and married at the age of twenty-one. He was said to be an uncommonly handsome man, with a good physique, a moving bass voice, and strength of character coupled with sensitivity and tenderness. As an itinerant singing schoolteacher, he hauled his little $20 folding organ on a cart pulled by his faithful horse. A naturally gifted musician, he excelled as a songwriter and as a vocalist with a wide vocal range. Eking out a living by teaching wherever he could, Philip emphasized hearty Christian music in church work. Moody and Sankey challenged him to leave rural teaching for urban evangelistic crusades. Thus in 1874, he became soloist and song leader for Major DW Whittle's evangelistic campaigns.

On December 20, 1876, at the age of thirty-eight, Philip and his wife, Lucy were traveling by train to Chicago to fulfill an engagement at the Moody Tabernacle. While crossing a ravine near Ashtabula, Ohio, the train bridge collapsed and their locomotive plunged into an icy river bed. Wreckage burst quickly into flames as the screams of the injured pierced the bitter cold air. It is said that Philip survived the initial fall. Climbing out through a coach window, he escaped the flames. However, he reentered the danger zone almost at once looking for his dear wife, pinned in the blazing wreck. Reunited, they died together with nearly one hundred other passengers.

Barely three decades later, Bev was aware, even as a boy, that many hymnal gems came from Philip Bliss' creative pen: "Man of Sorrows," "I Gave My Life For Thee," "Hold the Fort," "Dare

To Be a Daniel," "The Light of the World," "Jesus Loves Me" and "Whosoever Will," among many others. Bliss pioneered and promoted the idea of family gospel groups that were to proliferate particularly in the Southern states of the USA. Philip once declared, "I do believe that every Christian family should be a praise-giving band, and if possible, psalm singers!" Throughout the twentieth century countless family groups followed in his footsteps including the Blackwood Brothers, the Speer Family, the Rambos, the Goodman Family, Second Chapter of Acts, the Martins and the LeFevres. Bev considered that few gospel singers had Bliss' wonderful gift for reaching out to individuals, condensing all the hopes and sorrows of life into a lucid song.

THE WAR CRY

Across the Atlantic in the generation that proceeded Bev, came news of the fame of another great pioneer of popular gospel song: General William Booth. As a boy, young Bev likely heard how William was born in Nottingham, England and, after training for the ministry, passionately took up the position of minister of the Methodist New Connection Church in 1852. He left in 1861 to serve in evangelistic work in the very deprived, poverty stricken East End of London. Four years later, William founded the Christian Mission that sought to take the gospel of Jesus Christ to the poor and needy while at the same time getting involved in helping them in practical ways. In 1878 the Mission changed its name to the Salvation Army. William became its leader, taking the title by which he became universally known, General Booth.

By the time Bev was born, the songs and work of the Salvation Army were spreading around the globe. Salvation Army soldiers pioneered the use of popular Christian music in their open air meetings. The General also started the Army's famed newspaper entitled *The War Cry* that female Salvation Army volunteers would take into the pubs and streets to sell, much to the disapproval of the very conservative members of the established church!

When Bev was a toddler in 1912, General Booth died leaving his son Bramwell to succeed him as General of an establishment that became one of the world's largest Christian organizations. Through the years, Bev often dipped into the Salvation Army songbooks for his repertoire. Songs such as "The Old Rugged Cross" and "Sing Me a Song of Sharon's Rose" had their roots in the Salvation Army.

Chapter 3

The Old Rugged Cross
1909-1916

"Effective, true blue gospel music like the word of scripture should be "full of grace and truth!" What a wonderful description too of the gospel music ministry of George Beverly Shea! Full of grace and truth is an appropriate description of his lifelong, humble service. His deep, resonant tones for decades lovingly called people to their individual "Hour of Decision." His wonderful sacred songs have always been high in doctrinal integrity, which is truth. But I commend my friend most of all for never failing to share the amazing grace of God found in our Saviour the Lord Jesus Christ!"

—Pat Boone, Los Angeles, California

PROFILE OF A LEGEND

Many believe a person's basic personality is developed in childhood experiences. This is as true of George Beverly Shea as anyone. Words such as sincere, earnest, honest, shy, humble and dedicated describe his personality. But there is so much more to the man than one may see on the surface. His perceived shyness is really not what it initially appears to be. Rather, it is an expression of his genuinely humble nature arising out of his great love for his God. When one first meets him not only are you struck by his large stature, but also his large character. His strong six foot two inch frame conceals within it the gentleness of a man who has learned much from his Master, Jesus Christ. Indeed, this is the overwhelming impression of Bev—he's a person truly and genuinely dedicated to his Lord.

Since childhood, Bev evolved a most marvelous sense of humor and fun as anyone who had the privilege of knowing him will tell you. He will often interrupt a serious impromptu concert at the domestic piano by breaking into a rousing rendition of "The Great Profondo," a comedy song learned from his dear mother and his opera hero, John Charles Thomas. His sense of humor often has the ability to surprise and give rise to great hilarity in an assembled audience!

CANADA

Cheerful by nature even as a child, George Beverly Shea cannot be claimed by any single country. Although he is a Canadian by birth, he is an adopted favorite of people in many nations of the world. Canada is a gigantic, uncrowded, unpolluted territory full of mighty green forests, chilling north winds, vast icy lakes and gracious, friendly people. Proud of his heritage, Bev loves to render due tribute to his Britannic ancestry, the majestic beauty of Canada's wilderness, and her small but warm-hearted population.

Nostalgia flooding his thoughts, Bev shares a lot of enthusiasm for his birth place. As a schoolboy, his geography and history books about Canada left him with adventurous perceptions of brave pioneers among snow, pine trees, and huge mountains. As a boy, he started a long time fascination with Canadian Indians and the Royal Canadian Mounted Police heroes. Canada's great expanse of untouched land, particularly north of his hometown, seemed so full of possibility and new horizons.

The first European settlement was the brief one of the Vikings in Labrador around 1000 AD but white settlement came in earnest with the arrival of John Cabot in 1487. For the next century or so, it was the French who did most colonizing. They established a permanent settlement at Port Royal on the Bay of Fundy in 1605. Many early French colonists building the 'New France' sought freedom and prepared to risk their lives to develop their new colonies. They met severe persecution from Jesuit quarters in 1635.

English-speaking British colonists prospered from 1713 in the maritime states of New Brunswick, Nova Scotia and Prince Edward Island. The decisive battle between the French and the British came in 1760 and led to more British immigrants to territories like Ontario, Bev's home province. More came as a result of dispersal caused by the American Revolutionary wars of 1776-1783. In their wake came the gospel.

Revival swept Nova Scotia and New Brunswick in the late 1770s and early 1780s under the preaching of Henry Alline. Alline's influence left a strong Baptist presence that is evident to this day. Nineteenth century Ontario saw Methodists and Presbyterians make great gains in church planting and membership growth. In 1861, over 55 percent of Ontario's population attended Methodist or Presbyterian churches. Indeed, by Bev's birth in 1909, sixty percent of Canada's English-speaking population classified themselves as evangelical Christians.

In his late nineties, Bev philosophically still appreciated his Canadian Christian heritage and the quiet solitude of its wilderness of forests and lakes to which he retired at times for respite. Life in Canada could be tough as there was always a very real threat from the untamed elements and wildlife. One could still travel for several miles without seeing another human face. Somehow, Bev considered Canada to be a wonderful mixture of the best of the old and new worlds. Its stories, cultures, history and folk held a simple beauty and charm. Unashamedly, he always readily admitted to being Canadian, "and proud of it!"

As a boy, never for a moment did he imagine that he would one day, be known as such a credit to his country. For the best part of a century he promoted the Christian gospel and his Canadian musical heritage worldwide. Indeed, his hometown civic fathers would deem to erect a tribute sign on the edge of the Winchester city limits in Ontario announcing "The Birthplace of George Beverly Shea" to the whole world. At the unveiling, Garth Hampson, in the brilliant uniform of the Royal Canadian Mounted Police sang "O Canada." Flattered, grateful, and yet unfazed by the municipal honor, Bev took it all in his humble stride.

Winchester was and is a small town of modest churches. Yet these local fellowships were and are significant to the social fabric of North America. Most encourage congregational singing spiced up with special music of homegrown choirs, quartets, and soloists. Small town church music ministries, a very popular means of learning the basics of singing, still produce today many aspiring singers and musicians. Church soloists become practiced at techniques such as putting feeling, emotion and conviction behind the words.

HOW FROM INFANCY...

The words of the Apostle Paul, written while a prisoner awaiting execution in Rome, Italy, applied not only to young Timothy in ancient Ephesus, but also to young Beverly Shea in Edwardian Canada. The weary Apostle Paul wrote, "I have been reminded of your sincere faith, which first lived in your grandmother... and in your mother... and, I am persuaded, now lives in you also... and how from infancy you have known the holy Scriptures, which are able to make you wise for salvation through faith in Christ Jesus."

It was said of Bev's grandfather, Reverend George Whitney that he could "no more constrain his passion for hymns than he could for breathing." Born on the cold first day of February 1909, Beverly Shea was the son of a hardworking Methodist preacher named Adam J. Shea. Bev was raised in Winchester, near Ontario on Gladstone Street, a street named after William Gladstone, the beloved British Prime Minister of the previous century. Bev's earliest recollection of sacred music was in his father's church, the Wesleyan Methodist Church and in the loving family home.

Starting off as a school teacher, Adam Shea was called to the pulpit, becoming a dedicated Methodist minister and earning a modest wage. Initially, he studied under Reverend George Whitney of Prescott, Ontario who allowed him to preach as a student. Ultimately, Rev. Whitney felt that Adam was ready for wider pulpit and pastoral responsibilities. Adam met Rev. Whitney's attractive daughter, Maude, fell in love and married her on the first day of 1900. He conscientiously toiled and lovingly provided for his dear wife and later for their large family. One of the first purchases for the modest home was a Bell piano imported from England. Of conservative Christian stock, the household took their Christianity seriously. Reverend Shea could often be heard to quote Scotland's renowned preacher, Robert Murray McCheyne: "Watch against lip religion. Above all, abide in Christ and He will abide in you!"

Adam's first pastorate was to the lumberjack community of Northern Ontario. For two years, he worked with preacher "Big John" Scobie, a giant Irishman with a large physique and booming voice to match the bigness of his reputation. Never afraid of confrontation or hard work, Adam resourcefully tackled to the tough task of leading a church even though the income from his first year of ministry was only $4.05... and as many vegetables as he could eat! Clearly, that wage had to improve because soon he would be raising his eight fast growing children. When they arrived, they absorbed and duly inherited their parents' sense of dedicated commitment to the concept of family, the ethos of hard work, and love of God, king and country.

In times past, the name Beverly was a common name for boys in Canada and other parts of the English-speaking world. The new Shea male was one of three boys in Winchester named after Dr. Beverly Carradine, a famous Methodist preacher and author who often visited the Shea home. Later "Bev," was affectionately renamed by Cliff Barrows.

MIGHTY IN INFLUENCE

Bev's mother played piano in church and was named Maude Mary Theodora Whitney Shea. Her lengthy handle was the cause of so much teasing that she generally opted to be known simply as "Mrs. Shea." Most days, she dressed in an unadorned gingham frock, her silvery hair tied back in a bun. She was unpretentious in stature but mighty in influence. The epitome of her nineteenth century's pioneering stock, she ardently appreciated the scriptures and deeply embraced their principles.

Bev knew the importance that his mother put on what she called "written revelation." Texts of scripture were mounted in picture frames in almost every room of the home. Bev recalls one of his dear old mother's favorite texts in old King James English. It was one that she often quoted to her children.

> "But continue thou in the things which thou hast learned and hast been assured of, knowing of whom thou hast learned them; And that from a child thou hast known the Holy Scriptures, which are able to make thee wise unto salvation through faith which is in Christ Jesus. All scripture is given by inspiration of God, and is profitable for doctrine, for reproof, for correction, for instruction in righteousness: That the man of God may be perfect, throughly furnished unto all good works"
> (2 Timothy 3:14-17, KJV).

Young Beverly and his brothers and sisters adored their darling mother. Her devout Christian life performed a powerfully decisive and crucial part in their early development. With tender devotion, her prim frame would reverently kneel, slowly she'd open her well-used Bible and read from it sometimes aloud to the backdrop of the birds and the crickets. Then, usually without warning, she would gently roll into sacred song. Early on glorious Ontario mornings, with her time of thanksgiving and worship over, she would take special time to tearfully lift up her friends and family to the Lord. She would gather up her concerns and cares in prayer. As she would say to her watching children, she was "getting priorities right before the Lord in prayer at the start of the day!" Spiritual priorities met, she was stimulated and ready for whatever the day would bring. The work at the Gladstone Avenue home was challenging. But she had learned, as she often said, that a positive, optimistic outlook was the best way to meet her daily duties and Christian service.

GLADSTONE AVENUE

Beverly was the fourth of eight brothers and sisters, preceded by Pauline, Whitney, and Mary and followed by Alton, Lois, Ruth, and Grace. His dear mother was the greatest single influence during his very early days. His earliest memories go back to hearing the sweet sound of her voice awakening the family early in the morning with the words of one of her favorite hymns. She would always sing the first verse in full accompanying herself on the upright Bell piano in the parlor, "Singing I go along life's road, praising the Lord, praising the Lord, singing I go along life's road for Jesus has lifted my load." The habit of singing and playing a Christian song to awaken the household is one that Bev carried on into his own home, as many unsuspecting guests found out, many times at the crack of dawn!

Christian music was an important and integral part of his childhood and made a profound effect on his future life. On Sunday mornings, Mother Shea's choice of song was one that she thought much more appropriate to the start of the Lord's Day. She would sing out heartedly in her sweet soprano voice,

"Lord in the morning Thou shalt hear my voice ascending high, to Thee will I direct my prayer, to Thee lift up mine eye."

Bev remembers, "My father used to tell my brothers, Whitney and Alton and me, 'There will be many times, boys, when you don't feel connected. But the Lord is still with you. Just look up—keep that vertical relationship. Practice His presence in your life.'"

Bev's very eventful childhood days were happily spent in the unpretentious, white-clapboard building on Gladstone Street. Being the son of a parson meant that one did not have all the material things that other children might have. But what was lacking in wealth was more than compensated in the love and devotion that came from having Christian parents. Bev says, "My parents walked out their Christian life in faith and showered their family with love and warm understanding. At home, God was a very real person in the life of the Shea family." Often Father would lead the family devotions in his deep, rich vocal tones with scripture readings such as "Choose you this day whom ye will serve... but as for me and my house, we will serve the Lord!" (Joshua 24:15). A short application of the Word was followed by prayer. This strict pattern was followed conscientiously and Bev and his brothers and sisters learned the importance of daily fellowship with God. Father taught Bev the benefits of obeying the Ten Commandments including the ones about honesty, honoring God, parents and others.

Their Edwardian generation dressed soberly, stressed that hard work was a God-ordained lifestyle ethic, and earnestly tried to foster love and Christian values in their children. Highly conservative, the church strongly stressed the necessity of personal sincerity and faith for salvation. The church nurtured young Bev not only in the disciplines of faith but with a passion for Christian music.

As a wide-eyed toddler in the Sunday gathering he would listen attentively to the beautiful hymns. Naturally too young to read the words, the toddler's hands beat time as he hummed constantly, adding a humorous dimension to the choir's chorus. Often the bemused families in the seats around the Sheas' regular pew would revolve mid-song to beam at the toothy toddler whose rudimentary accompaniment caught their ears. Thus with a penchant for beating time, humming and then singing, toddler Beverly would amuse the mothers in the local stores with his performance of church melodies. Although tickled by his talents, no one ever visualized this toddler would someday arise to the heights of the world's gospel music profession. Never straying far from those beloved hymnal favorites of his boyhood church, he introduced the songs to millions of people around the globe.

HYMNS AND CATCHY CHORUSES

Without doubt, Christian music made a significant contribution to his emotional development. Continuously, he was drawn to this musical genre. It was all around him from the start. His mother's sweet, hymnal tones were familiar to him as a snug infant in his warm cot. Then, catching on to the words and melodies of his first Sunday school songs, he cultivated an enthusiasm for the majestic hymns and catchy choruses. He recalled that most people in his Winchester community were eagerly involved in church activities in one way or another. Culturally, the Christian music of those days blended godly values with leisure. When Bev was a boy, everything seemed very faith-orientated. Bev says that he was always very beholden to the legacy of those old sacred songs in his life.

Traditionally, his boyhood hymns were passed down through several generations. During his lifetime, he saw a variety of entertainers and evangelists bring many gospel songs, like "Amazing Grace," into the vast continually flowing river of popular music. Today there is much cross-pollination of musical styles and traditions. Bev called upon all these diverse traditions to form his own unique repertoire.

Mr. and Mrs. Shea raised their eight children with loving discipline. They instructed them in the wisdom of the ancient scriptures' pronouncement, "Children, don't let the excitement of being young cause you to forget about your Creator. Honor Him in your youth before the evil years come when you will no longer enjoy living. It will be too late then!" (Ecclesiastes 12:1-2).

Disciplined from the very start, Bev and his brothers were generally well behaved, polite young men rarely causing embarrassment to their parents. Bev's good behavior seldom slipped as a stern look or word from his parents usually sufficed.

Soon music became his first love and passion. He recalled with a wistful, yearning sigh that his dear parents understood and encouraged their growing son's musical propensity. He says that it is to his mother that Bev owes the greatest gratitude, as far as his love of music is concerned. From about five years of age, she taught him to pick out chords on the old Bell piano from England. Along with his sisters Pauline and Mary, he took turns to learn. Later under his mother's encouragement, he began singing and playing the piano at the age of ten. Unfortunately, he evolved the handicap of sometimes painful, introverted shyness. Like most kids, the growing adolescent-to-be was a blended mixture of his parents' qualities. But the acute shyness did not appear to be something that he inherited from either of them. "I had a happy home with loving parents. It was not a home where lots of no's were said. We received a great deal of encouragement and a lot of love. My mother and father were always independent in spirit, kind of serious and quiet yet they had special ways! They never guessed that their son was destined to become a gospel singer especially knowing that I was so shy!"

A SONG TO SING

Slowly, more and more, Bev came to value local church life. It was there that he first learned about God the creator, sustainer of the universe, and Jehovah Jireh. Later, it was there in the sanctuary that he in due time discovered Him as the personal God of his Salvation. He learned to adore Him for himself, personally maturing in what the Apostle Peter described, as "his holy faith." Despite the dire situations for some less fortunate people in the depressed post-World War I era, the quality of life was generally good for the Sheas. Family unity was strong and there was always, it seemed, a song to sing even in times of trouble!

Early in their marriage union, Mr. and Mrs. Shea had committed themselves to the Christian lifestyle despite the provocations that would ebb and flow. Dressed in smart but simple small-town attire, Bev's mother and father were robust in moral influence, the epitome of their conventional and conservative Christian stock. As they grew, the Shea children adored their dear parents.

He remembers his father as a gentle, philosophical individual, one to whom siblings would turn for sound counsel. An early riser, he would often wake first, taking time for Bible reading. In later years, Bev proudly validated his deep appreciation of his parents. Their Christian lifestyle played a crucial part in his early development.

Looking back, he recalled their humble parsonage home on Sunday morning. The family never missed Sunday services. The Sheas' Sunday worship was their time to declare their personal praise and thanksgiving. One special memory of church that Bev treasures is of his grandmother. 'Frequently my dear old grandmother would start up a song. It was always 'Welcome, Welcome' and other people in the congregation would join in sweet harmony."

After Sabbath worship was over and spiritual priorities met, mother and father were refreshed, ready for whatever tiring, daily chores the week ahead would bring! Mid-week too, in prayer, each would lovingly remember family and friends in need. Other times, while cooking or doing the family laundry, the young children would observe their mother focusing her eyes on her Saviour. Then she would sing her praises with a song like "What a Friend."

British in origin, the instantly singable hymn was written in 1857 by Northern Irish Joseph Scriven for his mother's use. But it could well be written for Bev's mother! The songwriter knew sorrow at close quarters enduring the tragic death of his fiancée on the eve of their wedding.

What a Friend we have in Jesus! All our sins and griefs to bear!
What a privilege to carry everything to God in prayer!

O what peace we often forfeit! O what needless pain we bear!

All because we do not carry everything to God in prayer.
—Words: Joseph Scriven (1820-1886)

Engraved in the observant Shea children's memory forever was their dear mother. To her watching children, she would regularly say, "Whatever happens, children, take all your burdens to the Lord in prayer!"

WHOLE-HEARTED AFFECTION

Cared for with whole-hearted affection, such a clear, optimistic, parental attitude rubbed off with engaging effect on the nest's young brood. At dusk in the sinking sun's summer twilight, or in the chill of the winter snow, with their everyday chore and household duty met, the united family customarily assembled around the crackling, stone fireplace and the Bell piano. No matter how weary they were, either parent would devotionally read the earmarked portion from the family Bible. The inspiring scripture reading terminated, the family would casually break out in well-versed song!

Come, let us sing of a wonderful love, tender and true;

Out of the heart of the Father above, streaming to me and to you:

Wonderful love dwells in the heart of the Father above.
—Words: Robert Walmsley (1831-1905)

Spontaneous and worshipful sentiments surged without hindrance as the family sang unchanging truths of the timeless classic hymns. Back in the family home, mother and father nurtured Beverly's growing personal relationship with his Maker with loving affection. These firmly held family convictions were hammered out in the crucible of experience, nourished by dedicated, disciplined adherence to the faith plus regular attendance at their local church. His parents encouraged him more and more to use his God-given talents for the good Lord, both in his local church and later in his multiple recordings and concerts. In later years, as a celebrated gospel singer, he gained noteworthy fulfilment expressing and sharing this faith through his giftings.

After seeing his parents' decades of sturdy, contented marriage, Bev deduced that they furnished the right kind of attitudes and attributes essential in a good marriage. Having been married for a lifetime, they were qualified role models. Mother and father understood the need to keep the gates of communication open, being willing to talk they discovered the art of forgiving each other with a good sense of humor.

Both believed that their ability to compromise was one of the keys to strong marriage. Lastly, but not least, they believed that praying together about everything was the most essential part of their marriage. The stalwart pair shared an active Christian faith, a very meaningful rallying point in their marriage. The outward sign of the inward reality was shown through their love of people. Often needy folks came into the Shea home, uplifting both them and blessing the hosts also.

OLD FASHIONED HOME

One of Bev's earliest song favorites was "The Old Fashioned Home." Reminding him of his boyhood habitat, it retold the story of Jesus' joy in visiting the old fashioned home of Mary, Martha and Lazarus in Bethany. The Christian ethos of the old fashioned home on Gladstone Street was scorched deep into the memories, motives, and meaning of young Beverly's life. In good times and bad, that seasoned, realistic, down to earth piety of "The Old Fashioned Home" fully prepared Bev for life's conflicts. The beloved nest crafted by his parents was festive and fulfilling.

Home was a typical, everyday Edwardian abode where the winsome aroma of mouth-watering home cooking stimulated appetites as his hardworking mother would faithfully make ready her unequaled Canadian dishes. She took rightful pride and delight in her culinary specialties. The residence was a sturdy, sheltering tower. Tough times were outweighed by the nonchalant periods of delight, song and laughter. Bev's transparent affection for his childhood and the uplifting teaching he tenderly acquired from his parents were reverberated in his life. It was manifested in the songs he loved to sing on albums such as *Through The Years*. His personal choice of song repertoire would be the inspirational kind boldly speaking up for God, country, home, freedom, integrity, marriage and solid relationships... the kind of things that Bev believes really matter.

With grateful emotion, an elderly Bev fondly and nostalgically recalls parental sacrifices of years ago. That dear old fashioned home always lovingly stood out in his cherished memories. That was where he and his brothers and sisters were all taught life's most significant lessons by deeply caring parents. Mother dearly loved to quote the Apostle Paul.

"Be strong in the grace that is in Christ Jesus and the things that thou hast heard of me...the same commit thou to faithful men, who shall be able to teach others also.

"Thou therefore endure hardness, as a good soldier of Jesus Christ!" (II Timothy 2:1-3).

FUN-LOVING PALS

Bev recalls that he came to simple child-like faith at the age of five or six years. Throughout his carefree childhood, the sound of sacred music captured his keen attention whether at home or in church. It was always his first love. During winter months, music filled many happy hours. At an early age amidst great encouragement, Beverly paraded his vocal talents before his friends around the living room's mahogany piano. "Come on Beverly, please give us a song. What about 'Safe In The Arms Of Jesus?'" friends requested, "Let's hear you sing it!"

He still remembers the assembled relatives before they became engrossed in discussing other things. It seemed as if the lights went on for him when he found something that mattered. It seemed to make an impression on others too, which secretly pleased him. Music now gave him something to offer at family and church get-togethers. However, despite persuasive enthusiasm from many quarters, the super shy youngster declined to sing for services. He never wanted to be a performing peacock. Yet at Sunday meetings, he boldly sang his heart out among the anonymity of the congregation on the old Ira Sankey hymns! Many years later Bev received an old hymn book inscribed by the wife of Major Whittle. She said it was a copy of the one Sankey so often used saying, "we like the way you sing the hymns."

Many were his favorites, particularly the tender, plaintive invitation songs such as "Just As I Am" that he identified with, even as a young man. He understood the hymn writer's heart-tugging message urging the wayward wanderer to come home to the heavenly Father. Like many others in his well-worn hymnal, such precious songs he took to heart, building up personal convictions regarding the needs for forgiveness of sin and personal salvation. His insecurity grew. Yet shyness caused him to fear the act of public confession.

The cold winters of Ontario were not endless. In better weather, glad to be outdoors, Beverly and his buddies headed for the sports field. Those years nurtured in him a spontaneously uninhibited sense of humor. Young Beverly loved to spend hours and hours of those boyhood days in Canada's fresh lakes paddling, boating and fishing with his fun-loving pals. Then they would turn their playful attention to climbing the majestic, leafy trees of his beautiful, green province. Many a late summer afternoon, he would revert to his family abode exhausted with wet and muddy trousers. Naturally, he loved frolicking outdoors and particularly enjoyed boating, a pastime he still enjoys to this day. Ontario's gorgeous pastoral landscapes also provided free-flowing waterways and lakes. Rivers, ponds and lakes were ready-made playgrounds for the adventurous youngsters. In all seasons, there were multitudes of exciting pursuits.

Back in town, Beverly occasionally got up to mischief with one of his best buddies, Asa MacIntosh. On summer evenings, hiding in the bushes of Bank Street, they delighted in planting an empty lost wallet in the path of pedestrians. Retaining their hideout, they waited for an unsuspecting finder to notice and reach down for the wallet. Then with the aid of some fishing line attached to the wallet, they reeled the booty in with a jerk, running away in laughter.

GREAT INNOVATIONS

During those boyhood years, he recalls overhearing tales of great innovators in the area of evangelistic meetings who were achieving worldwide fame. Born in 1867, Charles M. Alexander, song leader for the evangelist J. Wilbur Chapman, popularized "The Glory

Song" that was often sung around the Shea piano. His approach was to use simple joyful songs to set the mood for the gospel message.

Born in Tennessee, Charles M. Alexander trained for the ministry at the famed Moody Bible Institute. Nicknamed "Charlie," his sociable personality warmed up audiences. Despite his jovial exterior, it was said that he was very earnest about the gospel message of Christ. He and Wilbur Chapman's new evangelistic initiative in 1909, the year of Bev's birth, in Boston, Massachusetts was known as Simultaneous Evangelism. Dividing the city into zones and evangelizing with different teams at the same time proved very effective. Charlie died in 1920 when Beverly was only eleven years of age.

In 1914, the Shea family's Winchester home was visited one weekend by a special guest, Reverend John Vennard. That Saturday morning, seated at the piano, the visitor sang and played to the Sheas two new gospel songs, penned by George Bennard. John said they were written in 1913. The first was "The Old Rugged Cross" which he preceded with a quote of the Apostle Paul's words in Galatians 6:14 saying, "But God forbid that I should glory, save in the cross of our Lord Jesus Christ, by whom the world is crucified unto me, and I unto the world".

Young Beverly listened at the piano engrossed in the beauty of the new composition. Later, of course, the new song became one of the greatest hymn classics of the century. John then played and sang a song entitled "Speak My Lord." That, too, was to go on to be sung worldwide. Wide-eyed, five-year-old Beverly was intrigued again with this impromptu performance on the red mahogany Bell piano. Mother caught a glimpse of how much Beverly adored gospel music as he leaned over the keyboard of the parlor's piano. That evening she told his father accordingly, but he already astutely noted his son's inclination towards music.

Years later, Bev personally met and learned much about the writer of "The Old Rugged Cross" and "Speak My Lord." George Bennard was born in 1873 in Youngstown, Ohio to a family of modest means. Moving to Albia, Iowa and then to Lucas, Iowa, the Bennards were initially unsettled. At the age of sixteen, George lost his coal-miner father. Sadly, death forced a burdensome strain on the teenager. To support his mother and five brothers and sisters, he was forced down the coal pits. Responding to the 'gospel call' at a Salvation Army meeting, he was converted to Christ while still young. Simultaneously, he received what he described as a summons to the gospel ministry.

Financial restrictions hindered George Bennard from higher education but undeterred, he diligently studied under other local ministers. He learned all that was required by hands-on experience and personal private study. Joining the Salvation Army, he served faithfully for many years in leadership before serving as an evangelist for the Methodist Episcopal Church. Public fame came via the campaigns of the animated evangelist Billy Sunday. Following the death of his first wife, George Bennard married Hannah Dahlstrom.

Bev Shea met up with George Bennard in the early forties while visiting the beautiful Winona Lake in Indiana, 110 miles from Bev's Chicago home. Bev remembers the famed hymn-writing preacher being white-haired, short, and wearing glasses. George died at the age of eighty-five in Reed City, Michigan on October 10, 1958. He bequeathed to the world a legacy of about 300 compositions. Often through the years, Bev and his wife and family were reminded of him as Albion, George Bennard's hometown, was on route to the Sheas' summer cabin in Quebec. "Listen kids," Bev would say as the Shea car slowed through town, "we're passing through the Albion city limit sign that I think should proudly announce 'The Home Of George Bennard, Composer of America's Favorite Hymn, The Old Rugged Cross!' One of these days, we are going to tell the folk in the Chamber of Commerce office that that's what they should do!" And now they have.

OPTIMISTS MAKE HISTORY

Particularly among visitors, young Beverly Shea remained painfully shy. But his music abilities could not be hidden forever. It was not long before the quality of his young singing voice was recognized in his father's church. More and more, he quietly appreciated his Christian music heritage, determining within himself never to stray from the sacred repertoire. He observed how the message in song turned depression into delight, no matter what the exigency. "The words of the Apostle Paul were being burned into my young heart: 'Let the word of Christ dwell in you richly in all wisdom, teaching and admonishing one another in psalms and hymns and spiritual songs, singing with grace in your hearts to the Lord. And whatsoever ye do in word or deed, do all in the name of the Lord Jesus, giving thanks to God and the Father by Him.'"

Mother Shea progressively taught young Beverly piano chords and showed him how to pick up melodies. Later came lessons from his father on the mouth organ and then on Beverly's prized $13 violin. Conveniently, practice took place in the solitude of the fields down the hill from the Shea house, amid the oil rig drills that rhythmically clanged time for the fledgling musician. It was a private world that highly suited his painfully shy disposition. All this practice stimulated his growing interest in the music at the church. He recollects how at the Winchester Presbyterian Church on special occasions, he became enthralled by their wonderful sounds emanating from their great pipe organ. Going home Beverly asked his mother, "Why doesn't our Methodist church have one of those wonderful instruments, mom?"

His mother patiently explained to the youngster that their small reed organ was perfectly suited to their smaller church building. Realizing her young son's fascination, she bought a mouth organ for his birthday. Bev would play behind the barn to his heart's content in the company of his imaginary horse called Midnight. Needless to say, his brothers and sisters, and anyone else in the nearby vicinity, were not quite so enthralled by the repeated harmonica sounds of "Home Sweet Home." Nevertheless, his mother and father continuously nurtured their young son's love of music and a sense of optimism about life. "Always remember, son," the experienced pastor would say, "only optimists make history. No monument was ever built to a pessimist! Pessimism is an investment in nothing but optimism is an investment in hope!'"

Starting in England, the Salvation Army's promotion of brass band music was spreading across the world during Bev's formative years, gaining great popularity. In small town Canada, there were few Salvation Army band recitals to speak of, but Bev does remember being taken by his father to listen to the Saturday night performances by Winchester's secular brass band. Being so young, Reverend Shea wisely restricted his son to just the first half of the performance. But how they were thrilled to hear the hit songs of the day such as "Wait Til the Sun Shines, Nellie" and "In the Good Old Summer Time." Father and son usually left during the intermission, walking home as the band was beginning the second half of the program in the background.

It was after one such performance that the whole family was called together to a family meeting. Reverend Shea announced that after twenty years of service to the Winchester Wesleyan Methodist Church, there was now an impending move south to Houghton, New York. From this new base, he intended to take the opportunity to go back to preaching on the road. Young Beverly was heartbroken at the thought of leaving his hometown where he had spent such happy days. He remembers sobbing himself to sleep on their last night with the sounds of the Saturday night band concert still ringing in his young ears.

Chapter 4

Take My Life, and Let It be Consecrated, Lord, to Thee

1917-1938

"Frances Ridley Havergal's song 'Take my life, and let it be consecrated, Lord, to Thee' reveals the motivation behind George Beverly Shea. More than a beautiful sentiment, it's a beautiful goal for any Christian singer. Like millions of others around the world and throughout history, most of my gospel singing has been in the local church. Yet we feel that we can identify with Mr. Shea. His music ministry has gone beyond the pew and pulpit. He is a worthy role model for us all as he too shares the unsearchable riches of Christ via music. 'Take my voice, and let me sing always, only, for my King. Take my lips, and let them be filled with messages from Thee.'"
—Judy Leigh, Sikeston, Missouri

CHURCH PLANTING

Six of the Shea children were born in Winchester, Ontario and George Beverly Shea was eight years of age when they moved to Houghton in Upstate New York. From there his enterprising father developed not only a local pastoral ministry but also a successful church planting program. It took him away from home to seemingly exciting parts of the wild frontier with exotic names such as Moosejaw and Medicine Hat.

The anticipated move south to Houghton in 1917 that appeared so ominous to the fearful youngster was in no way as traumatic as the boy expected. Moving as a family en-masse had its advantages. Everyone pulled together to ensure that the move went efficiently and settlement was swift. Soon the Sheas were enjoying meeting new friends and the proximity of the larger stores full of exciting products not seen in small town Canada. As an eight-year-old, Bev recalls one such shopping trip in the company of his father and mother. On the round of the shops, Reverend Shea greeted and tipped his hat to a tall, elderly lady, Mrs. Clara Tear Williams. They all exchanged hellos and chatted for several minutes. What impressed young Beverly was that this elegant lady, a stranger to him, was according to his father, a prominent hymn writer.

"Fancy," he thought to himself. "We have a real life, famous hymn writer living in our town!" Returning home, Beverly promptly made his way to the parlor piano and scouted through the songbooks in the piano stool until his eyes fell upon "All My Life Long I Had Panted." Loudly, he announced the discovery to his mother busying herself in the kitchen, "I've found one, Mom! I've found a song by Mrs. Williams!"

Entering the sunny room, Mrs. Shea smiled, sat on the stool and played through the melody in the book that Beverly placed on the rack. The scene basked in the sunbeams of the late afternoon as the melody of "All My Life Long I Had Panted" filled the air. "Oh, Beverly this is a beautiful song. Mrs.

Williams wrote the words and sent it to Ralph Hudson who's a publisher and a fine gospel singer in Ohio. He added the melody, son."

'Riting, Reading and 'Rithmatic

Beverly's sister, Pauline and brother Whitney were soon enrolled at the local educational academy while Beverly and Mary attended public school. At school, as his report cards testify, his grades were reasonably high. But about this time, he contracted a mysterious throat infection of the tonsils that kept him out of school for much of his third and fourth grades. His troublesome tonsils were eventually removed but the nasty poison seemed to spread through all his system, remaining for several months. Rest in bed was the stern doctor's order. There was no penicillin back then so people relied on the body's own resilience to bounce back to normality. His nurse and teacher was his dear hardworking mother who, between the chores of home, served him with the three basic R's: reading, 'riting, and 'rithmatic at the kitchen table. In a very real sense, commencing with nursery rhymes and children's Bible stories, his basic education had already started years earlier at home on his mother's knee.

Principled and loving, his mother delighted in quoting scripture to her children. Young Beverly marveled at her memory. The words of wisdom seemed to flow from her tongue when the family sat at the supper table. "Remember children," she would spontaneously remark, "the Holy Spirit inspired King Solomon to write that a good name is rather to be chosen than great riches, and loving favor rather than silver and gold! So let's be sure that we in the Shea family live up to our Christian calling!"

As a growing schoolboy, he seemed to be totally lacking in self-confidence or self-belief in his own abilities and brainpower. Being considerably taller than anyone in his class, it was difficult to remain inconspicuous when a teacher was looking for volunteers to read aloud from the Charles Dickens' novel Oliver Twist in the English lesson. He deliberately developed a hunch to conceal his height, but the ploy seldom worked. Despite this excruciating shyness, he usually enjoyed his lessons particularly the exciting stories about history's men and women of admirable exploits. One of the greatest heroes was President Abraham Lincoln. Many of the older generation in his local community enjoyed personal memories of Civil War life under his presidency. One of his history teachers repeatedly delighted in telling his class, "Always bear in mind, boys, Mr. Lincoln was once a poor country boy like some of you but he became president. He said that it was his resolution to succeed that was more important than any other thing in his success! So you all need to apply yourselves, boys, and determine that you'll succeed at whatever you decide to do! In this country any boy can aspire to be president!"

His foundational Christian education endowed Beverly with a highly positive attitude at home and at school despite his unnatural shyness and genuine humility. So it was no surprise that the resolve to succeed, planted in him from his boyhood by his parents and teachers would prevail in later life. Then, with his beloved music lessons, it seemed as if the lights went on for Beverly. He found something that mattered to him and seemed to make a favorable impression on others, too, which secretly pleased him. It gratified him that often, when it came to music, he was admired as a high achiever and the center of attention. In pleasure, he remembers that not only was he the piano soloist, but "We had a family of eight singers who made a choir around the table."

ON THE ROAD AGAIN

After four years in Houghton, the enterprising Reverend Shea was offered another pastorate back in Canada. Soon the family and all of their belongings were on the road again, heading north to Ottawa's Sunnyside Wesleyan Methodist Church. It was yet another new start for the twelve-year-old Beverly.

As a pre-teen kid, he was certainly domestically secure yet also self-conscious, clumsy, and lanky. Suddenly in his teens, he came more alive than ever with his music lessons. By his mid teenage years, Beverly's great passion for musicology was fully developed. At the age of fifteen, he stood six feet one inch and weighed a hefty 170 pounds and more confidently viewed the world behind chunky horn-rimmed spectacles. Music now gave him something to offer at household and church get-togethers.

He received friendly and persuasive encouragement from others and his vocal skills developed. Although still no performing peacock, at Sunday meetings he boldly and loudly sang his heart out among the congregation on the old Methodist hymns.

Never laying stress on his obsession, Father Shea lovingly nurtured his young son's affection for music and encouraged a sense of positive optimism about life. Soon the Shea family members were making harmony together—Dad on violin, Mother and Beverly sharing turns at the keyboard and all the children joined in joyful vocal accord. Beverly was becoming very proficient on the organ, too. Soon he was playing his first public solo, debuting on the Estey reed organ at the Fifth Avenue Church of Ottawa.

Practice arrangements were made by his buddy and Fifth Avenue member, Asa MacIntosh who loved to sit in on the private practice recitals. "Beverly! That may be a small, modest ole organ but it sure sounds great when you play 'Hiding In Thee.'"

Then tragedy struck. The brevity of life and the distressing reality of death came home to Beverly when his healthy, fun-loving young pal, Asa suffered some heart malfunction. Predictably like all Asa's friends, Beverly was, of course, shocked to the core. Beverly, 15-years-old, fulfilled the request of Asa's mother that he play Fanny Crosby's "Safe In the Arms of Jesus" on the organ at the funeral, one of the toughest assignments ever.

CAMPGROUND SINGING

During Beverly's teens and twenties camp meeting and convention-style singing blazed across the New World's denominations. Initially from the American Southland, it was initially promoted by the deeply spiritual and charismatic school teacher, James D. Vaughan. His ground-breaking quartet, initially consisting of him and his three brothers, popularized Christian music immensely. After music school, taught by ET Hildebrand, Vaughan practised his song writing to the full, going on to write hundreds of tunes such as "I Feel Like Travelling On." *Gospel Chimes* was Vaughan's first published songbook embracing the shaped note techniques. Conceived several hundred years ago users could recognize the Fa, So, La or Mi by reading the shape of the note on the staff.

In Canada and the US particularly, churches of many denominations burgeoned in number in the first quarter of the twentieth century as a result of the great revivals. Beside their unremitting outgrowth came an appetite in the public for contemporary gospel songs. To meet common demand, Vaughan set up a publishing and marketing business in Lawrenceburg, Tennessee with a network of energetic quartets to advance the new sacred songs. By 1912 when Bev was three-years-old, they were selling eighty-five thousand songbooks per year and by the mid-twenties there were no less than sixteen quartets on the road. Then Vaughan expanded into fresh, daring offshoots of operation such as radio stations, phonograph records and singing schools. Expansion came geographically too, as the organization extended into four other states including Texas.

Basically of Southern Baptist and Calvinistic theological persuasion, it was in Texas that the Stamps' gospel enterprise prospered most under the astute auspices of VO and Frank Stamps in the second quarter of the twentieth century. Subsequently, their empire joined with the Baxter empire to form the renowned joint Stamps Baxter empire. For many years, the Stamps Baxter quartet-style of music was slower in gaining acceptance among mainstream, denominational churches like Bev's family church. However, their influence spread eventually north even to the quiet pastoral back waters of New York State and the province of Ontario. Slowly, Beverly Shea territory embraced the camp meeting and convention-style singing repertoire, too.

Young Beverly's church culture incorporated many serious evangelicals. Such conservative Christians proliferated particularly in the northern states, Canada and the United Kingdom. Generally, they were distrustful of songs that had a beat. Some felt that the message-in-song was not deep enough and Pentecostal theology too emotional. Soloists and groups, failing to sing in strict tempo that churches anticipated, were treated with some suspicion. Many were also distrustful of songs when substance wandered away from the well-trodden orthodox trail. The Pentecostals were the first group to make widespread use of modern gospel music. Their emotional enthusiasm-flavored worship was perfectly suited to the day's contemporary songs with a beat.

In Beverly's youth, this newer classification singing was heard increasingly at Summer Camps, All-Day Sings, Brush Arbor Meetings and Festivals of Male Voice Praise. These events were joyful evangelistic occasions when eager Christians of diverse denominations rallied together. Such events of enchanting music prospered influencing the impressionable Beverly Shea. He applied for his drivers license at the early age of fourteen years. The world was changing due to the invention of new technology. The explosive arrival of the electronic media, including phonograph records and radio, detonated globally, propelling the expansion of gospel music. Inside the time span of merely a generation, gospel music inevitably stretched to all corners of the world.

COAXED AND PERSUADED

Soon the opportunities arose for the quickly-maturing Beverly to play the organ and even his violin at such services. In August 1926 he was invited to a month-long camp meeting at Westport, Ontario by his parents' friends, Fred and Kitty Suffield. They commanded his deep respect and attention. For years, he looked upon them as an honorary uncle and aunt. He fondly remembers Fred, a traveling preacher who was converted under Reverend Shea's ministry, and Kitty, a soprano and gifted pianist, as a great source of personal inspiration. Their God-given creativity provided the Christian world with gospel music classics such as "Little is Much When God is In It" and "God is Still On the Throne."

At the month-long camp meeting at Westport, the Suffields coaxed and persuaded Beverly to sing some solos, such as "He Died of a Broken Heart" for the first time. Predictably, all these musical duties were performed by Beverly with characteristic shyness and modesty. But now from the age of seventeen at this August camp, personal confidence grew steadily with practice and by wisely pitching future solos only in the most suitable keys. Overjoyed to be requested to sing at camp meetings, he finally consented to singing on home territory in his father's church, as he recalled nostalgically. "As a young teenager it was always a vital joy and privilege, being asked to go up to the wooden platform and sing a solo in our church. These were my first experiences of singing before crowds."

Through the beginning of the Sabbath service at Ottawa's Sunnyside Wesleyan Methodist Church, Beverly sat nervously in the front pew before the pulpit. Then at the appointed moment with song sheet creased in his hand, Beverly made his way up the steps to the wooden platform. Making sure not to catch any girl's or mischief-making buddy's eye as he stood on stage, he gave a nod to the organist and took a deep breath. As the first notes rang out, Beverly felt sure that the congregation could see his crazy heart leaping beneath his white Sunday shirt. Then out it came—thankfully on pitch! The first words of the song, they brought with them the peace of knowing that he was doing his best for the Lord—and mother sitting proudly in the fourth row pew. In an instant, the sacred song was on its last note, and feeling relief, exhilaration, and pride, young Shea returned to his seat, to subdue his racing heart rate.

Now enthused, Bev started taking more interest in some of the colorful gospel singers of the time such as Gypsy Rodney Smith. *The Christian Press* in Canada told how Gypsy Smith tearfully sang gospel songs such as "If I'm Dreaming Let Me Dream On" and "Where He Leads Me I Will Follow" with his beautiful tenor voice. The newspapers reported that he had the rare ability to seemingly move with emotion every listener in his audience.

The son of gypsies, he was born in 1860 in a gypsy tent in the parish of Wanstead, England near Epping Forest just northeast of London. Since the gypsies did not attend school and few of them could read or write at the time, it is small wonder that Gypsy Smith was at a severe educational disadvantage. Recognizing this, he enterprisingly began the task of educating himself by constantly reading. The result was that Gypsy Smith developed for himself a style of vocal delivery unique in its force and beauty.

He was converted to Christ in 1876 in a Methodist Chapel in Fitzroy Street in Cambridge, England. Later he worked with the Christian Mission headed by the Reverend William Booth, who became General Booth of the Salvation Army. Gypsy Smith was the founder of the Gypsy Gospel Wagon Mission and became the designated missionary of the National Free Church Council in 1897. His evangelistic meetings took him all over the United Kingdom and further afield to Africa and America where his meetings grew large crowds with many people making personal commitments to Christ. Gypsy Smith died in 1947 at the time that Graham, Barrows and Shea were hitting the evangelistic trail. After seeing such great fruit from the Billy Graham team's labors, Bev loved to quote Gypsy Smith "If I'm Dreaming, Let Me Dream On."

TOUCHED EARLY BY GOD'S SPIRIT

An elderly Bev says that he came to a personal childlike faith in Christ at the early age of five or six. But, as he recalls, there were later many times in growing up when he needed to renew his vow. "When I was eighteen, my dad was still pastoring in Ottawa and I was not feeling too spiritual. The church was having revival services with Kitty and Fred Suffield—a special effort, as they called it, for a week. I attended all the services moved by the Evangel call and the invitation hymns but avoided any public commitment. Then I remember that on Friday night, Dad came down from the pulpit and tenderly placed his hand on my shoulder. He whispered, 'I think tonight might be the night, Son.' Whatever Dad did or said, I listened to him and respected him. And yes, that was the night!"

Beverly's fear of public confession was conquered on that significant evening during the altar call and the singing of "Just As I Am," a song any attendee of a Billy Graham meeting in later years will know as the invitation hymn. In quiet emotion, Beverly nodded determinedly and quietly shifted out into the aisle to join the others making their way forward in repentance and faith. Taking their leave of the modest chapel after the service with the Suffields, beaming from ear to ear, the pleased pastor and his wife expressed their deep gratitude to God. More and more, Beverly started sensing and responding to nothing less than a divine musical calling on his life.

Touched early by God's Spirit, his tender love affair with sacred music grew. The proud Shea parents heard positive feedback from various members of the congregation. "You good folk ought to be mighty proud of that boy of yours! He's maturing into a fine young man! When he was singing today, my heart was really stirred. The good Lord's surely gifted him. I'm glad to see Beverly's now using his gift as a blessing to others!"

The obvious success of those first Beverly Shea solos at campgrounds and churches, his first introduction to performing, brought immediate rewards. He relished the joy of forming a vocal quartet with college friends including Alonzo Scharfe.

Beverly initially studied at Annesley College in Ottawa along with a hundred or so other students. Their curriculum was a general study, although it majored highly on Christian values. The college building had a fated future as a venue because a couple of generations later it was demolished and turned into a gas station. The college quartet, however, was a modest success story at school and church functions. Memorably, they were platform guests, dressed in their Sunday best, at the opening dedication of the famous Christian Missionary Alliance Tabernacle. They sang a song that advocated deeper commitment, "Come Over Into the land of Corn and Wine." Singing at such a prestigious event gave the boys a deep thrill and a great sense of fulfillment. Mingling with the large congregation after the special service, Beverly chatted with Alonzo Scharfe. A pretty girl drifted into Beverly's view and captivated his attention. It was a magic moment that he never forgot. *Who was this irresistible girl?* That was the question that later the next day he put to Alonzo in excited terms. Beverly was unprepared for his friend's jovial answer. "Why Beverly, didn't you know? She's my sister, Erma!"

Whoso Findeth a Wife…

Predictably, at a Sunday morning service, the distinguished Reverend Shea's sermon topic was from time-to-time on the subject of Christian marriage. Clearly, looking over to the teens and twenties assembled as usual in their favorite wooden pew, he surprised Beverly and his friends as his booming voice rang clear with authority. "Whoso findeth a wife findeth a good thing, and obtaineth favor of the Lord! House and riches are the inheritance of fathers and a prudent wife is from the Lord!"

The powerful sermon certainly seized attention. Bev knew that he was now at the age where he started to notice girls, particularly the attractive ones like Erma Scharfe. Born in Ottawa, she too shared Beverly's passion for music. She attended Houghton College followed by New York's Juilliard School of Music and the Toronto Conservatory of Music. When the special church meetings and socials rolled around, it was usual for the young guys to invite and escort their best girlfriend. Beverly recollected the first time that he plucked up courage and approached pretty Erma, knocking on her door on Clemow Avenue. She was somewhat surprised to see him as it was a long walk from his Patterson Avenue abode.

Erma was developing a soft spot for the handsome, coy, long-legged teen. Dates between Erma and Beverly became regular as they saw more and more of each other. The couple was undoubtedly catching the love bug, becoming more than merely fond of each other. Yes, he was beginning to fall. She had a sweet, trusting personality that made her well-liked and excellent company.

Walking to and from church, Beverly and Erma found time to chat. It was the opportunity for him to express his seriousness about her as he gazed into her hazel eyes. Naturally, like everyone, always afraid of rejection, he feared hearing her response. But he reasoned that he had nothing to dread. Confidently, he came to realize as the months passed that she was the only one for him!

The humble mode of transport in those early days for Beverly and Erma was a car that would sometimes stubbornly refuse to start! Like a scene from a Laurel and Hardy movie unfolding, Beverly sometimes pushed it off to start it, much to Erma's amusement. Every new venture and outing was fun! He knew and liked her personality, she was now his sweetheart. Often a smile would come across his face as he overheard his friends commenting about the handsome singer and his Erma. Erma's folks had long known Beverly as a friend of Alonzo's and very soon after his attention had started to fall on Alonzo's little sis, her parents began to gently tease her about it. Privately, they were happy for their daughter to be seeing someone who seemed so respectable.

THE GREAT DEPRESSION

Although not knowing what career path he should follow, Beverly enjoyed his education at New York's academically strong Christian institution. His brief spell at Houghton College commenced in the autumn of 1928. Also, signing up was Erma. Sadly for Beverly, however, he only lasted a year at Houghton as the family's college fund dried up. Still timid when it came to public speaking, Beverly knew he'd never follow his father's footsteps into a preaching ministry. Yet, nevertheless, with his solo singing, services, and fellowship meetings at the church now took on a delightfully different dimension for him. He also particularly reveled in singing with the famous Houghton College Glee Club, an extracurricular activity, under the direction of Wilfred C. Bain.

Also from Winchester, Wilfred became Beverly's new college roommate. They enjoyed fun times at college and developed a lifelong friendship. (Wilfred went on to fulfill a successful musical career at North Texas State University and Indiana University.)

Beverly's first formal vocal coaching was at Houghton with the invaluable help of Professor Herman Baker who auditioned him for the Glee Club and the school orchestra, as a violinist. Beverly credits the professor specifically for injecting expression and sincerity into his bass-baritone style. He also helped him battle with the self-consciousness by emphasizing preparation as a sure foundation for confidence before an audience. However, Beverly never imagined in his wildest dreams that in decades to come, he could sing gospel music as a career to millions of people. More and more spirituals and hymns such as Philip Paul Bliss' favorite "I Will Sing of My Redeemer" became his well-requested party pieces.

A fellow student, Fred Mix, was so impressed by Beverly's violin skills, he persuaded his mother to hire Beverly to teach him. After some quick thinking, Beverly consented and a deal of seventy-five cents per hour was struck. This credit would be paid in exchange for laundry services from Mrs. Mix. Thus Beverly gladly secured a treasured year's free supply of washing and ironing, a crucial God-send as his budget was balancing on a knife edge. Indeed, the financial situation for the tall Canadian student was so grave that he still had to resort to doing odd jobs in his spare time such as digging ditches at fifty cents an hour. Nationally, the clouds of economic depression were hovering low across the nation. Erma knew that the gold pin birthday present from Bev that year did not come without much sacrifice. What she did not know was that the full cost was in sweat, blisters and calluses along with the

$3.50 price tag. Funds were so stretched that cold winter, Beverly was very glad to receive in the mail a secondhand, blue serge suit from his understanding uncle, Paul Whitney. Erma said it fitted fine and he looked a picture. That boosted his ego!

Meanwhile, new employment opportunities arose for the 56-year-old Reverend Shea when he was called to yet another new church—First Wesleyan Methodist in Jersey City, just across the Hudson River from Manhattan. Timing was opportune and Beverly agreed after Houghton College to rejoin the Shea family in the new urban environment. Indeed, he helped to facilitate the move with his father and brother Alton amid the uncomfortable humidity of a July heat wave. With disruption of relocation settled, the rest of the Shea brigade moved in a month later. But Beverly felt lost without Erma. Having reluctantly left Houghton College, he secured a promising job but it was so hard to say goodbye to Erma. Their temporary parting was to last longer than either wished.

The distressing period that followed was the economically-troubled days of the Great Depression. Tremendous suffering ensued among the working class unable to find employment after the Wall Street Crash of 1929. The chilling wind of privation continued to blow strongly across the continent for many years. It forced every working family, including the Sheas, to resourcefully adapt to the pragmatic realities of, or threat of, unemployment. Merely the fearful thought of it brought considerable stress on every home's breadwinner. Looking back, Beverly is most grateful to his faithful parents for the constancy of Christian example they displayed even when times were bad. They not only took him and his brothers and sisters habitually to church on Sundays, but they walked their talk throughout the week too. Slowly, the Sheas settled as a team into the new church, First Wesleyan Methodist in Jersey City. All became engrossed in the fresh work and new community of believers.

A HARD DAY'S WORK

It was all such a vast contrast from the open spaces that Beverly had previously enjoyed. The Big Apple was noisy, brash and overcrowded. In New York City, Beverly's medical secretary job lasted for nine years. Although he was the boss, Beverly described Harold Voege as "a dear Christian gentleman." Beverly worked diligently in Mutual Life Insurance Company's head office in the busy part of the downtown city. The 21-year-old's task was to assist the medical examiners in the acquisition and checking of the health histories of insurance applicants. The brevity and fragility of life that his father often preached on was coming home to Beverly in a new and relevant way as he perused the life-expectancy tables in the office.

For vocal training in his spare time, initially, he rode the uptown subway to be coached by a well-qualified teacher. However, his tuition charges were grossly expensive at $10 for twenty minutes, and the teacher was unsympathetic to the Christian cause to boot. Other teachers followed, including Emerson Williams— the big, tall bass-profundo with NBC's Revelers Quartet; and Price Boone, tenor in the Calvary Baptist Church choir and a one-time contender for a staring role at the Metropolitan Opera before the death of Herbert Witherspoon, the Met's general manager. Beverly recalls, "I sang for a while in a quartet with Price Boone, Hassie Mayfield and William Miller on the Erling

C. Olsen WHN and WMCA broadcasts. The beautiful theme song was 'May Jesus Christ Be Praised' that starts off with 'When Morning Guilds The Skies.'"

When Morning Gilds The Skies my heart awaking cries: 'May Jesus Christ be praised!'

Alike at work and prayer to Jesus I repair: 'May Jesus Christ be praised!'

Does sadness fill my mind? A solace here I find: 'May Jesus Christ be praised!'

When evil thoughts molest, with this I shield my breast: 'May Jesus Christ be praised!'

To God, the Word, on high the hosts of angels cry: 'May Jesus Christ be praised!'

Let mortals, too, upraise their voice in hymns of praise: 'May Jesus Christ be praised!'

Let earth's wide circle round in joyful notes resound: 'May Jesus Christ be praised!'

Let air, and sea, and sky, from depth to height, reply: 'May Jesus Christ be praised!'

Be this while life is mine. My canticle divine: 'May Jesus Christ be praised!'

Be this the eternal song, Through all the ages long: 'May Jesus Christ be praised!'

—Katholisches Gesangbuch

The pre-dawn radio program introduced Beverly to an impressive array of edifying Christian teachers and preachers including Harry Ironside, Wilbur Smith, Will Houghton and Donald Grey Barnhouse. In his training sessions, a priceless piece of advice seeped deep into Beverly's memory. It came from his teacher, Emerson Williams. Beverly had rendered a heartwarming version of the "The Love of God" when Emerson remarked thoughtfully, "Stick to the heart songs, Beverly. They suit you best and give spiritual uplift to your listeners." Sadly, Emerson died suddenly of a heart attack after giving Beverly only a few months training.

CELEBRITIES OF THE DAY

Back then, Erma ably displayed her musical abilities by acting as Beverly's accompanist. Previously, she studied at the Toronto Conservatory of Music. For a couple of years, Beverly also guest-starred as the vocalist on J. Thurston Noe's Friday evening organ broadcasts on an FM station entitled *Sundown* that had "Thou Light of Light" as its theme song. Thurston was considered by Bev to be a classy composer as well as being the competent organist and director of the Calvary Baptist Church choir. The historic church was situated across the street from the famed and sophisticated Carnegie Hall. It was at the Baptist church that Beverly first met a contributor to the radio show and the minister of the church at the time, Dr. Will Houghton. An important contact in the future chain of events, Will went on to serve as president of the Moody Bible Institute in Chicago. Years later, he was responsible for organizing Beverly's opportunity to enter full-time Christian work.

From time to time, Beverly's insurance job presented him with opportunities to meet celebrities of the day. One such personality was the composer Sigmund Romberg who had a splendid 1100 pipe Skinner organ for sale. Beverly privately thought to himself, "That'll be fine for Dad's church!" Plans were made to visit the famous composer's opulent penthouse with the insurance agent. "Try the organ for yourself, Mr. Shea," said Mr. Romberg.

Dying to get his hands on the instrument, Beverly needed no second invitation. Sitting at the grand instrument, he skillfully played Romberg's "When I Grow Too Old To Dream." The impromptu rendition impressed the composer who then announced to Beverly's shock, "I'm happy to sell it for $10,000!" Needless to say, sadly, the Sigmund Romberg organ never did make it to First Wesleyan Methodist in Jersey City. By now Beverly was enjoying alternating weeks with his mother on the faithful old motorized reed organ even though it lacked any subtlety of expression.

Now taking whatever opportunity he could, Beverly sang throughout his area at church meetings, socials and such. His piano accompanist was either Erma or a volunteer drawn from a pool of local pianists. The gospel bass-baritone knew that he had to additionally hone his natural talents to achieve greater impact. With his mind focused and fixed on the discipline required to succeed, he developed an ever-widening repertoire of songs. Strenuously practicing his concert skills, he meticulously nurtured his great love for the unadorned gospel-singing genre. Paradoxically, it was the golden heyday of a new musical genre that generated great ballads from beloved crooners such as Bing Crosby, Al Jolson, Gene Autry, Perry Como, Jo Stafford and Frank Sinatra. But Beverly would not, as he said, be tempted from his chosen role.

I'D RATHER HAVE JESUS

In 1933 at the age of 23, the cement of commitment hardened. That year Beverly wrote the music for one of his best-known songs, "I'd Rather Have Jesus." It subsequently became one of the Christian world's most beloved hymns. Mother Shea realized that the maturing young man was still making significant choices. He was also full of questions about what do with his life and talents. One noteworthy Saturday night, she conspicuously left a hand-written poem by Rhea Miller on the piano for her son to see the next Sunday at his morning keyboard practice. The devotional lyrics had earlier caught the attention of King George VI of England. During the Roosevelt Administration, President and Mrs. Roosevelt entertained King George VI and Queen Elizabeth at the White House. On that occasion native Indian American Chief White Feather, an opera singer, was asked to sing from his repertoire. For the encore he asked, "May I sing something from the heart?" The song was "I'd Rather Have Jesus." After a moment of silence, the young Queen responded, "This song bespeaks the sentiment of my heart, and that of my husband."

Some forty years later Bev was singing at a School of Evangelism held in Toronto, Ontario. The visiting Vicar from England, Bishop Baughen told of speaking for her Majesty, now the beloved Queen Mother at her private chapel at Sandringham. He had been in touch with the Queen's secretary asking if he could relate the tender event in Washington DC and if he might repeat her remarks. She remembered and gave her permission to relate that moment and her words concerning "I'd Rather Have Jesus."

The words of the poem also caught Beverly's attention on the piano that day. "But what is more important," Bev explained to me, "the sentiment captured my heart. With my fingers moving across the keys soon I composed a melody. Then I felt her hands on my shoulder and I turned and there was Mother standing behind me with tears in her eyes. When married to the lyrics, the song became well-known, included in many hymn books. What a privilege to be associated with this meaningful poem."

In the long years that followed, the fervent stand taken in the lyrics of his song became increasingly real to Beverly as he turned down one secular radio and recording contract offer after another. He was determined to remain true to Christ and the Great Commission. It was a momentous stand that he never regretted because he said he was later offered better positions of God's choosing. Such opportunities were presented in radio stations and record companies. There he mightily used to the full the gospel songs he loved.

Hundreds of recordings of his classic song "I'd Rather Have Jesus" have been minted, performed by every conceivable style of Christian music artist. Yet, as country star Wanda Jackson explained, every Christian artist seems to claim personal identification with the song's sentiments. "It would be impossible to count the number of times Mr. Shea has sung 'I'd Rather Have Jesus.' Whenever it is heard, the sentiment comes over so powerfully especially the line that says 'I'd rather have Jesus than men's applause!' As an entertainer who has now found my salvation in the Lord Jesus Christ these words from Mr. Shea's song express how I feel deep down inside! How can the world and its acclaim adequately be compared to the untold riches of Christ? I would like Bev to know that I am so grateful to him for faithfully sharing and indeed co-writing this classic sacred song. 'I'd Rather Have Jesus' seems was written for people like me. His song has become my heartfelt testimony!"

"Among the later stories about the song," Bev recounts, "my favorite came from an American infantryman in Europe's World

War II. He loved to play the pipe organ whenever he'd get the chance. A German village had just been bombed and almost everything was leveled but the local church. He saw one wall and part of the roof was gone. The thought struck him, 'I wonder if the organ is still there?' He ran inside. It looked okay. He threw the switch and it came to life. In a few moments this fine old instrument burst forth with the message: 'Than to be the king of a vast domain, or be held in sin's dread sway... I'd rather have Jesus than anything this world affords today.' Yes, the world often holds sway with conflict. In the midst of deep trial the Christian may not be happy. But he can feel an inward sense of peace... the peace that Jesus gives."

In the late fifties, a heart-warming letter arrived from a distressed lady in Australia. At the end of her courage, she was initially focusing serious attention on suicide. Then, she said, listening to the radio, she heard the warm deep tones of Bev Shea's "I'd Rather Have Jesus." Strangely, faith was sparked into fire and thoughts of suicide were dissuaded.

SING AND TRAIN

Bev possessed an ongoing passion to sing and train. From one audition at a CBS radio network came a subsequent offer of a desirable contract. "The audition by CBS radio was accepted. The money offered was three times what I was receiving in the insurance office. So I was reluctant to turn it down."

"Sir," Beverly asked, "could I sing gospel songs on the radio? They are my first love!"

"No son, CBS network needs to have you singing the songs from the Hit Parade. You might though use one gospel song occasionally."

Misgivings flooded Beverly's troubled mind as he pondered the tempting offer all the way home. What should he do? Should he compromise his stand about singing exclusively from the sacred song repertoire? His mother understood her son's plight and was praying for him. Still deeply committed, he resolved to remain true to the Great Commission, to what they saw as his gospel music calling.

"The music they wanted me to sing was contrary to what I loved." Often his convictions would return him to the sentiments of Frances Ridley Havergal's prayerful words of commitment.

Take my life and let it be consecrated, Lord, to Thee;

Take my moments and my days, let them flow in ceaseless praise.

Take my voice, and let me sing always, only, for my King;

Take my lips, and let them be filled with messages from Thee.

—Frances Ridley Havergal (1836-1879)

The Wedding

What was supposed to be a short separation between Erma in Ottawa and Beverly in New York was much longer than either wished or anticipated. They endured five long years of waiting. The parting was sweetened by regular letters and meetings two or three times a year when he rode the New York Central train to see his beloved. Friends and kin were not surprised when the loving couple became engaged, committing themselves to each other for life. That night alone in her bedroom Erma pondered silently, fighting back the emotion and the tears. The couple's decision was rational and the subject of marriage was maturely approached. Turning to her Bible, she read the moving words of Song of Solomon 2:10-13.

"My beloved spake, and said unto me, 'Rise up, my love,
my fair one, and come away. For, lo, the winter is past, the
rain is over and gone; The flowers appear on the earth;
the time of the singing of birds is come, and the voice of
the turtle is heard in our land; The fig tree puts forth her
green figs, and the vines with the tender grape give a good
smell. Arise, my love, my fair one, and come away."

The engagement was not so much popping the question or
rushed impulse of the moment! Rather it was two Christian
individuals, much in love, sitting down and entrusting themselves
to each other and devising their future as a pair.

Erma and Beverly visited the jewelry store and picked out an
endearing diamond ring. Financial restraints, however, delayed the
wedding for four long years. Excited as the day drew closer, she
kept her nails well-manicured so that she could show off the new
wedding ring that would make her the future Mrs. George Beverly
Shea. Finally in 1934 on June 16th, the sun shone, the bells rang,
and the flowers bloomed. The long-awaited special day arrived.

Erma's brother Alonzo, acting as the best man, speedily drove
the groom in his spotless Chevrolet to Ottawa's Sunnyside
Wesleyan Methodist Church. Beverly felt particularly smart
in his black, double-breasted suit that cost him an outrageous
$17.50 in Howard's store in Times Square.

Dressed in a beautiful long sleeve, high-necked, white wedding
gown, Erma glided down the aisle to meet her handsome fiancé
dressed in a stand-up collar, his hair smoothed down to the left.
The wedding venue was, of course, the Shea family's old church
and many old friends were there to witness the special event.

Her long white dress, trimmed in delicate lace, was perfectly complimented by a dainty bouquet of roses. All invitees agreed that it was a delightfully happy wedding followed by a reception at Erma's parents' farm. Then the couple honeymooned at Niagara Falls. Later in their week of vacation, while visiting the Churchill Tabernacle, they were thrilled to meet the famed sacred songwriter, BD Ackley. The honeymooners could not have guessed that in the years to come Beverly was to record many Ackley numbers.

WIND-UP VICTROLA

Hymn-writers were to be huge influences on Beverly especially in the decade before World War II. One of the most impacted was Homer Rodeheaver. Born in 1880, the composer and performer became evangelist Billy Sunday's song leader in 1909. Homer said that he realized early on the importance of gospel singing as a vital part of revival meetings. This new emphasis was to change the face of evangelistic meetings. At the age of fourteen, Beverly recalled the great thrill of hearing Homer for the first time on record singing "Sunrise." The inspiring sound came from a wind-up Victrola phonograph, a mahogany instrument that was highly prized at the time. It belonged to the Beardsley family who lived opposite the Sheas on Metcalf Street in Ottawa. After the wedding, years later, Beverly remembers his meeting with Homer at Winona Lake. "I found him to be a short, smiling man whose sincerity was infectious. In his years of service, Homer developed to the full the art of audience participation in gospel singing. His innovative style and his God-given ability to draw even the most reluctant individuals into taking part in the services was a totally different style to that of other song leaders before his day. He would often prelude the meetings with a musical quiz or parts singing drawing on the audience to participate. An accomplished trombonist, like Cliff Barrows, Homer's trombone with piano accompaniment, provided dramatic background to gospel singing not heard of before in revival meetings."

Beverly followed closely the team of Sunday and Rodeheaver, examples of a more relaxed version of revival meetings. He openly gives credit to the gospel music pioneer for his distinctive way of singing. "I loved to listen to Homer Rodeheaver singing. He was an early inspiration. Homer would sing every week, on the radio when the radio was America's only source of entertainment. Homer died in 1950 but in his days, America wanted to hear oldies like 'Amazing Grace' and 'Blessed Assurance' plus his new favorites like 'Then Jesus Came' and 'Precious Memories.' The Dust Bowl and the Great Depression left folks simple in their joys and pleasures. They did not want the taint of Hollywood's values or news of approaching world war."

Radio Stations

Returning from their honeymoon, the young couple visited Ottawa to pick up Erma's belongings and their wedding presents. It was a strange feeling for Erma as she boxed up all her familiar possessions that she had held for a lifetime in her parents' home. Inevitably, some boxes were left temporarily in the attic, but every parent knows they will sit there for several years. Then putting the borrowed suitcases and cardboard boxes in the trunk and backseat, Erma hugged her old life goodbye to start her new life as Mrs. Beverly Shea. They headed south to their small studio apartment at 1275 Palisades, Fort Lee located on the subway line just thirty minutes from Beverly's office in New York City.

With the landlord's duties dispatched, the newlyweds entered the tiny apartment. Two fresh cups of coffee were made on the unfamiliar stove and the couple flopped onto the sofa. Sparsely decorated with the bare bones of furniture, they looked around, soaking up their new home. Their love nest, however, cost $47.50 a month in rent and the couple struggled unsuccessfully over the months that followed to balance their finances. Fortunately, Mr. and Mrs. Hopper who were members of Beverly's parents' Jersey City church, learned about the newly married couple's needs. They invited them to move into their property with them. The Great Depression was still taking its toll nationwide.

Back at his office desk, Beverly was grateful for the secure job that he had held for ten years. He didn't want to rock the boat. Nevertheless, deep inside there was the nagging feeling that it was not his life's passion as far as he was concerned. His greater sense of fulfillment came when given opportunities to sing for his Lord.

About this time, he buddied up with a young lay preacher called Jack Wyrtzen who was employed in the insurance business. He was a fire insurance clerk on John Street, a few blocks from Beverly's office. Jack had an evangelistic passion to reach the young people of his generation via youth rallies. He and Beverly met regularly to share plans and experiences over a sandwich and coke at lunch. Soon Beverly and Erma were becoming involved in Jack's evangelistic enterprises. Meanwhile, Beverly's parents were on the move again, accepting a call to pastor the Willett Memorial Church in Syracuse in upper New York State.

Each summer, Erma and Beverly spent an enjoyable vacation week at the Pinebrook Bible Conference in the Pocono Mountains as he sang solos and she played piano. His popular gospel songs were gaining in appeal and stimulating more and more inquiries about whether he had any records available for sale. He chatted the matter over later with Price Boone. "Why don't you ask Jack Kapp of Decca Records whether his label has any openings? The label is doing really well nowadays with Al Jolson, Bing Crosby, Jimmy Davis, Ernest Tubb and others… you never know, Beverly."

Sure enough to Beverly's delightful surprise, Jack Kapp responded positively to Beverly's proposal of doing some gospel music recordings for the Decca label. On the designated day, with Ruth Crawford at the organ, he minted his first ever recordings, namely "Lead Me Gently Home," "I'd Rather Have Jesus," "Jesus Whispers Peace" and "God Understands." Finally a pleasing 7,000 copies were sold. Despite Beverly's natural flair for singing, he still remained petrified when it came to public speaking. Radio, however, held no fears.

Insurance still offered a good secure job but secretly, Beverly's real desire was still to sing. Such a lofty career as a professional singer, however, was seen as a temperamental, poorly-paid choice. So despite the unglamorous nature of the insurance business, he decided to stick with it for the time being. Thus with no real plans to be a professional singer, he was content working as an amateur retaining his employment near Wall Street for $34.50 per week. One spring weekday morning at his desk, the phone rang. On the line was one of his singing pals speaking in excited tones. "Beverly, have you heard that the Lynn Murray Singers are holding auditions this afternoon at CBS? Come on down and give it a try! The job's worth $75 a week and will give national exposure."

Bev's interest was stirred enough to check out the opportunity. He got off early from work to meet the audition time. Nervous before the famous, inscrutable Mr. Murray, Bev rendered "Suwannee River" and "Down By the River" with flair. Murray's smile and gentle nod of his head indicated he was satisfied. "Let me hear you sing the 'Song of the Vagabond,' Mr. Shea!" said Lynn Murray handing Beverly the sheet music. "My choir will be singing it at the upcoming Texas Centennial."

Beverly rendered the tricky number well enough to pass this tough audition, but something was wrong in his inner spirit. The line of the song "...to hell with Burgundy," from a Broadway show, was sticking in his throat and challenging his conscience as a committed Christian. He felt to sing such words would be compromising. It was a tough choice but he decided he must make a stand! Consequently, when the invitation to join the Lynn Murray Singers came, he graciously turned down the offer. It was not the first or the last time that he chose to take the higher moral ground despite the misgivings of some friends who said he was crazy.

A few weeks later, he entered a top talent contest that was part of comedian Fred Allen's coast-to-coast radio show. Talk among the talent organizers was how Beverly's voice reminded them of a young Paul Robeson. Robeson was beginning to hit stardom worldwide via the emerging media of Hollywood's talking movies. On that day of the talent competition, Beverly sang live before a studio audience of 1500 plus those out in NBC's radio-land, the spiritual "Go Down Moses." He was accompanied by a simple piano but his efforts won him the second prize of $15, the first prize going to a yodeler. Beverly was still determined not to sell his soul to the world of show business by going secular.

Later Bev recorded a 1950's Hit Parade song, "He." Bev asked the publisher if he could change the closing words of the song from *He will always forgive* to *He is always ready to forgive* taken from the Psalms and was given permission.

The Great Depression was taking its tragic toll. One lunch hour, Beverly remembers the shock of witnessing an ambulance screaming to a halt just outside his office. Nearby, a depressed victim of the economic blight jumped to his suicide from a skyscraper. Days were dark for so many but fortunately, Beverly's music study and radio openings prospered through those days. He was never afraid to face sheer hard work and never lacked the determination to overcome.

Opportunities arose when Jersey City's preacher, Elmo Bateman, on radio station WKBO, invited him to be a guest on his near crack-of-dawn show. Live radio in those days was the scene of many hilarious hiccups that went out on air, but it was invaluable experience for the young Canadian. Beverly recalls candidly, "In the early thirties, I just still never dreamed that I would be a gospel singer. I was actually training in New York just to do radio. I was preparing, but I didn't know what for. Manley Price Boone, who was teaching at the old Metropolitan Opera, would say, 'Bev you should take every opportunity to let people know that you love to sing.'" Natural restraint caused the modest Bev to retort gently, "Price, I can't do that!"

Persistently, Price pressed home the point and said, "Listen Bev, Dr. George Palmer is speaking at Calvary Baptist Church, and you know he's got a network program. Why don't you go up there and tell him that you'd like him to consider you as a singer to sing on his broadcast?"

"But I can't do that, Price!" Nevertheless, Beverly went to hear Dr. Palmer, as he recalls. "When I got in the line of people to shake his hand, I thought of what Price advised. But I knew I wasn't going to speak of it. Reaching the preacher I said, 'Dr. Palmer, we hear your broadcast *Morning Cheer* from Philadelphia, and we enjoy it so much... and your message tonight blessed our hearts. God bless you, thank you.'"

Smiling, Beverly returned up the aisle, his heart rejoicing that he didn't succumb to the temptation to push himself forward. Since the victory of that day, when asked by young people about developing their own ministry in song, he replies, "I suggest that you don't put your hand on the knob to open the door—let God do it! He will! I feel that it was right to wait for God to open the radio doors while still working as a daytime clerk in the New York insurance office."

For many years at 6:30 a.m. he jumped on the Bergen Avenue bus to sing on WKBO from 7:00 to 7:30 a.m. Then he took the tube or ferry to the MONY offices on Nassau, near Wall Street. After a hard day's work he undertook more voice lessons or practiced alone in the evening.

Establishing New Circles

"Please sing more for us, Mr. Shea!" That was a suggestion in the radio station correspondence that he and the sponsors loved to hear. Yet despite the overnight radio success, his focused mind told him that he should further sharpen his talents to achieve greater impact. He auditioned for radio networks but refused two more offers that would have required the singing of non-religious songs because, as he said, he dedicated his life to the service of Christ. In the hot summer of 1938 at the enjoyable, edifying Pinebrook Bible Conference in the Poconos, Beverly met again with Dr. Will Houghton now president of the Moody Bible Institute.

"Beverly, have you ever considered full-time Christian radio as a vocation?"

"I didn't know such an opportunity existed."

As they shook hands Will said, "I will be in touch with you about it."

With its historical origin, perspective and outlook, the Moody Bible Institute and its non-commercial radio station was an ideal ground for further training. Beverly's interest was certainly stirred and after prayer, he and Erma felt that it was right to accept the opportunity to become an announcer and soloist on WMBI Chicago.

Relocation, of course, had its disadvantages. They were very happy in the Big Apple and singing opportunities were steadily increasing. Contacts, friends and relations were all in the east so they would have to establish new circles in Chicago. He moved a month or so before Erma, to prepare the way. His overnight train trip from the Grand Central Station was spent sitting up. He chose to save some cash rather than spend more on the sleeper car. By the end of August 1938, the Shea couple were both in Chicago. Despite his lack of relevant experience, Beverly's first six months were spent promoting the availability of 1400 student vacancies at the institute's evening school with the help of Russell Hitt, later to be editor of *Eternity Magazine* and Robert Walker, later to be editor of *Christian Life Magazine*. In March 1939, he became staff announcer on WMBI. Soon he was guesting on the Wendell Loveless' broadcast, *Let's Go Back To the Bible* and hosting a fifteen minute long broadcast entitled *Hymns From the Chapel* with the familiar favorite of his mother, "Singing I Go" as his theme song.

While in Chicago, he commenced studies under Gino Monaco, recommended to him by the opera star John Charles Thomas of whom Beverly was a lifelong fan. Gino's studio was located at the Fine Arts Building in South Michigan Avenue. His training focused on improving Beverly's diction and voice placement. Where sacred songs were concerned, Beverly developed an almost a missionary zeal. The tall Canadian with the kind, intense eyes poured his heart into his gospel singing for evangelistic purposes.

Looking back and surveying the seven decades and more of his gospel singing career, he had risen almost as far as anyone could go from his humble, middle-income family man to that of international opportunity. In his twenties and thirties, it seemed preposterous to imagine himself as a professional gospel singer, but in Chicago he got the chance. And little did he know that soon he would form a friendship and ministry that would take him around the world, singing in front of more people than anyone in history.

Chapter 5

It Is No Secret What God Can Do
1939-1949

"Bev, I'd like to say, you'll never know. No, you'll never know just how much you move a person's heart. You move mine when you sing that song, 'It Is No Secret What God Can Do.'"
—Stuart Hamblen, Los Angeles, California

RALLYING AROUND THE FLAGS

George Beverly Shea is fully aware that history records the incalculable debt that North Americans of early pioneering days owed to Christianity. Faith granted consolation, confidence and direction in heart-breaking calamity and strife in the new frontiers of wasteland. In the brave new world an individual's faith flourished amid tension, exertion, misfortune and loss.

Like their forebearers, generally, Bev Shea's experience is such that he is convinced that modern Americans still deeply appreciate hymns and gospel songs. Last century's broadcast media made them part of popular culture and emotional development. Americans hear gospel music from childhood to adulthood. Many today still like to relax to it in their homes. It is their harbor of rest while relaxing in an armchair at the end of a frenzied busy day. There they repose to the honeyed uplifting and inspiring sounds of gospel music. An elderly Bev says, "Quality gospel music dissolves the gloom of daily headlines picking up flagging spirits and edifying souls with spiritual optimism! Back in the early days, singing was a growing hobby and a secret ambition for me, but I didn't really expect that I might have a ministry in song. I discovered that happiness really is finding God's individual plan for your life, getting in step with it, utilizing the talents and opportunities He provides, and then really making the most of them! I asked God to direct my steps... He led me into the ministry of song. It's wonderful because I couldn't have arranged it myself. I believe that He'll do that for anyone!"

George Beverly Shea contends that providentially, his Christian music often meets an individual at the crossroads of life, at a time of great crisis. He explains, "People meet many crossroads on the highway of life. Modern days present innumerable perplexities, but it is nothing new. Our forefathers, too had their crossroads. The same divine guidance and His precious promises are still to be found in the Bible today. We can approach our crossroads with confidence in His Word which says, 'In all thy ways acknowledge Him and He shall direct thy paths.' That was the direction our forefathers knew and, in our day, millions still rely upon God's never-failing word. Yes, as we love to sing—'with Him as your guide you have nothing to fear; His Word is the light and His presence is cheer!'"

Cautiously at first but steadily during Beverly's early radio career years, Uncle Sam started climbing out of the shadow of economic depression that had persisted for a decade. Then just when it seemed like better times were back again, sadly, greater international stresses were just ahead. Politically, the growing nation hopefully, but vainly, tried to cling to an isolationist foreign policy, prudently reluctant to exercise itself as a major power in world affairs. In 1941 George Beverly Shea became an American citizen.

Fearful storm clouds of possible US involvement in World War II hovered unavoidably. Violent war was already being waged all over Europe and the Far East. That same year, on the otherwise peaceful Sunday morning of December 7th, the voice of President Roosevelt made the dreadful announcement that the US was engaging in a world war. Protectively, Beverly held his wife close as an inner chill took hold. The mortal security of millions was smashed by the horrific announcement that day over domestic radio sets. Japanese aircraft had bombed the Pacific USA naval base. It was an earth-shaking catastrophe that sent nauseating waves around the USA to affect every aspect of life. Beverly knew that Uncle Sam would put the full consequence of his manufacturing and military might behind the beleaguered John Bull and his British Empire in their sole fight against fearfully robust, determined Nazi and Japanese aggression.

The Sheas knew that external circumstances beyond its control had propelled the US onto front and center stage of global politics, shattering domestic peace and growing prosperity. Suddenly on the world front, the thunder-and-lightning of whole-scale global war broke out with great fearsome vengeance. Yet busy, but peaceful Chicago—despite its Al Capone gangster reputation—seemed a blissful eternity away from the vexed troubles of the foreign nations.

But to some, it seemed that the end of the world was definitely at hand. Politicians, preachers and journalists, progressively warned of the severe political calamities to come. For most of the nation, specific involvement in the new war was not yet personal despite the urgent rallying around the flag. This unreal domestic scenario had been abruptly shattered.

Beverly knew that most people in America reluctantly found themselves fully involved in war. He understood too, however, why Prime Minister Winston Churchill was delighted now to have them behind the British Empire's war machine. In church on that eventful December Sunday evening, the dramatic declaration of war proclaimed by President Roosevelt was high in people's prayers, thoughts and fears. Darkness had fallen swiftly on that chilly evening in the pastel-painted sanctuary of the packed church. Many faces not seen for months attended. The shocking radio newscast of the day stimulated worship attendance and tremendously dramatized the impact of the sermon. From that first momentous day and for the duration of hostilities, the vexed subject of world war was top of everyone's conversation roster and prayer list.

CALL-UP DEFERRED

In 1943 while still serving as radio announcer on Chicago's WMBI's *Hymns From the Chapel*, Beverly helped his old friend Jack Wyrtzen, a fellow fugitive from the insurance business administration, in his evangelistic work with Word of Life. It lasted for three months and took the Sheas back to the New Jersey, New York and Connecticut areas. The previous regular soloist, tenor Carlton Booth was moving to California. Beverly was delighted that the Word of Life meetings saw thousands of young people turn to Christ under Jack's preaching with Beverly Shea in support.

About that time, national call-up for World War II duty was looming nearer. Beverly was soon expecting to hear from Uncle Sam's draft board. Sure enough the long anticipated letter came, but surprisingly the board asked Beverly whether he should be classified as a "religious minister" and duly considered for deferment from military duty. He replied negatively as he said he was not a religious minister strictly speaking. He saw no reason, although he was 37-years-old, not to serve his country like many others. The draft board, however, unilaterally decided on reclassification despite his reply.

His call-up was deferred. Meanwhile, increased wartime insecurity was stimulating desires among the public for more spiritual answers. Accordingly, Beverly and Erma returned home after the Word Of Life meetings for more youth meetings in Chicago. Reaching the youth of the windy city with the claims of Christ became a heartfelt passion for Beverly. Consequently, he enthusiastically promoted evangelistic ideas to several contacts including Torrey Johnson of the Midwest Bible Church. Later, the elderly Bev cheerfully recalled the 2,900 attendance at the initial launch of Youth For Christ. It took place in Chicago's Orchestra Hall on Michigan Avenue with Torrey and a young new pastor from the Village Church in Western Springs, Illinois called Billy Graham. The meeting went well and Bev recalls with a chuckle some humorous words that caused more than a few smiles in the interdenominational congregation:

Give me that old time religion,
Give me that old time religion,
It's good enough for me!
It makes the Baptists love the Methodists,
Makes the Methodists love the Baptists,
Makes the Presbyterians love everybody!
It's good enough for me!

Some days later, Beverly heard some useful news from the grapevine via Robert Walker. The Christian businessman Herbert Taylor's *Club Aluminum* was possibly interested in sponsoring thirteen weeks of daily hymns to be broadcast on WCFL Radio and needed a resident soloist. Beverly was more than interested but there was a major quandary to consider. WMBI Radio staff policy outlawed second contracts of such a nature as Beverly held. After prayer, he and Erma were convinced that he should resign from WMBI to sign for WCFL. Thus in June 1944, Beverly Shea debuted on *Club Time*. It was a calculated gamble that the married couple prayerfully accepted and turned out for the good. But, of course, he did miss the fellowship at WMBI.

The broadcast went nationwide on ABC network in September 1945. It gave Beverly even greater confidence in the promises to Christian believers found in scripture. "The Bible says that the steps of a good man are ordered by the Lord so I'm confident that because of prayer we made the right decision." It became the second oldest hymn program on commercial US radio and was carried for eight years over ABC, the Armed Forces network, and many independent stations. He feels that professionally, *Club Time* had a class and dignity to it. For the

First time in the Shea's marriage, it also provided a little more financial security. As the singing host, from time to time Beverly featured his distinctive versions of the favorite hymns of famous celebrities who visited the Chicago studios. He recalls that the parade of star picks included John Charles Thomas' "Softly and Tenderly," an Ira Sankey standard; Kate Smith's "In the Garden," penned by C. Austin Miles; and baseball superstar Babe Ruth's "God Is Ever Beside Me." The musical director of the series was Don Hustad, who was by then the head of the Moody Institute's music department. Other gifted colleagues included Jack Halloran, choir director and later an orchestrator for RCA; Bill Cole, later a soloist and executive for Light Records; and Forrest Boyd, later with the White House Press Corp.

TWO BEVERLYS

About this time, the name Beverly, as he was known, became a problem. It was a common name for a boy in Canada at the turn of the twentieth century, but in a mid-century big American city it sounded strange. Amplifying the problem was the postal mixup in the radio station where there was a lady called Beverly on the same show! Backed by piano and organ, Beverly Taylor, daughter of the program sponsor, regularly read the scriptures. The advertising agency believed having two Beverlys on the show, one male and one female, to be too confusing for the public. Although now a radio star with much experience and professionally-known since 1938 as Beverly Shea, the Canadian conceded accordingly. He consented to go by his full name of George Beverly Shea from then on.

A humorous incident once confirmed the public's confusion with the name Beverly when used for a male. One year Bev was surprised to receive an invitation addressed to him as "Miss Beverly Shea" from the American Federation Of Radio And Television Artists asking him whether he would like to participate in a beauty contest!

PREACHER PRODIGY

Back in 1945, Bev met one of the men who was to be a lifelong friend and with whom he would be forever linked. Bev's Sunday evening presentation broadcast weekly called *Songs In the Night* was conceived and originated by Torrey Johnson but because of increasing Youth For Christ duties, Torrey handed over the reins to his young preacher prodigy, Billy Graham. In turn he approached Bev about the continued radio broadcasts. Despite traveling far, Billy found it difficult to see Bev at the radio station because of the security policies. Eventually, he succeeded. In Billy's eyes, Bev was already a star and was somewhat bashful with his request. "Mr. Shea, your wonderful ministry in song seems so Spirit blest, I'd sure appreciate it if you'd prayerfully consider singing regularly on the *Songs In the Night* broadcasts."

"Well, Mr. Graham, I'm very heavily committed with other duties, but I sure enjoy your fellowship and the broadcasts. So how can I say no to you?"

Later Bev and Erma were impressed to learn that Billy and his wife Ruth had voluntarily consented to go without salary for a time, to help finance the initiation broadcasts. Joined by the King's Carolers, Bev was thrilled to open up with the Wendell Loveless composition "Songs In the Night," inspired by Job 35:10, "Where is God my maker who giveth songs in the night?"

Unfortunately for Bev, along with success and fulfillment, personal misfortune hit the tranquility of the Shea household. His beloved Erma was critically and suddenly struck with pernicious anemia. She was rushed to hospital and blood transfusions followed swiftly. For several days, the outcome was uncertain as friends and relations rallied around in practical and prayerful support. Bev praised God for answered prayer as she improved. Doctors then prescribed lots of fresh air and rest, the kind that could only be sensibly obtained by moving from an urban area into more country surroundings. Later, after befriending Billy and Ruth Graham, the Sheas decided to move to Western Springs, Illinois. Thus, they house-hunted with the helpful Grahams, although the Sheas were painfully aware that they had only about $500 surplus to spend. It was proving difficult, if not impossible, to find a residence that would suit their budget. Then thankfully, an old friend from New York, Will Ebner volunteered his help with a $2,500 loan. So the Sheas said goodbye to their Deming Place apartment in Chicago and hello to Western Springs. On the doorstep when the Sheas arrived, were their new friends, the Grahams, anxious to help the move go smoothly. In the evening, the Sheas and the Grahams ate supper in the Graham home in Hinsdale and joined in prayer to seek the Lord's blessing on the move and the future.

Providentially for Bev, Billy loved Bev's hymns on *Songs In the Night* and made another inquiry this time to obtain him as team soloist for his evangelistic meetings. That was the beginning of a long association between Bev and Billy that carried the gospel into the third millennium to every state in America and then to every continent on the planet. Thus at the age of thirty-one and twenty-one respectively, Bev met and became friends with Billy. Decades later, Bev remembers how striking a character he seemed to be even at that young age. "With a shock of blond hair and a winning smile, Billy was a young student from Wheaton College. Very clean-cut, there was something special about him, very much a Southern gentleman. Four years later, began the lengthy career as soloist for Dr. Graham's crusades, held since 1947. Often I'm asked whether Billy and I always were in harmony. I answer that question with the rhetorical question asked by Amos, the Old Testament prophet: 'Can two walk together, except they be agreed?'"

Since the very beginning of national and international acclaim, Bev has been Billy's chosen featured vocalist in crusades, radio shows and TV programs. He continued to record elegantly unpretentious traditional hymns and gospel songs for RCA that confounded music critics as he received increased air play. By the late forties, gospel music radio stations were plentiful, filling the crowded airways continually with the Christian message in both word and song. Bev considered that this Christian media explosion was a wholesome influence on society, making a positive social impact on morals. Many people now procured their soul food and spiritual drink, not only from the local church but also from the airways. Bev's sincerity, spontaneity and fervent expression of the Christian faith through song was increasingly appreciated.

Another lifelong friend, Cliff Barrows first met Bev in the summer of 1943 at the WMBI radio studios. Cliff says that by then Bev was a famous local radio star. Cliff was singing in a college quartet and was heading into his senior year of college. His mother had given him a copy of Bev's song "I'd Rather Have Jesus" when he went away to college. "I'd always hoped that I'd have the privilege of meeting Bev," Cliff recounts, "and now believe it or not, there I was standing next to him in the same studio.

How gracious and kind he was!" Neither Cliff nor Bev could have realized that this meeting would lead to a lifelong association in just a few short years.

God Bless Our Boys

In the conflict of World War II, after many initial tragic defeats and disappointments, the determined allies steadily accrued victories. During these days, Bev received many listener requests for special hymns and gospel songs that brought comfort and assurance for loved ones parted by the conflicts. The mail was filled with testimony after testimony of how his songs were agents of divine blessing. Often he'd finish broadcasts with the prayer-in-song written by Louis Paul Lehman entitled "God Bless Our Boys." The peace that Christians prayed for started to dawn in people's hearts. Newspaper headlines announced a first welcome victory, secured in North Africa, then in Europe, and finally, in the Far East. Ultimately in 1945, came the collapse and surrender of Nazi Germany followed a year later by the surrender of Japan forced by the dramatic impact of two atomic bombs. Bev and Erma headed to church to give thanks for the eagerly awaited victory and peace. Later, laughter and tears of joy were plentiful as the much missed normality of peacetime returned. Those discharged from military service and the returning prisoners of war gleefully rejoined their delighted communities. Bev could not fail to be affected by the dramas of those memorable days. Ominously, however, the dangerous atomic age had dawned with the Cold War.

BURNING BUSH

Billy Graham was born in Charlotte, North Carolina in 1918, the same month that World War I ended. As a youngster his job was to milk the family's cows but he loved sports, particularly baseball. His personal commitment to Christ came about as a result of a 'Burning Bush' experience—the visit to his hometown by the colorful evangelist, Mordecai Ham. Billy attended only one of Mr. Ham's tent meetings and immediately realized, under Holy Spirit conviction, that he was a sinner who needed Christ's forgiveness. His life changing decision for Christ was also to transform the direction of his life. He began preaching as a teenager, practicing on the poor cows in the fields. Sensing a divine call, he then began to study hard for the ministry and attended Wheaton College. To help pay his way through college, he became a top salesman for the Fuller Brush Company outselling all the other salesmen in the area! Following his graduation in 1943 he married beautiful Ruth Bell. Her father, Dr. Nelson Bell, was a creditable medical missionary to China for twenty-five years. Eventually, Billy became the pastor of a church in the suburbs of Chicago.

Bev noted that one of the characteristics of Billy's relationships with people down the years was his knack of easily being able to make lifelong friends even at the first encounter. At the close of World War II in Asheville, North Carolina, Billy met an aspiring 22-year-old song leader named Cliff Barrows at the Ben Lippen Bible Conference. Although on his honeymoon, Cliff was urged that day to conduct the singing for the youth night service at which Billy was to speak. This first surprising encounter is recalled by Billy with a smile, "Any doubts were instantly dispersed by his skill and sunny disposition! Aided by a fine voice, a trombone, and the piano playing of his beautiful wife, Billie, soon he had the audience singing to their fullest capability!"

Cliff became a lifelong confidante to both Billy and Bev. So began the historic association as Cliff, the song leader; Billy, the preacher; and Bev, the gospel singer, hit the road as an evangelistic trio. Their heartfelt quest endured more than half a century taking them worldwide. Charles H. Spurgeon, the famous Victorian Baptist minister of London, England was right when he said that, "It needs more skill than I can tell, to play the second fiddle well!" Perhaps, the trio's durability has been their individual willingness to play second fiddle to each other whenever necessary, never craving the center stage. Only eternity will reveal the full extent of their fruits! Many thousands bore grateful testimony to the life changing message the trio shared. Historically, when the trio teamed up together, a new chapter on church evangelism was to be written from that time.

EVER POSITIVE EXTERIOR

Bev enjoys giving great credit to his musical colleague. "Cliff's song leading expertise is world renowned but he is also a first class songwriter, a masterful MC, and an excellent preacher. He is a person of many abilities but on every continent of the globe it is as a song leader that he has taken to heart the most! He has single-mindedly devoted his time and effort into declaring the Good News via a wide variety of media varying from radio, television and movies to recordings, books and concerts."

With many decades of vast personal experience behind him, Bev is solidly confirmed in his view that he does not believe the twentieth century ever saw a more commanding song leader than his colleague, Cliff. With his proficiency in gospel music and his loyal devotion to the responsibility of worldwide evangelism, he has undoubtedly left his personal mark on history. Like Bev and Billy, never one to covet the limelight, Cliff would often repeat the lyrics of his famous choir song. "We in the Billy Graham team can't take any praise. In the words of the blind Victorian poet, Fanny Crosby, 'To God be the glory, great things He has done!'"

Bev says that Cliff's ever-positive exterior always contradicted his deep sensitivity and discernment. With his ever youthful looks, he was more than just a genial host and song leader. He was a loyal friend and confidante of both Billy and Bev. For the worldwide Billy Graham Missions, he was actually the leader until the evangelist himself stepped forward to discharge his gospel message. Able to oversee and display authority among his peers, he was fully equipped for his exacting responsibility.

Born on the sixth day of April in 1923 in the little town of Ceres, California, inappropriately named after Ceres, the pagan goddess of the harvest, Cliff's immediate family enjoyed a rural background. His dear father was a farmer, cherishing the soil and his undertakings in the fields. Boyhood days in the country held affectionate memories for Cliff as he remembered how he toiled alongside his father. "It was a precious time although I didn't think so at the time! As I reflect back in later life, I respect my dad's work ethic, his love of creation and his work in the fields of harvest and faithful labor for many years in several countries with the Gideon Ministry. His love has been a great challenge and inspiration to me!"

Conversion came at the age of eleven as Cliff responded to Christ in his local church. The preacher zeroed in on the necessity for everyone to personally identify with the "whosoever" of John 3:16. "For God so loved the world, that He gave His only begotten Son, that *whosoever* believeth in Him should not perish, but have everlasting life." In repentance and faith, Cliff says that he personally experienced God's salvation. Soon full-time Christian service beckoned that would extend, like his buddies Billy and Bev, to his sunset years. An enthusiast all his lifelong ministry, Cliff stated, "The Bible says, 'Sing unto the LORD; for he hath done excellent things: this is known in all the earth. Cry out and shout, thou inhabitant of Zion: for great is the Holy One of Israel in the midst of thee!' (Isaiah 12: 2-6). I believe that in history every great moving of the Spirit of God has been accompanied by great singing and I believe it always will be!"

Multi-talented, Cliff is also a quality songwriter as "May God's Blessing Surround You Each Day" demonstrates. Cliff dedicated his youth to the service of God and continued to spread the gospel into adulthood. He will be lovingly remembered for his choir leading and his powerfully effective narrative skills with scripture and poetry. One of Cliff's best known recited poems is the meaningful *The Touch of the Master's Hand*, also known as *The Old Violin* and popularized by cowboy movie star, Tex Ritter. He excelled too with great sing-a-long songs and hymns. Country singer George Hamilton IV, who recorded Cliff's "May God's Blessing Surround You Each Day" says, "How can anyone forget the wonderful, majestic melodies of praise that have personified the engaging Billy Graham missions of the second half of the twentieth century led by Cliff Barrows?"

As a lifetime co-worker, Billy summed his partner up well when he said, "Cliff's dedication and sincerity are immediately evident!

He gives Christ the chance to live out his life in Cliff, and the results in terms of Christian witness are wonderful to see!" The other lifetime co-worker with Cliff, his friend Bev says, "Publicly, Cliff's Christ-centered dedication to his song leading and choir directing ministry has given him a much deserved worldwide reputation. He was inducted into Nashville's Gospel Music Association Hall of Fame in 1988 and into the Religious Broadcasting Hall of Fame in 1996. Surely, a man of many skills, his winning smile and enthusiastic charm motivated millions to lift their voices in praise of God in song. His majestic choir sounds were great musical blessings. Privately, no one has helped me to relax and overcome my shyness on the platform like Cliff. His sincerity, warmth, grace and sense of humor have helped me time and time again."

FRIGHTENING CURVES

By 1945, travel for Barrows, Graham and Shea became more and more time consuming and routine. Bev also traveled to a series of meetings between Los Angeles and Seattle with preacher Bob Pierce, founder of the world-famous charity World Vision, and organist Don Hustad. Much of the exhausting tour was via the Greyhound bus system, riding all day to their next destination. On the stretch between Portland and Klamath Falls, Bev recalls that he struggled with sleep that night on the bus while Bob and Don slumbered sweetly. The mountainous terrain with its frightening curves was scary. He arrived weary and wrinkled hoping for a good breakfast, a hot shower and a comfortable bed to catch up on his sleep. Instead, within fifteen minutes, he was ushered swiftly to the local radio station for a live appearance.

Meanwhile, Torrey Johnson was facilitating the continued growth of the Youth For Christ organization. About this time, Billy was commissioned as an army lieutenant awaiting a position as a chaplain. Then in October 1944, he was struck down with a bad case of mumps that put him out of commission for about six weeks. But, thankfully, he was on the mend. Eventually, Billy was released from his army commitment in 1946. This freed him to go initially to twenty-seven towns and cities of the United Kingdom with Cliff Barrows for six exhausting months of 360 Youth For Christ meetings. This starting point would lead to decades of evangelistic service worldwide. Leaving the Sheas, the Billy Graham family found themselves on the move again, house hunting this time in Montreat, North Carolina. Their stay in Western Springs was extremely short despite the Sheas move to the same Chicago area.

That year, Bev's Father, 73-year-old Reverend Adam Shea was by then too frail to stand in the pulpit. Reluctantly, he decided that it was time to retire. But before he left he delivered a farewell sermon to which the large group of extended family members were invited. The eventful day came and Reverend Shea bravely mounted the platform to deliver his final message while seated. Although the flesh was evidently weak, the fire and anointing were still there. Before another year expired, the beloved warrior was, as the Salvationists often say, promoted to glory!

People often commented as they have watched Bev that he never attempted to draw attention to himself even when performing. Asked about it, Bev replied, "I came to the Crusades at a terrific period of shyness in my life. When I would sing, I would have to hang on the pulpit and just do the best that I could. My parents had taught all eight of us Shea children not to put ourselves forward. So I just have never had a desire to do that."

Prominent preacher and teacher, Charles Swindoll stated at the end of the twentieth century that the longevity of the working relationship between Bev, Billy and Cliff was outstanding. He said that it was just about unique in any sphere of activity, religious or secular. He paid tribute to the trio's creditable integrity and evident deep commitment to each other.

Honor In His Hometown

In November of 1947, the age old question about whether a prophet has any honor in his hometown was addressed. The answer was a resounding yes. The evangelistic trio, Graham, Barrows and Shea, boldly went to Billy's hometown of Charlotte, North Carolina to witness for three weeks of evangelism in the first of their city-wide crusades. They won many friends in the process. By later standards of the Graham team, Bev remembers that the attendance numbers were modest at the armory. "The ministry started so small, about 2,000 to 3,000 but it was a great privilege for me to sing songs centering on the person of Christ. My first solo was "I Will Sing the Wondrous Story." Among my fondest memories are those wonderful meetings."

Joining them in the work was one of Billy's old classmates, Grady Wilson. The meetings soon outgrew the First Baptist Church premises on Tryon Street and were, therefore, moved to the armory. The milestone event introduced Bev to a man who became one of his precious lifelong friends, a meeting of kindred hearts. Arthur Smith in his strong Southern accent remembers, "Although I was familiar with his singing, the first time I heard George Beverly Shea in person, was at the Billy Graham Charlotte Crusade—the first one. I heard him sing and we became close family friends in 1947."

A great professional showman, Arthur invited Bev to sing on his popular secular radio show. An established singer, songwriter and instrumentalist on the RCA and MGM record labels, Arthur was known professionally as Arthur "Guitar Boogie" Smith. The "Guitar Boogie" nickname came after his celebrated instrumental hit that was country music's first million-selling instrumental. In Europe, it was popularized by the English guitarist, Bert Weedon in the early rock 'n roll years of the late fifties. Born on April Fools' Day, the first day of April 1921 in Clinton, South Carolina and raised in nearby Kershaw, Arthur was a multi-instrumentalist and record producer. Bev recalls that years later, many prominent country and Christian artists came under his skilled studio direction. Arthur also penned and recorded "Dueling Banjos" under its original, legitimate title of "Feudin' Banjos" on MGM. He auspiciously validated claim of the tune, winning an important litigation dispute with the makers of the Hollywood movie, *Deliverance*, which was used without any permission.

Arthur later owned a quality recording studio on Sardis Road in Charlotte that gave Bev some backing on an album released on the Homeland label. Side-stepping the magnetic tug of Nashville, by the time that Bev met Arthur, he was a hugely successful business person in the North Carolina area with radio interests and coast to coast TV. He also fronted his Crossroads Quartet and Crackerjack Band for many years. A quality songwriter, many country and gospel artists utilized the Smith repertoire consistently.

For many years along with the legendary Hank Williams Senior, Arthur shared top billing on the prestigious MGM record label. Among his best known songs are "Acres of Diamonds," "The Shadow of a Cross," "You Are the Finger of God," "The Fourth Man" and "I Saw a Man." Bev is fully aware that many big time artists recorded Arthur's tunes including the Statler Brothers, Pat Boone, Johnny Cash, Connie Smith, George Hamilton IV, Paul Wheater and the Blackwood Brothers. Indeed, Bev knew that he could rely on Arthur's songs to be based on scripture so he recorded almost twenty-five of his songs over the years. For all these years, Arthur was well-known locally as a conservative Baptist and a Sunday school teacher. Although a household name as a TV star on WBTV aired from Charlotte, in his home town Baptist church he was sincerely motivated in evangelism. Bev developed a high regard for Arthur and his wife, Dorothy. In short, he respected Arthur's renown as not only a fine entertainer but also as an outstanding Christian gentleman.

MONTANA SNOWSTORM

After the Charlotte Crusade, invitations to the Billy Graham team proliferated and Bev joined them for about three campaigns a year while still maintaining his *Club Time* radio broadcasting duties in Chicago. By the late forties, the name George Beverly Shea was fast becoming revered nationally for his sincere interpretation of hymns and gospel songs on radio and at the Billy Graham meetings. From those busy days, the local Assemblies of God music leader and internationally known steel guitarist Bud Tutmarc of Washington remembered Bev accordingly. "By the end of the forties, George Beverly

Shea was already a much beloved Christian singer of the truths of God's Word. His performances were always a blessing because listeners sensed that his singing came from his heart, not just from his vocal chords and mind. His singing of the great hymns and his self-penned songs richly blessed millions leaving a lasting impressive legacy."

Big Bud remembers well his interesting first meeting with Bev. "Our first meeting was back in 1948 or 1949 when my Harmony Quartet was asked to fill in at a Friday night service because the train bringing Bev and Billy Graham to Seattle was stalled in a Montana snowstorm. We did the music for the service and then went to the train station at midnight and picked Bev up and drove him to his hotel. His singing has always been a blessing to me. To reach a listener's heart, the singer must sing from his heart. Bev's singing of great hymns like "Great Is Your Faithfulness" was always from the heart, making lasting impressions upon me and others!"

Back home in Western Springs, Bev was delighted when Erma presented him with a bouncing baby boy on February 11, 1948 whom they named Ronald. Later the couple prayerfully decided that they should also adopt a girl. Gladly, they welcomed Elaine, nicknamed Lainie, into their growing family circle as their adopted daughter. She was two years younger than her brother Ronald who was soon nicknamed Ronnie. The original Shea duo of Bev and Erma was, therefore, within a couple of years a quartet. Busier than ever, that year Bev was back on the road to places as diverse as Augusta, Georgia; Altoona, Pennsylvania; and Modesto, California, close to Cliff Barrows' birthplace.

MODESTO MANIFESTO

While the Graham team was holding evangelistic meetings in Modesto, Billy decided to meet with Cliff, Bev and Grady Wilson. They prayerfully determined a binding team policy on how they personally conduct themselves and their meetings. Their sincere desire was to be completely above reproach in the public eye. Before their time, mass evangelism had not always maintained a creditable reputation. The uncomplimentary Burt Lancaster movie portrayal of Elmer Gantry in the early fifties illustrated the way many people perceived matters. The Billy Graham Evangelistic Association (BGEA) was formed accordingly to provide the team with an agreed constitution of stability and accountability. The team's resulting Modesto Manifesto, while not written down as a formal document, became the accepted standard for accountability that the team followed.

Resolutions covered the important matters of honesty, integrity, purity and humility. In unison they agreed that no communications to the media and to the churches would be inflated or exaggerated. The size of crowds and numbers of inquirers would not be embellished for the sake of making the Billy Graham Evangelistic Association look better. Financial matters would be regularly audited and submitted to a board of directors for review and facilitation of expenditures. Every local crusade would maintain an open book policy and publish a record of where and how monies were spent. Members of the team would pay close attention to avoiding temptation, never being alone with a woman and remaining accountable to one another. Wives would be kept informed of team activities and often attend and feel a part of the crusades. Members of the team resolved to never speak negatively of another Christian minister, regardless of his denominational affiliation or differing theological views and practices. The team said that the mission of evangelism included *strengthening* the Body of Christ as well as *building* it.

At the time, the team's bold stand was a unique position, recognized widely by the skeptical media who regularly sought their opinion on topics that affected contemporary living. In the decades since, in spite of the considerable pressures of constant, transparent fish bowl existence, with God's grace, they were able to live out almost unaffected lives. They managed to say just the right things and maintain just the right balance at all times. Against tremendous odds, over seven decades, they achieved enviable public respect from both the media and society as a whole. The unique longevity of their successful association is the very stuff of which it can be said, legends are generated.

So how does Bev in particular keep his feet on the ground, acutely aware of the real world? He is, of course, no super hero! He does not pretend to know everything or have the answer to all of life's problems. But he readily and publicly declares that he knows One who does! This is the open secret of how he maintained his common touch and balanced perspective. Bev was never one to be bulldozed. Seeking good solid foundational Bible teaching and wise counsel from mature Christians, Bev's decisions about his career were based on the premise that God wanted him to remain out of the secular music world. "My first calling is to sing about Jesus and the change that He can bring to a life. I love to talk and sing about Him when I get the chance to do so! My privilege is to carry and raise the Christian flag in places where it might not otherwise be seen. I never say that I am a Christian entertainer!

In the words of the scripture, we are challenged to let our light so shine before men that they may see our good works and glorify our Father which is in heaven!" The sound, godly advice received before and after his conversion proved robust enough to weather all the storms subsequent years inevitably brought. Many others in the public eye who said that they found faith in God fell flat on their faces because of immaturity, fickleness and poor advice. Against huge odds, George Beverly Shea demonstrably managed to grow spiritually mature on the public stage and walk worthily in his Christian vocation.

CATAPULTED TO FAME

By the latter forties, the fledgling evangelistic trio worked together in increasingly larger missions after Charlotte. In September 1949 came the famous Los Angeles tent meetings that catapulted Dr. Graham and his associates, including Bev to national media attention.

It was a short cab ride to the tent pitched at the junction of Washington Boulevard and Hill Street. It became known as the Canvas Cathedral. Once inside the unpretentious tent, he was rushed through his cues with Cliff and the instrumentalists. The choir performed magnificently as the minutes ticked by before the lights and press cameras flashed on this clean cut Canadian chosen to sing before the preacher spoke.

It was Billy's first major city crusade and overnight the team trio was making national headlines. It caught the attention of James Blackwood of the Blackwood Brothers in far off Memphis. He told me, "The meetings were headline news even in the South. Apparently, the famed newspaper publisher William Randolph

Hearst in Los Angeles was so impressed by the Billy Graham phenomenon that he gave the instruction to all his newspapers to 'puff Graham' nationwide! That meant provide positive nationwide media publicity!"

Because of the fruitful success, the three weeks of LA meetings were extended to eight weeks and Bev sang every evening. Then he was traveling by a DC-4 airplane between LA and Chicago on a weekly basis to do his *Club Time* broadcast on ABC radio network coast to coast. "It was most exhausting," Bev commented, "but very worthwhile!" Bev was pleased too that his wife Erma and young son Ron were able to join him in LA.

News of Billy's powerful evangelistic preaching spread to every corner of the US, and even abroad. Invitations came in swiftly for crusades in Boston, Massachusetts; Columbia, South Carolina; and Portland, Oregon. That same year the *Hour of Decision*, named by Ruth Graham, was broadcast. Grady Wilson, Billy's childhood friend and now close buddy, read the scriptures on that first broadcast. Cliff hosted, Bev sang and, of course, Billy preached.

Attracted to the hyped newspaper publicity of the LA event was the locally well-known cowboy singer, Stuart Hamblen. Born on October 20, 1908 in Kellyville, Texas, he was about the same age as Bev. As Stuart grew, he loved the freedom of the open Texas range and the songs of the cowboys. Show business beckoned and soon he was making a name for himself as a very popular singer on the west coast radio circuit. He came to great broadcasting fame in the thirties and forties during the golden age of Hollywood's singing cowboys. Movie stars such as Gene Autry, Roy Rogers, John Wayne, Tex Ritter, Rex Allen, and Randolph Scott were his close buddies. He rode alongside with them in their movies usually playing one of the bad guys. Songs such as "Remember Me, I'm the One Who Loves You," "Texas Plains," and "My Mary" penned by Big Stu became established standards. Indeed, Hamblen material was regular repertoire for all the silver screen cowboys, the country stars of Nashville, and the great crooners of the time.

Stuart's dear long-suffering wife, Suzy knew that tempting passions led Big Stu into various moral pitfalls. She prayed that somehow he would be convicted in his conscience of his sin and waywardness of life. Intrigued by publicity, he attended a Graham meeting. Angrily stomping out of the tent, he initially responded to Billy's call to repentance by literally shaking his fist in the face of the young blonde evangelist from the hills of North Carolina. Troubled, unable to sleep that night and deeply challenged in his conscience, Big Stu eventually decided to yield to the claims of Christ. In the middle of the night he phoned asking Billy to pray and counsel with him. The Graham Crusade and the Hamblen conversion hit the national headlines. As far as Stuart was concerned, his friends and foes were bitterly cynical! *How long would it last?* was their question. Bev recalls with a smile, "But last it did! Into old age. The Hamblen lifestyle was radically converted, changed dramatically for the better."

In latter years, Stuart wrote quality sacred songs such as "How Big is God," "Until Then," "Known Only To Him," "My Religion's Not Old Fashioned," and "He Bought My Soul at Calvary." Top personalities including Elvis Presley, Tennessee Ernie Ford, Kate Smith, Stu Phillips, Pat Boone, Slim Whitman, Jo Stafford, Hank Snow and many others recorded the songs. His best known composition was "This Old House" that hit the charts on both sides of the Atlantic, decades apart via Hollywood's Rosemary Clooney and Wales' Shakin' Stevens. Movie star John Wayne gave his friend Stuart the idea for the song "It is No Secret." While they sauntered together down Hollywood Boulevard, John turned and smiling broadly at his friend said, "Say, Stuart, what's this I hear about you hitting the Billy Graham sawdust trail?"

"Oh, John my ole buddy, it's sure no secret what God can do! What he's done for this ole cowboy, he can do for you!"

With the well-known, broad beaming smile widening, Wayne narrowed his eyes and spoke in all seriousness in his familiar deep tones. "Stu, you need to write a song about it, Pilgrim!"

That night back home, as the chimes of his grandfather clock struck midnight, Stuart later told Bev that he was creatively inspired. Taking pen to paper, words and music of "It is No Secret" came to him with ease as he sang over to himself. "The chimes of time ring out the news another day is through. Someone slipped and fell. Was that someone you? It is no secret what God can do! What He's done for others He'll do for you !"

From 1949 to his death decades later, Stuart became a dear friend to Bev and the team. Since those days, top class acts recorded from the Hamblen songbook including Sir Cliff Richard and Mahalia Jackson. Significantly, Bev notes that his friends Bill and Gloria Gaither devoted a complete album to Hamblen material. Rarely—if ever—does one find songwriters of Gaither status hailing another song writing legend. In the era of austerity in the fifties when Western Europe was still recovering from the economic crisis of World War II, UK Prime Minister Harold Wilson's government legislated for the outlawing of the transfer export of British money in large quantities across UK borders.

This curtailed the payment of European song royalties to Stuart in the US for the sales of product such as Rosemary Clooney's "This Old House," plus the Elvis Presley and Bev Shea versions of "It is No Secret." In response, he told me that he purchased several brand new Rolls-Royce limousines in England with UK royalty money. He then duly shipped the cars to the US where he resold them at a handsome profit thus circumventing the British government's decree. On another occasion, he demanded an answer of the BBC bosses as to why they refused to broadcast his hit Christian songs on national programming. They replied that as his songs mentioned God by name so often, that made them unusable by the BBC broadcasters. Stuart's comical but pointed retort was, "Does that mean that you no longer sing your national anthem, 'God Save the Queen'?"

After his song successes, Stuart and his wife Suzy settled in the Hollywood Hills in a mansion that they purchased from the Hollywood heartthrob, Errol Flynn. Mrs. Hamblen said jokingly that, throughout her life, she had to compete with Big Stu's horse for Stuart's affections. She told me when his dear horse finally died, he insisted on burying the mare in the front garden of their mansion, against the wishes of the neighbors, the environmental health officials, and the police. After heated debates, they relented and, according to Suzy, the cowboy's will prevailed.

Singspiration Recordings

After those early Los Angeles meetings, soon Billy Graham was receiving invitations to travel all over the world. In the years that followed he met with kings and queens and prime ministers and presidents of many countries as he presented the gospel message. The Billy Graham Evangelistic Association was duly consolidated and later created Worldwide Pictures to produce Christian movies followed by *Decision Magazine.*

Predictably, the first Shea album sessions were clearly reflective of his personal taste, but he saw that the songs were of sufficient quality to outlive the generation that produced them. The dictionary describes a classic as a work of lasting quality. Among the ranks of inspirational music are some outstanding works and performances that justly deserve more than a place on the archive shelves of the great recording companies gathering dust. Indeed, scriptural history documents that man's longest lasting songs are about God. At the dawn of the new millennium, Bev surely found it hard to believe that the first of his many records were minted way back in the Cold War days of the late forties and early fifties.

He is aware that history's irrepressible advances will condemn the vast majority of mankind's art and industry to be lost forever in the sands of subsequent generations. But Bev's recording legacy has had a timeless quality from the beginning, as his *Singspiration* archives show. He sought to subjectively and objectively select his special inspirational songs on merit, those deserving of longevity. Remembering his mother, father and home, he chose "Singing I Go" and "I'd Rather Have Jesus." The Negro spiritual heritage was represented by "Roll, Jordan Roll." Through the succeeding years many of the other fairly new songs became associated with the Bev Shea contribution to the Graham missions such as "The Love of God," "He the Pearly Gates Will Open," "Jesus Whispers Peace" and "God Leads Us Along." Also represented were favorites associated with Homer

Rodeheaver, such as "Then Jesus Came," and Ira Sankey, such as "The Ninety and Nine."

On a trip to England in 1949, Bev recalled hearing about how "The Ninety and Nine" had its start. In Victorian times, evangelist Dwight L. Moody and his gospel soloist Ira Sankey were riding the steam train one cold crisp morning from Glasgow to Edinburgh. Stopping briefly at a station for more passengers, Ira took the opportunity to hop off the train to buy the morning newspaper from a platform newspaper stand. Back in his train seat, browsing through the pages of the paper, his eyes became transfixed on a new poem entitled *The Ninety And Nine* by Elizabeth Clephane. Touched by the theme, he clipped the section out and put it into his wallet. That evening, Mr. Moody's exciting public sermon was based on the Good Shepherd. Once the message was over he turned to Ira for a suitable closing song as an altar call. Pulling the newspaper clipping from his wallet, he placed it on his folding harmonium. Breathing a prayer, he struck up the chord of A flat and began to sing. Divinely anointed, the tune came to him as he sang. Tears flowed freely from both Moody and Sankey and from many in the audience. It was the time for the evangelist to give the invitation to the lost sheep to return to the Great Shepherd of their souls. Years later, in 1955 when the Graham team visited Scotland, he and Cliff visited the Carrubbers Close Mission in Edinburgh. There Bev was invited to play the very harmonium that Ira Sankey played so long ago. It was presented to the Americans as a gift and is today on show in the museum of the Billy Graham organization in North America.

SOFT SPOT FOR ORGANS

Back at home in Chicago, Bev's continuing passion for organs was infectious. It even indoctrinated and excited Erma at times. One morning just after breakfast, Bev perusing the small ads in the Chicago Tribune, spoke up as Erma cleared the table of the coffee cups. "Say, honey! There's a guy here in the paper who lives on the north side of Chicago wanting to sell some reed organs. What do you think about seeing what he has?"

Erma smiled knowingly at Bev and answered positively, happy to indulge her husband's soft spot for organs. The old man's basement was an Aladdin's Cave of reed organs. What caught Bev's eye immediately was an Estey—the same model that he played for Asa's funeral at Ottawa's Fifth Avenue Church. Sitting at the majestic instrument, he surprised the old man with his spontaneous rendition of "Safe In the Arms of Jesus."

"Mr. Shea, the instrument is yours for $65!"

The prized possession was installed in the Shea basement and became the source of great musical fulfillment and satisfaction.

Chapter 6

How Great Thou Art
1950-1957

"I know no one who has tried harder to attain perfection in his work and all facets of his life. To my way of thinking, he has come close! I'm proud to be his friend."
—Chet Atkins, Nashville, Tennessee

ONE MOTIVE MUSICIAN

The Billy Graham team was joined in 1950 by the skilled Canadian pianist, Tedd Smith. He was followed into the team by a succession of organists. Loren Whitney, Paul Mickelson, Don Hustad, John Innes, Bill Fasig and Ted Cornell provided additional accompaniment in the succeeding decades. Slim and quiet in disposition, virtuoso Tedd was clear about his Christian motivation. "The ministry I have as a musician has one motive—to constantly praise and honor our Lord Jesus Christ through my musical instrument. No matter what the mood—be it happy, solemn, or meditative—it is because of Him and for Him that I will praise Him."

Born in London, Ontario, Tedd began his piano studies at the early age of five with Marjorie Dudgeon and later with Dr. Harvey Robb. When he was nine-years-old he won the first prize gold medal in piano at the Peel Music Festival in Canada. He later continued his musical education at Toronto's Royal Conservatory of Music with the distinguished Canadian teacher, Mona Bates. Before joining the Billy Graham team, he was director of music at Toronto's Avenue Road Church and at the Youth for Christ rallies in the same city. He also directed several vocal ensembles and a five-piano group. Residents of Silver Springs, Maryland, Tedd and his wife Thelma parented Howard and Glenn. Bev states, "Tedd had so much musical ability, he could easily have progressed in a classical concert career if that had been his choice. He chose instead to faithfully serve his Lord in the fulfillment of the Great Commission. He's been a blessing to millions. I've known him longer than any other musician in the crusade work and I take joy in his longtime friendship and support."

A London native, Colin Simpson is now a busy church pianist in the old English town of Dunstable. Back in 1954, Colin was a shy but impressionable young teenager at the time of the London Crusade. He recalls Tedd Smith with particular interest. "I first heard Tedd Smith accompanying Bev Shea when, at the time, two piano teachers had given up on me as being useless at playing the piano. But the remarkable thing was when I heard Mr. Smith I realized that I understood the harmonics of his keyboard style. It was from then that I went on to play for many decades in church services and in larger Christian rallies. If it had not been for the Smith and Shea team, I would not have my interest in music today.

So I owe them a great gratitude. In the mid-sixties I wrote to Tedd at his New York home and told him so!"

To his credit, Tedd has completed at least five albums for RCA Victor, six for Word and Light and seven for other labels. He has written thirty-two piano arrangement publications and several movie music scores.

Joining Tedd in London, England in 1954 as the London Crusade organist was Paul Mickelson. An ordained minister, he was born in California and began studying the piano at the age of eleven and the organ at fifteen. He started his gospel music career in his teens and rose to soloing at New York's Radio City Music Hall. From organist for the Graham crusades he went on to become the president of his own record company Supreme Records. His wife, Jo served as producer for many of his big orchestration recordings. Following Paul, down the decades came other fine organists including Loren Whitney, Don Hustad and John Innes.

His Master's Voice

The BGEA radio broadcast, *The Hour Of Decision* debuted on the air on December 5, 1950 initially via 150 stations. It received a staggering 178,000 letters in its first year. George Beverly Shea's apt repertoire choice on that first broadcast was "I'd Rather Have Jesus." By then his bass-baritone singing was fast becoming well known from coast to coast, live booking invitations increased in multitude. In the early fifties, he appeared in an exciting Christian event at Philadelphia's Convention Hall. It also included his new cowboy friend from LA, Stuart Hamblen. Next day in the hotel coffee shop over breakfast, Bev and Big Stu chatted enthusiastically about their music. "Tell me Bev," Stuart asked, "what's your recording situation? Are you signed to any label yet? In my view, you ought to be! Did you know that Paul Barkmeier, Vice President of RCA was impressed by your songs last night?"

The now legendary RCA Victor producer, Steve Sholes was astutely responsible for bringing a very wide and impressive range of talent to his RCA Victor label during the forties, fifties and sixties. Sholes scouted popular talent that included Harry Belafonte, Stuart Hamblen, Perry Como, Hank Snow, Eddy Arnold, Chet Atkins, the Blackwood Brothers, and Elvis Presley among many others! Born in Washington DC, the Sholes family moved to Camden, New Jersey when Steve's dad secured employment with the Victor Talking Machine Company. As a youth, Steve experimented with the clarinet and saxophone and joined the Radio Corporation of America (RCA) in 1929 as a part-time messenger, the same year that it took over the Victor record label. In 1933 he graduated with a degree from Rutgers University and in 1936 he initially acquired a clerk's job in the record department because of his musical interests followed by a job in recording. Victor's Eli Oberstein embarked young Steve down jazz tracks. At the time, the label was recording jazz greats such as Sidney Betchet, Mezz Mezzrow and Jelly Roll Morton. Steve soon followed with Dizzy Gillespie, Earl Hines and Coleman Hawkins.

In 1939, Victor's vice president, Frank Walker asked the portly Steve to set up portable recording equipment in a hot stuffy Atlanta hotel room with a sound engineer for auditions. World War II followed and Steve honed his recording ability with recordings aimed at the military serving overseas in combat. Later when

Frank Walker left RCA, Steve shouldered the responsibility of the folk and race division of the company under Eli Oberstein.

In 1951, aware of Bev's growing international fame and potential, Steve Sholes contacted him saying that he would like to sign him up. It was a unique offer for a Christian soloist to be presented with such an inviting deal and opportunity from secular origins! This was doubly amazing, remembering Bev's personal aversion to and stand against all things that seemed like show biz.

Since world peace and freedom were reestablished in 1946, some Christian artists modestly did custom recordings for their own labels, but the practice was still rare in the gospel music field. None of them were on secular labels. The RCA Victor pact was not only a major boost to Bev's career but also for Christian music as a whole! It gave positive, evangelistic exposure to America and beyond via the vast RCA marketing network. It was a dream come true for Bev. Bev pioneered the way for other gospel artists including Cliff Barrows, the Billy Graham Choirs plus Chet Atkins, Perry Como, and many more. But the Bev Shea gospel recordings were among the first!

HISTORIC RCA RECORDINGS

RCA emissaries Sam Wallace and Elmer Eades were dispatched to meet Bev in Atlanta and over a business lunch offered him a recording contract. Before accepting, he politely told the two gentlemen that he would first discuss the matter with his BGEA colleagues. They must have agreed because recording commenced in the spring of 1951 with the Walter Winterhalter Orchestra. Bev's first two ten-inch LP albums for RCA Victor were entitled *Beautiful Garden of Prayer* and *Evening Vespers*.

These first historical RCA recordings were captured with the best equipment of the day, yet compared to modern equipment, it was basic. Steve Sholes presided and each album boasted arrangements that were perfected before the session. On *Evening Vespers* several beloved British hymns were paraded including John Newton's "Amazing Grace," George Matheson's "O Love That Wilt Not let me Go," and Joseph Scriven's "What A Friend We Have in Jesus." From more modern North American sources came "The Old Rugged Cross," "Life's Railway to Heaven," and "When They Ring the Golden Bells." The restful album *Beautiful Garden Of Prayer* soon followed with fairly country material such as Homer Rodeheaver's "Sunrise" and "Farther Along." "Farther Along" was a true standard in Southern gospel territory. It was originally credited as being sung by the Burnett Sisters, a ladies act from Texas. In 1940 after the Blackwood Brothers sang in a high school in Greentop, Missouri, James Blackwood was introduced to the real writer. He was Reverend WB Stevens, an elderly Methodist minister. After that proper credit was given. Also on the album was Thomas Dorsey's "Take My Hand, Precious Lord" from the black-gospel arena.

Bev learned later that Thomas Dorsey was ten years his senior, born on July 1, 1899. He was raised in poverty in rural Georgia. The state in many quarters still resented and begrudged the freedom from slavery granted to his parents following the Civil War. When he left his deprived boyhood home, he rubbed shoulders with some of the legendary blues and jazz artists of his day such as Bessie Smith. Morally, he struggled between such unwholesome influences and the pull of the Holy Spirit. Finally, he surrendered to heaven's claim on his wayward life. Later as the pastor of a Chicago church, he wrote "Take My Hand Precious Lord." The song came from his personal experience of tragedy. Booked to go to a St. Louis church meeting, upon his arrival after his long journey he was given the devastating news of the death of his dear wife in painful childbirth. Heartbroken, he immediately drove homewards arriving back only to receive another blow. The newborn baby had also died. Greatly distressed he drove aimlessly around the streets of the big city as he musically conceived, under divine guidance, the now renowned prayer in song, "Take My Hand Precious Lord." The composition is accepted today as standard fare with plentiful recordings available.

SAFE IN THE FOLD

Bev was aware that down through the years, the Christian influence on RCA boss, Steve Sholes was considerable in view of the lineup of Christians that he signed up. He was not a tough talking businessman but a true gentleman and a fine musician in his own right.

His prime task, of course, was to ensure that RCA made acceptable profits after paying musicians, vocalists, arrangers, songwriters and such. Many years after Steve signed him up, Bev enjoys recounting the event when, at a Billy Graham meeting in Pittsburgh, he was informed that Steve had responded to the evangelist's call. It had taken many years for the gospel seeds to germinate. Years later in New York, Bev attended a testimonial celebration in honor of Steve's twenty-five years in the industry that the National Association of Recording Arts and Sciences organized. In attendance were many notable RCA artists including

Eddy Arnold. The next day in Steve's office, Steve commented favorably on Bev's soulful and regal version of Fanny Crosby's "Safe In The Arms Of Jesus," just produced. Radiantly smiling, Steve indicated to his pleased Canadian friend that the lyrics reminded him that he was personally now safe in the fold! Bev remembers well his mixed feelings when later he heard of the heart attack and death of Steve on Monday April 22, 1968, at the age of fifty-seven. Steve was driving from Nashville's Metropolitan Airport to a meeting at the Country Music Foundation when the heart attack came as he crossed the Silliman Memorial Bridge. In Australia at the time, Bev heard of his friend's sudden death. "I received the cable in Sydney, during the Australian Crusade, which told me of Steve's passing. Surely, I thought, remembering the day in his office, Steve Sholes is indeed, now safe in the arms of Jesus!"

Astute Choice of Songs

Released in 1955, the repertoire choice for the 12-inch album entitled *Inspirational Songs* conducted by heavy-set, serious-faced Hugo Winterhalter was heartwarming. Originally a saxophone player from Pennsylvania, he was a hit maker for the Columbia label in 1949 with "Blue Christmas." A year later he was lured to RCA by his friend Joe Csida. Soon Hugo was making hits in the RCA studios for Eddie Fisher, Perry Como and Eddy Arnold. He specialized in the lush, relaxed sounds of multiple French horns, cellos, violas, saxophones and such, plus rhythm and vocal chorus backing. Hugo's outstanding talents were now focused on George Beverly Shea.

Diverse and challenging, *Inspirational Songs* included "It Took a Miracle" penned by John W. Peterson and popularized by the evangelist Percy Crawford in Philadelphia. Unaccompanied, Bev sang the Christmas spiritual lullaby "Sweet Little Jesus Boy" by Robert MacGinsey. Also included was some popular twentieth century hymnology "Ivory Palaces," written by Henry Barraclough in 1915 after hearing Wilbur Chapman preach in Montreat, North Carolina, and "In The Garden," written by C. Austin Miles in 1912.

Without doubt, the ditty, "He" was early-fifties inspirational hit material initially sung by Al Hibbler. Despite the rhythm, bounce and marketability of Bev's rich commercial sound, there was never any conscious effort by him or RCA in those days to attempt to impact what was then known as the Hit Parade. With hindsight that now seems surprising for several reasons. Firstly, in view of the national publicity given at the time to the Billy Graham team. Secondly, there was a definite grassroots popularity for some of Bev's inspirational songs like "How Great Thou Art." Lastly, the public was not averse to making inspirational songs into hits. Included in Bev's LP session were two newer sacred songs associated with Billy Graham soon to become all–time favorites: "It Is No Secret" and "How Great Thou Art."

"Lead Me, Guide Me" was an interesting inclusion by the then unknown new writer, Doris Akers. Bev remembers decades later in the nineties, just prior to her death, Doris Akers was still displaying her great senses of vitality and humor. In a live *Homecoming Friends* taping of her songs, she playfully pushed the host Bill Gaither from the piano stool, replacing him with herself. There amid light-hearted banter and laughter, she showed Bill and the amused cast how her songs were intended to be sung. Throughout the years her songs received hundreds of interpretations ranging from Bev to Elvis Presley to Pat Boone to the Statesmen. For many years, she made her home in Columbus, Ohio although she was born on May 21, 1922 in Brookfield, Missouri, one of ten children. As a child she enjoyed music and poetry, writing her first gospel song when she was merely ten years old. Despite her lack of any formal training, Doris learned her skillful trade the hard way but, she said the best way was by practical experience.

Now an established and respected RCA Victor artist, Bev's program of hymns, sponsored by *Club Aluminum*, was broadcast from 1946-1953. *Songs In The Night* began in 1944 with Don Hustad as organist and is still being broadcast under the auspices of Chicago's Moody Church with the current organist John Innes. Now free to become even more committed to the BGEA, Bev was busier than ever. He was heard more constantly on radio, both nationally and internationally via the Billy Graham programs. From the first thirteen weeks, *The Hour Of Decision* was broadcast on ABC network and on TV slots across the nation. With Cliff Barrows, the music of Bev and Crusade choirs, and the preaching of Billy, the show continually reached record-breaking audiences.

In these early days, as the crusades moved from Washington DC to Memphis to Dallas to Detroit, Bev started to rub shoulders with many personalities from the Southern gospel field. The outspoken singer and preacher, Hovie Lister of the Statesmen Quartet used to laughingly joke that "God never intended for Christianity to sing the blues or wear a long face." The Statesmen recorded for RCA Victor, the same label as Bev. Hovie recalled with a smile his Quartet's spirited back up vocals on Bev's lead version of Stuart Hamblen's "Open Up Your Heart and Let The Sunshine In" and Doy Ott's "Mercy Lord." In the mid-1990s, Hovie arranged for each prison in Georgia to have copies of the *Bill Gaither Homecoming* videos in the library for prisoners to check out and hear. At the time of his death, he was involved in a project to have videos in each parole office for parolees to check out and take home for their families to hear. On the Saturday night before his death, Hovie called some friends together to a favorite eating spot and ended the evening by playing and singing "He Touched Me." It was his last performance. He died of leukemia on December 28, 2001 at age seventy-five.

MANY WONDERFUL STORIES

In the fifties, living in Western Springs, Illinois, Bev was deeply in love with his wife and devoted to his ten-year-old son, Ronnie and eight-year old daughter, Elaine. His only lament in being on the Graham team was being away from home so much of the time. Now he was on the road for so long doing such great distances. Down through the years he was asked often whether this was a struggle for the family. "Well, the children always seemed to accept it. They said good-bye warmly always knowing that dad would be coming back. In the old days, of course, we'd be away longer than we were in later days. Back then we'd be away a month at a time but the family coped well. Once I remember my son Ronald saying, 'Why can't you come home every day like Jimmy's father does?' I explained to him what I was doing helping Billy. He was about six at the time. I asked him if he wanted me to resign with Mr. Graham and go home every day. He replied, 'No dad, please stay with Uncle Billy!'"

Whenever possible, however, Erma and the family joined Bev on the tours. He recalls particularly how they were with him through the British Crusades of 1954 to 1955. He says jokingly that he sang a little better when they were there with him. He says, "I have warm memories of the Greater London Crusade gatherings at Harringay in 1954. The meetings lasted for nearly three months and we speak of those days so much. Cliff, pianist Tedd Smith and all of us were so taken with the way the English people sang. They would put their heads back and really sing out on hymns such as 'To God Be the Glory'."

These crusades were the real beginning of the BGEA Team's expansion into a worldwide ministry. Now a key Anglican minister in Central London, The Reverend Richard Bewes remembers the spiritual influence of those dizzy days. "I first saw George Beverly Shea in action at the great Harringay mission when I was a teenager. He and Cliff Barrows and Billy Graham were like film stars to us young people. I went night after night to Harringay—which was as formative an influence for my future ministry as anything else in my life."

Cliff was now well established as BGEA choir director, platform MC and radio director. He recalls, "The Harringay statistics are impressive—more than two million attended and 30,000 people registered as becoming Christians. A choir of 4,000 voices sang for twelve weeks backing up Bev at times."

Interestingly, many heard the crusade meetings in venues other than Harringay such as the White City Stadium, Trafalgar Square and a mass rally in Hyde Park on Good Friday. Five hundred scattered auditoriums heard the team via the old World War II telephone land lines that were installed throughout the UK as part of the national defense administration. Bev's engineering friend, Bob Benninghoff from Chicago remembered the existence of these land lines and inquired about them with the post office authority in charge. Sure enough, the lines were still in good working order and permission was granted for this unique means of communicating the gospel across the nation.

Bev loves to recount some of the many wonderful stories of those Harringay days. "I remember one gentleman who came to the London meetings, brought by his neighbor. He came thinking that he would just sit and make fun of everything. When I got up to sing, he was talking out loud and probably criticizing as he heard me singing "He's Got The Whole World." But when I got to the line that says 'He's got the tiny little baby in His hands' the man slumped in his seat, probably thinking of his little one, who was ill at home. During Mr. Graham's invitation, the man stood, came forward and gave his heart to the Lord Jesus!"

Opening on March 1, 1954, Billy said that he and his wife Ruth could not see anybody waiting to get in when they arrived at the 12,000 seat indoor Harringay Arena. They thought nobody had come until they were stunned to discover that the arena was already filled. The London Crusades captured the attention, it seemed, of the entire United Kingdom including the fairly recently crowned Queen Elizabeth II and the legendary Prime Minister, Winston Churchill. Both had meetings with Billy and established enduring friendships. Billy remembers how three months later, the team bus slowly made its way through the waving crowds after the closing meetings at West London's White City and Wembley Stadiums. He recalls, "The entire team couldn't help but join with George Beverly Shea as he softly sang 'Praise God From Whom All Blessings Flow.'"

Returning home in 1954, Bev was duly summoned to Washington DC to sing "What A Friend We Have in Jesus" before President Eisenhower at the Presidential Prayer Breakfast. What a thrill that was for the shy boy from little Winchester, Ontario! Each generation of the Shea family was immensely proud. Bev stood tall and stately as he sang. On the stage that day were many dignitaries that included Chief Justice Earl Warren, Senator Frank Carlson and Vice President Richard M. Nixon. The next day, across the nation on the TV newscasts, Bev could be seen with the President as he testified to the friendship of his Lord. To his delight and surprise, Bev remembers that the President knew all the words of "What a Friend" and dutifully sang along. A short time later, in the National Christian Endeavor meeting again in Washington DC, President Eisenhower spoke and Bev sang "I'd Rather Have Jesus." Afterward, the President greeted Bev with a warm handshake and thanked him for the song. In the years that followed, Bev sang before Presidents Johnson, Nixon, Carter, Clinton and George H.W. Bush and George W. Bush on more than one occasion each.

DISCERN QUALITY SONGS

Gaining in professional stature daily, his unique recording artistry was universally evident even in those early, almost experimental, RCA LP recordings of the fifties. Highly acclaimed was the orchestral wizardry of Hugo Winterhalter as he enhanced Bev's vocals. It seemed that every RCA album that Bev created in the mid-fifties until the early eighties became instantly popular. Throughout the years, he skillfully negotiated the musical terrain of song choices enduring subtle shifts in public taste. There was, however, always a clear thread of consistency in his professional work, a singular ability that stood out over time. Between his producers and himself, they shared an ability to discern quality songs that reflected their knowledge of the art form and the marketplace as illustrated by the albums *An Evening Prayer* and *Sacred Songs Of George Beverly Shea*.

The song, "An Evening Prayer," was written by CM Battersby and Charles H. Gabriel. By the time of Bev's recording, it was becoming a standard. In contrast, "Day by Day" was a traditional song from Sweden and "I Found a Friend" was a new song from Roc Hillman and Barclay Allen. Bev tells how Barclay was an aspiring pianist in the successful west coast orchestra of Freddy Martin. The pianist sadly lost his livelihood in a car wreck when he damaged his hands. Bev remembers how in the hospital, Barclay was visited by a Christian minister who led the injured man to faith. The "I Found a Friend" song, was his testimony. In 1985 in the foreword to the book entitled *Lord Of Song* by Ronald B. Allen, son of Barclay Allen, Bev recounted, "I'm not sure how many times I've sung the comforting words of 'I Found A Friend' in evangelistic crusades around the world with the Billy Graham team. I lost count years ago. But I know that wherever hungry ears have ached to hear and believe in the love and grace of a faithful God, the song has had a mighty impact. It seems, the song speaks to everyone and I am so grateful for the privilege of bringing to people its tender words. "

Heading the *Sacred Songs* album pack was Bev's co-penned classic, "I'd Rather Have Jesus," Thomas Dorsey's "Take My Hand, Precious Lord," and two songs by Stuart Hamblen: "The King Of All Kings" and "He Bought My Soul at Calvary."

Among the newer songs were "The Beautiful Garden of Prayer," "Take Time to Pray," "If You Know the Lord," and "I Walked Today Where Jesus Walked." Bev also chose to include country songs including Cindy Walker's "Beloved Enemy" and Redd Harper's "Each Step of the Way." About that time, Cindy and Redd were together, chosen to star in the new Billy Graham World Wide Pictures films—the world's first two Christian westerns—entitled *Mister Texas* and *Oil Town USA*.

Bev remembers the cheerful red-haired Redd Harper in *Mister Texas*. Born in Nocona, Texas on September 29, 1903, he was raised in the beautiful, wide open ranges of Oklahoma. Most of his early life was spent in the saddle but instead of becoming a cowhand he entered the University of Oklahoma. After his studies, he had a short spell as a newspaper reporter. He later worked in a dance band then did radio work at various radio stations in Oklahoma City and Des Moines before eventually finding his way to Hollywood. There he worked in a Western swing band before World War II rudely interrupted his career for three years when he served in the Coast Guard. Returning home, he hosted a very successful radio western program entitled *Redd Harper's Hollywood Roundup* where invited celebrity guests would talk and maybe sing. If the guest was an actor, he would play a little scene from the soundtrack from his latest movie. He counted as his close acquaintants many western characters, Roy Rogers, Dale Evans, Tex Ritter, Stuart Hamblen and many more. So when word went around Hollywood that Stuart had become a Christian, Redd Harper thought he was a phony. But it was true! Not long after, Redd was invited to the Hollywood Christian Group where Stuart was giving his testimony. It was at a later meeting that Redd himself came to Christ. He went on to become a Christian singer and songwriter, later landing parts in *Mister Texas, Oiltown USA, The Gospel According to Some People* and *God Loves People.*

For three years following his conversion, Redd traveled extensively with the Graham team, going to Great Britain in 1954. In Glasgow's Kelvin Hall in April 1955, the Graham Team held a Greater Scotland Crusade. It drew a total of 2,647,365 people and registered 50,000 decisions. In the Hampden Park Stadium holding 90,000 people, 5,000 came to Christ. Bev remembers the first night well. After being down with a nasty bout of laryngitis, he could only sing one verse that evening, but he loved to hear how the bonnie land of Scotland gave the world a treasure of great hymns. For instance, intensely personal "Beneath the Cross of Jesus," full of biblical symbolism and imagery was written in 1868. The writer, Elizabeth Clephane, who also wrote "The Ninety and Nine," died one year later at the young age of 39. Born in 1830, she was raised in the beautiful countryside around Edinburgh. One of three sisters, she was known as the delicate, retiring member of the family. Nevertheless, she was always popular because of her helpful and happy nature. Cheerfully, she served the poor and sick of her underprivileged community. In her spare time, she loved to write Christian poems.

GOSPEL ENTERTAINMENT

In the entertainment industry of the fifties, cultural changes were heralded with much media hype. Teenage music ushered in a substantial social revolution that affected culture and even ethics. Typical music of the 'hip teenage generation' of the day came from Guy Mitchell, Frankie Laine, Tony Bennett, Patti Page, Johnny Ray, Teresa Brewer, Eddie Fisher and Perry Como—all were the rage. Conversely, as the revolutionary decade progressed, Bev's plentiful recordings became immensely acceptable in the growing marketplace, earning awards and nominations, a strong affirmation of the high esteem in which he was held by both the industry and grassroots music devotees. Yet, despite the early glamour and hype, he deliberately played things down choosing to remain essentially the regular everyday son that his dear parents wanted him to be.

As leisure time increased even for Christian people, the second half of the twentieth century ushered in the arrival of more contemporary Christian music in the entertainment sphere. Artists who expanded the genre to daringly embrace the risky new idea of Christian music entertainment were the likes of the Blackwood Brothers, Mahalia Jackson, Pat Boone and then surprisingly Elvis Presley. Bev's emphasis, however, remained staunchly in ministry—not entertainment. Since the beginning of crusade ministry, Bev and Cliff barrows remained unaffected, the nucleus of the Graham musical team.

Following the British Crusades of 1955, the Graham team visited several American military bases on mainland Europe including camps in France and Germany. Bev especially learned Fanny Crosby's classic "Pass Me Not O Gentle Saviour" so that he could sing it on the Berlin boundary line of the Iron Curtain at the historic Brandenburg Gate before a crowd of 50,000.

ACCOMPLISHED SONGWRITER

Not just a superb singer, Bev was also proving that he was a highly accomplished songwriter too. He tells how the inspiration came for the lyrics and music for "The Wonder of It All." "The man who inspired me to write the song was a Jewish music company executive. We met on the old *SS United States* sailing from the USA bound for Southampton for the Scotland meetings in 1955. We struck up a friendship because we were both in the music business. One day, my new friend asked me what really went on at those crusades. So I told him about the volunteer choir and how they rehearse for weeks ahead of the date. I explained how the visiting preachers including Billy Graham didn't receive a salary for doing these meetings. When I got to the point where I was trying to explain how Mr. Graham asks people to make a commitment of their lives to God, I think I ran out of words. Then I said, 'Oh sir, if only you could see it! The wonder of it all!' Since my new friend was a man of music, he commissioned me to write a song with that title. That's how I wrote the words, *There's the wonder of sunset at evening, the wondrous sunrise I see, but the wonder of wonders that thrills my soul is the wonder that God loves me!* Bev says that he struggled for several weeks in trying to achieve a rhyme on the second verse. Eventually, a phone call to Cindy Walker in her Texas home helped solve the quest and finish the masterpiece.

Bev first met Cindy at the Hollywood Crusade in 1951. The Graham team was invited to the home of YP Freeman, vice president of Paramount Pictures. Billy spoke and Bev sang to the group of sixty or so that included many Hollywood personalities. Cindy responded to the evangelist's gospel call. Several days later, as a testimony to the event she composed the song "Oh, How Sweet To Know" and gave it to Bev to consider recording. Cindy Walker was born in the little town of Mexia in Texas. From a very early age, she was surrounded by music. Her maternal grandfather, FL Eiland was the writer of the hymn, "Hold To God's Unchanging Hand" while her mother Oree was an accomplished pianist. Cindy was to follow in her grandfather's song writing footsteps. Before World War II, her song "Casa De Manana," which she wrote specifically for the Texas Centennial, was recorded by the Paul Whiteman Orchestra.

The Walker family moved to Los Angeles, a dream come true for a songwriter as LA was considered the mecca for popular music at that time. Cindy carried her compositions in a little briefcase on her lap for the journey. When they reached the city, her father looked for a suitable apartment to rent. They found themselves on the famous Sunset Boulevard. Suddenly, Cindy spied the Bing Crosby Building and decided there and then that the famous Mr. Bing Crosby would definitely be the right person to record her compositions! She persuaded her father to stop the car and clutching her briefcase in her hand marched with great audacity straight into the office complex. "Oh, hi! My name's Cindy Walker! I'm a songwriter just up from Texas. I've got some great songs that I think will be ideal for Mr. Crosby to record!"

The baffled secretary tried in vain to dissuade her from reaching her intended goal, but Cindy boldly made her way into the inner office where an amused Larry Crosby consented to listen patiently to one of Cindy's compositions, accompanied on the piano by her very star struck mother! She must have made a good impression because an appointment was made for Cindy to meet the great man himself at Paramount Studios. Cindy then proceeded to sing a Western song to him that she had just composed entitled "Lone Star Trail." Impressed with the song, Bing decided that he would record it. Recognizing her talent, Bing encouraged her to follow a musical stage career in her own right, advice which she readily followed. She went on to write songs for many remove famous artists such as Jim Reeves, Roy Orbison, Dean Martin, and many others. Her friend Redd Harper often helped her transfer her compositions into sheet music. Her acting career also took off and she starred with Redd in *Mister Texas* made by World Wide Pictures. In years to come, from her pen flowed numerous beautiful Christian songs many of which were recorded by Shea.

When Bev put a phone call through to Cindy to ask for help on the quandary of the second verse of "The Wonder Of It All," she listened to the words he sang down the phone. "How about this, Bev?" and she sang, "The wonder of sunset at evening, the wonder of sunrise *I see*. That rhymes now with ... *the wonder that God loves me*." Humming it over in his mind, the puzzle was solved. "That's it! Thank you Cindy, that bit flows much better now!"

FOREIGN LANGUAGES

After the very successful British meetings, invitations to foreign lands became plentiful for the Graham team. In Frankfurt, Germany the team drew 30,000 people, and in the Gothenburg Olympic Stadium in Sweden, 25,000 attended. Billy himself had an interpreter for the preaching. Therefore, Bev felt that he ought to make the effort to try to master at least one song in the languages of the countries visited. He practiced Fanny Crosby's "Pass Me Not" in German, "I'd Rather Have Jesus" in Finnish, and for Sweden he learned the Swedish classic, "He the Pearly Gates Will Open." "I'm not sure," Bev says, "how good or clear my accents and expressions were but what I do know is that the audiences appreciated the effort to learn the languages! Leaving the Helsinki port of Finland, some supporters kindly gathered on the quay's pier to see us off. Someone yelled from the shore in an echoing, loud tone. 'Please Mr. Shea, please sing your song 'I'd Rather Have Jesus' to us one more time in Finnish!'"

Tickled that they would ask for such an unusual request, he happily obliged. Pulling the Finnish lyrics from his jacket pocket, he turned and smiled at his pianist colleague, Tedd Smith. "Say, Tedd can I ask a favor, Brother? Please could you hold these words up as I try to sing?"

Tedd was, of course, delighted to help. Amid the robust sea breezes, he raised the paper to an optimum position where the vocalist could focus. Then Bev cupped his chilly hands and in that familiar deep-rich bass-baritone tone loudly sang the request to the delight of the crusade supporters and the many bemused onlookers on ship and on shore.

With competent coaching from Dave Barnes, Bev says that he just could not adequately phonetically master "The Love Of God" in the French language for the Paris meetings. After a less than successful French version one evening, ever the diplomat, Cliff approached Bev the next day with a new suggestion. "I'm told, Bev, that folks here in France love jazz and so they know and love many of the spirituals in English. How do feel about doing a spiritual tonight?"

Bev welcomed the inspired suggestion with enthusiasm and a broad smile. "Cliff, my dear brother, that's a wonderfully tactful suggestion. I'll do spirituals here from now on!"

Recognition of work well done, although never courted or solicited, came regardless to the Billy Graham team as the years progressed. In 1956, Bev was given a Doctor of Fine Arts degree by his old college, Houghton College in New York. A year later, the team would take New York City by storm. The Madison Square Garden Crusade lasted sixteen weeks and was attended by one million with 56, 000 recorded decisions for Christ! The rally in Times Square drew 150,000 people and Yankee Stadium was filled by 100,000, its largest crowd ever and 2,500 decisions were recorded. The unofficial anthem of the New York Crusade meeting was undoubtedly "How Great Thou Art."

AN UNFAIR QUESTION

Years ago on my BBC Radio show in England, I asked Bev to tell him what were his favorite songs. "Tell me, Bev, if you had to name your three or four favorite hymns what would they be?"

"Well Paul, I'd say 'Great Is Thy Faithfulness,' 'The Love of God,' 'In Times Like These' and, may I humbly add, 'I'd Rather Have Jesus.'" Then he lowered his eyes, smiled broadly and replied, "Paul, that's an unfair question, as I've loved so many wonderful songs." Then almost in the same breath, he continued, "But I don't get tired of 'How Great Thou Art'! That magnificent Swedish hymn, has a special history, too. I was presented with that song on Oxford Street in London in 1954. Mr. Gray, of the Christian publishers, Pickering and Inglis, was the man who walked up to me and asked us to consider this new song. Mr. Gray said that it was written in Sweden in 1885 and translated from the Russian version by a Londoner named Stuart Hine."

Later Bev discovered that the original inspiration for the author of the English text came when the peaceful greenery of an Eastern European countryside was struck suddenly by a violent thunderstorm. But decades before that event, it was originally written as a poem by Reverend Carl Boberg, a well known preacher and religious editor in Northern Europe. Carl served for fifteen years as a senator in the Swedish Parliament. An old familiar Swedish folk tune was later married to his nine-verse poem. A German version "Wie Gross Bist Du" was translated from the original Swedish by Manfred Von Glehn in 1907 and five years later in 1912, Rev. Ivan S. Prokhanoff, who was known as the Martin Luther of Modern Russia, translated it from German into Russian and published it in St. Petersburg. It was included in a collection of hymns entitled *Cymbals: A Collection Of Spiritual Songs Translated From Various Languages*. The unusual and wordy title of the book suggests that the compiler took it from Psalm 150:5 that says "Praise Him upon the loud cymbals: praise Him upon the high sounding cymbals!" To many people of various lands in Europe, throughout the bitter years of World War I, the hymn became an anchor of hope.

In 1922 several of Prokhanoff's hymn booklets in Russian were published in New York City by the American Bible Society in a large volume entitled *Songs of the Christian*. This book was then translated into Russian and widely used across Eastern Europe. The modern English version of this beautiful song, now entitled "How Great Thou Art," was written by Stuart K. Hine. Stuart was born in 1899 in The Grove, a leafy avenue of Hammersmith in West London. As a child, he was duly dedicated to God by his devoted parents at the local Salvation Army citadel. Brought up in a warm Christian home, Stuart dedicated his life to the Lord in 1914 via the ministry of Madame Annie Ryall. His love for the preaching of the London-based Baptist preacher Charles Spurgeon and of gospel music encouraged him to join the Tower Hamlets Choir in London. Later he was called up for World War I service in the British armed forces at the age of eighteen. He married in June 1923 and nine years later the couple dedicated themselves to missionary work in Eastern Europe.

During their spell as missionaries in the Ukraine, Stuart came across the Russian translation of the song, "O Great God" in the book of evangelical hymns from the American Bible Society. Immediately impressed by the song, Stuart set about translating the song into English adding to the original with verses of his own. He says that he took additional inspiration for his version of the song from personal experience. The first stanza came about after he experienced an awesome thunderstorm in Czechoslovakia that he said displayed God's awesome power. The second stanza was inspired, Stuart said, from peaceful walks in quiet mountain forests in Romania. In the third stanza, he drew upon Biblical theology and his own personal knowledge of what he called the saving grace of God.

After completing these verses, the Hines returned home to the UK in 1948 and began working with the countless refugees who were fleeing from the Nazi and Communist persecutions in Mid and Eastern Europe. Years later in a letter to me, Stuart said, "What struck me about the mass departure into England of large numbers was the fact that these refugees, in spite of having found greater freedom in their adopted British Isles, continually asked when they would be able to return to their beloved homelands.

These requests inspired me to pen the last stanza in 1948 that talks about the anticipated joy of Christians as they look forward to the second coming of Christ when He will take them to their 'home' to be with Him!"

Later Stuart Hine informed me that the song was first sung in America in New York in 1951 by the British missionary, James Caldwell on furlough from Africa. In 1951 to 1954, it became the theme song at the Inter Varsity Fellowship camps in New York State and at Wheaton College meetings. Other colleges used it, too as a choir song. Dr. Roy Nicholson informed Stuart that at the January 1955 General Conference of the Wesleyan Methodists, "the song inspired thousands." Roy added, "At the great 1957 New York Crusade, the Billy Graham team must have wondered why all New York asked for the song from the start, and for every night, for a total of 99 times! The reason was so many knew it already, but at the Crusade they could all sing it together. So it became the unofficial theme song."

Stuart Hine informed me that when the Bev Shea autobiography was issued in 1968, Bev was unaware of Dr. Roy Nicholson's involvement with "How Great Thou Art" and so it was not mentioned in the book. When Stuart informed Bev, he said that Bev's voice "showed much emotion. Bev was saddened to hear news of the omission in his book of his old pastor and his denomination's use of the song. 'I was brought up as a boy under the preaching of Dr. Roy Nicholson!' Bev explained, 'Dr. Roy and I and my father grew up together!'"

Earlier in 1954 Dr. Edwin Orr heard the song sung by Naga tribe members in India. He introduced it to audiences in

California where it was heard by Tim Spencer, of the Sons Of the Pioneers cowboy vocal group. Captivated by it, Tim, the owner and publisher of *Manna Music*, then secured the American copyright from the author Stuart Hine. Hine retained worldwide rights elsewhere. Bev always considered that "How Great Thou Art" was unique, its lyrics majestic and poetically powerful in the high note of praise they raise. In the mid fifties, as a result of his solos at the Graham Missions, the hymn gained worldwide popularity. It debuted at the Maple Leaf Garden Arena in Toronto, Canada in 1955. Bev remembers, "The response was unbelievable! 'How Great Thou Art' was thereafter appreciated by every audience after its exposure in regular crusades. Also, it was heard on *Hour of Decision* radio broadcasts that were by then on some 900 American stations and on shortwave in such faraway lands as Luxembourg, Ecuador and Monte Carlo."

One of the most popular modern hymns ever written, Bev and the Blackwood Brothers probably had the first recordings. Later, Bev noted to me, "Soon everybody was recording it. Elvis Presley, I'm told cut it nine times and during his last years, used it to sign-off on his shows. We did ask permission from Stuart Hine to change the lyrics slightly and he agreed. I preferred to sing about the *rolling* thunder rather than the *mighty* thunder."

Recorded numerous times by many other famous singers, both Christian and secular, Bev recalls how Stuart K. Hine always insisted that the "K" part of his name was used! Stuart went to be with his Lord on March 14, 1989, passing away peacefully in his sleep at the age of ninety-two. His memorial service was held at the Gospel Hall, Martello Road, in England at which his tremendous song was sung. For half a century, Bev has sung

"How Great Thou Art" thousands of times. Asked how he managed to keep it from being just a performance, he responded simply. "I never ever think of it as being a performance. But I do recall that one night during those sixteen weeks in Madison Square Garden in 1957, I went back to the hotel, got into bed and thought, 'Did we sing 'How Great Thou Art?' Well, sure we did but I didn't remember! I asked the Lord to forgive me for perhaps having done it like a parrot. I'm sure I never again failed to concentrate on these meaningful words."

SURPRISED AT THE SUPPORT

Many star-studded celebrities took time to attend Madison Square Garden in 1957. The list included Pearl Bailey, Richard Nixon, Jack Dempsey, Walter Winchell, Greer Garson, Dale Evans, Gene Tierney, and Ed Sullivan to name a few. Signing up as a member of the public for the New York Crusade Choir, the Graham team was surprised at the support they received in an unsolicited way from Ethel Waters. She was a famous jazz song-stylist and movie star of the early 'talkies'. Born in a sordid tenement and raised by her grandmother, Ethel knew severe poverty and strife from the start. Her mother, Louise, born from an assault at the age of twelve, was little more than a child herself. Brought-up in the poor tenement slums of Chester, Pennsylvania, Ethel thought that becoming a honky-tonk singer would elevate her from the ghetto. She went on to become an internationally famous jazz singer and stage/movie actress in productions such as *Member of the Wedding*. In 1957 she also starred in the BGEA movie, *The Heart is a Rebel* and Bev remembers her as a great character and a lady of winsome faith. "Late in life, Ethel surrendered to the claims of Christ. I guess you could say that Ethel did everything that a voice teacher would advise one not to do. Her special intimate vocal style mixed song and narration. Yet, she thrilled audiences leaving them utterly mesmerised. Her career spanned more than half a century during which time she won countless honors and awards. She told me that her favorite hymn, and that of her grandmother too, was 'His Eye is on the Sparrow' that she was always asked to sing at crusades. She was called home after a long illness on September 1, 1977."

Being resident again in New York City for the summer of 1957 was for Erma and Bev Shea a delightful return to home territory where old acquaintances could be revived. Nineteen years had passed since they moved to Chicago. With the public acclaim and press coverage now given to the Billy Graham team, it was inevitable that RCA conceived an album release in 1957 entitled, *A Billy Graham Crusade in Song*. Repertoire included "How Great Thou Art," Bev's newly written, "The Wonder of It All," and "The Old Fashioned Home," usually sung by Bev in connection with Mr. Graham's sermon on The Home. There was also "Balm in Gilead" and Lowell Patton's "Sunshine." All were musical expressions of comfort in times of pain and sorrow for those putting their trust in God. Next came Elizabeth Clephane and Ira Sankey's "Ninety and Nine," "I Must Tell Jesus," one of Mr. Graham's favorites, and Cindy Walker's "Oh How Sweet To Know." Cindy described the lyrics as a sentiment welling up from her heart, the experience of Christian assurance. To complete the session were some live crusade recordings such as "He's Got the Whole World in His Hands." This featured a very effective and moving change of key for the verse, *He's got the tiny little baby in His hands.* Then followed the patriotic anthem, "America the Beautiful;" Albert Malotte's "The Lord's Prayer;" and "Lord, I'm Coming Home," the song used to close the *Hour of Decision* broadcasts.

ANY LOVE SONGS?

Did Bev ever record any love songs? Well, the answer, surprising to most people, is yes! The 1958 release of *Through the Years* produced by Brad McCuen and orchestrated by Charles Grean was a wedding album of sorts.

Born in 1913, bass player and orchestrator, Charles Randolph Grean was a former copyist for the Glen Miller Band and served as an assistant to Steve Sholes from 1947. Charles assisted Steve in the securing of new Southern signings to RCA and in finding session musicians for recordings. He left his mark as an arranger with diverse classics such as Nat King Cole's "The Christmas Song," Vaughn Monroe's "Riders In The Sky," and "The Thing," a novelty song by Phil Harris. The *Through the Years* album by Bev was given a handsome production budget for Brad McCuen and Charles Grean to spend. Clearly, RCA was looking beyond solely the religious market.

Commenting on Bev's *Through the Years* album, Frank S. Brenner declared, "Life holds no greater gift than the mutual love of man and wife. In mature marriages, joys are magnified and sadness tempered by the knowledge of shared experience. George Beverly Shea reviews the whole wonderful cycle in this collection of grand songs and anthems which weave a story that Christians will never tire of hearing and living. The tender declaration of love, as expressed in Grieg's immortal 'I Love Thee' to the glorious wedding day so beautifully revealed in

'Because' and 'O Perfect Love,' is but the first short step on a long journey. The first true realization of marriage finds its voice in the wonderful awareness that 'I Am Not Alone.' The daily trials and difficulties of life are lessened by the hopefulness of two people finding courage in each other and 'Smilin' Through' their tears and troubles. The joys of having made a home together are felt in the benediction 'Bless This House.' Two great hymns, 'God Is Ever Beside Me' and 'Jesus Will Walk with Me,' are stirring testimonies of faith in divine guidance, and one may truly ask 'How Can I be Lonely." The beautiful song 'Thou Light of Light' is dedicated to Mr. Shea and it was America's great poet James Whitcomb Riley who provided the inspiring words of 'The Prayer Perfect.' And so, with the slow passing of time, two people, no longer young, perhaps not wealthy, can look back 'Through the Years' upon the true richness of love shared and a life well spent."

Chapter 7

The Love of God
1958-1963

"Mr. Shea is such an incredible man who has faithfully down the years reminded me that God is faithful. Sometimes, when I turn on the television and see such a servant as Bev Shea, or when I put on one of his many albums, I'm reminded that God is faithful and that I should be faithful myself. Faithfully, year after year—come hail, snow or sunshine—he has reminded millions that great is God's faithfulness!"
—Sheila Walsh, Nashville, Tennessee

ENTERTAINMENT MAGNET

George Beverly Shea was always clear regarding the criterion he used in selecting gospel songs for meetings and church services. "Of course, the singer or choir director should know the subject of the preacher's message and stay on target, relying on the Holy Spirit to bless the sermon in song too."

Outside the church scenario, however, his recordings were gaining popularity. In the late fifties, the public was still heavily buying singles while LP albums were slowly gaining acceptance. For a time, RCA Victor issued the same Bev Shea singles on both 78rpm and 45rpm speeds. It took a while for the public to switch. The next couple of years were made up of momentous album recording memories for the now very popular Mr. Shea.

As the featured soloist with the Graham team, he was fast approaching his twelfth year on the road. RCA Victor asked Bev to record another album. They booked him for three days with producer Dick Pierce and conductor Ralph Carmichael for *The Love Of God* album project. When Bev drove into Hollywood's Center Of The World studios, the radio newscast was announcing that the USSR's Premier Bulganin was still urgently calling for top-level talks between the East and West. In the context of storm clouds of war gathering internationally, Bev prayed that the new album project would provide every listener with a tangible sense of hope in God's sovereignty.

The sun shone brightly on that fresh, late summer day in Los Angeles. As he excitedly crossed the dusty sidewalk and entered the dimmed RCA studios, the well-marked calendar on the wall read September 16, 1958. Before them were three days of recording. It took very little time for them to focus on the repertoire to be achieved that day. Recognizing the first song, they all erupted into knowing smiles. Top on the list was, "Christ is a Wonderful Saviour" written by the versatile Tim Spencer in western style. Tim, a member of the Sons of the Pioneers, wrote the song in response to his conversion to Christ. Using the melodic tune of his hit number, "Room Full Of Roses," he substituted gospel lyrics to celebrate his experience being born again. It was a serious song but it was also a fun version for the musicians who heard the melody often on popular radio shows. Bev said brightly to his musician friends, "Tim Spencer is to be thanked for publishing and publicizing 'How Great Thou Art' via his *Manna Music*. The song is now popular worldwide"

Changing musical direction, "God is So Good" was written by Doris Akers. Not as familiar, "I Love Thy Presence, Lord" was a beautiful new song that Bev co-wrote with his brother, Alton J. Shea. Next was a challenging Mosie Lister composition entitled "How Long Has It Been?" Soon to become very popular, it was less rhythmic in style than Mosie's usual compositions. Bev knew Mosie as one of the greatest and most enduring of the Southern gospel writers. Born in 1921 in Cochran, Georgia where his father was a singing teacher and choir director, his first song was published at the age of eighteen. Soon after, he gained considerable radio experience. Originally part of an early Statesmen Quartet lineup, Mosie decided to quit and concentrate on song writing instead. Following national service, he was further encouraged by his wife to compose. Looking back, he says that he has written so many songs that he has lost count! Outstanding Mosie Lister songs recorded by Bev include "How Long Has It Been," "Where No One Stands Alone," "Then I Met the Master," and "Til the Storm Passes By." "His Hand In Mine" is perhaps Mosie's greatest song. When the songwriter was inducted into the Gospel Music Hall of Fame in 1998, the recorded version by the Blackwood Brothers' "His Hand In Mine" was included in the induction ceremony. It became the classic title-song of Elvis Presley's first gospel album for RCA. Artists who have recorded Lister materials through the years include The Gaithers, BJ Thomas, Jim Reeves, Faron Young, Jan Howard, Jimmie Davis, Jimmy Dean, Webb Pierce as well as Bev Shea. He now resides in Tampa, Florida and even in old age he still produces quality material. He is a frequent guest on the Gaither *Homecoming Friends* videos.

There were other great songs recorded that day in Hollywood. They included "Holy Spirit, Faithful Guide" penned by MM Wells and "I Asked the Lord." The writers, Johnny Lange and Jimmy Duncan, were two great Tin Pan Alley professionals. "Here's two numbers you'll know very well, Bev! One of them is sung every night at the close of all Dr. Graham's meetings. Let's sing them through a couple of times! Then if they sound okay, let's have you do the takes!" declared the breezy voice of Dick Pierce from behind the studio's glass partition.

"Okay, Dick, I'm ready!" Bev spoke as he moved closer to the microphone. "I'm so glad we've chosen Fred Lehman's 'The Love of God' and this 'Just As I Am' penned by Charlotte Elliott and William B. Bradbury. That invitation hymn is one of England's best exports. Both these songs are so beautiful."

COLD WAR SHADOW-BOXING

Remembering his humorous experience in France, thankfully for Bev, when the Billy Graham team traveled Down Under in 1959, there was no need of any new language. Generally, Australia was very sunny, hot and humid. What made the trip particularly bearable, however, for the BGEA team was that some of them, including Bev, had their families with them. Then the rain began to fall in torrents in Melbourne, Australia. Despite the adverse weather this particular crusade venue stands out in Bev's mind as an unforgettable highlight. "On a rainy night, our boy, Ronald, eleven years of age, left the area of the sound booth and took the long walk up to the front.

Grady Wilson followed him and counseled him, and that night Ronald gave his heart to the Lord Jesus."

The Australian crusade was three-and-a-half months in Australia and New Zealand and included the cities Sydney, Melbourne, Brisbane, and Adelaide. Over three million people attended and 146,734 persons said they committed or rededicated their lives to Christ. Press photos and stories were plentiful including Bev's early morning visit to Sydney's Taronga Park Zoo that produced appealing photographs of Bev cuddling a koala bear. The photo was aptly utilized by RCA for a special Aussie-only, extended-play record release entitled *George Beverly Shea In Australia*. It included songs typical of the Australian Crusade meetings, encompassing live recordings made at the Sydney Showground. Cliff Barrows joined Bev on friendly banter with the fun-filled "Old Time Religion." This was followed by the more somber Shea solos of "His Eye Is On The Sparrow," "The Lord's My Shepherd," and "Then Jesus Came." This album is now a rare collector's item. But it did find its way across the world to the collection of Northern Ireland's Stewart Hamilton who provided the information for this book.

At this time, *Christian Life* magazine pointed out that the Shea records were outselling rock 'n roll titles in Australia. Yet despite his high profile, he still remained amazingly indifferent to and detached from the entertainment magnet. His unsolicited fame was still spreading widely via the weekly *Hour of Decision* radio broadcasts and through his numerous personal appearances. His bass-baritone voice was now recognized worldwide.

At this time, at the height of public fears about atomic warfare, the armies of the nations of the East and West were Cold War shadow-boxing in diverse parts of the world. The collective mood in the West was the desire for a better sense of security at home and abroad. Into this mood Bev's new album *Blessed Assurance* in 1958, coined from Fanny Crosby's beloved terminology, seemed so apt and opportune.

> *Blessed Assurance, Jesus is mine: O what a foretaste of glory divine!*
> *Heir of salvation, purchase of God; Born of His Spirit, washed in His blood.*
> *This is my story, this is my song, Praising my Saviour all the day long.*
> *This is my story, this is my song! Praising my Saviour all the day long.*
> —Fanny Crosby (1820-1915)

Before the inspiring recording, Bev's Bible reading of Isaiah 12:2 assured him of God's presence and protection. "Behold, God is my salvation; I will trust, and not be afraid: for the Lord Jehovah is my strength and my song; He also is become my salvation!" *Blessed Assurance* was brimful of confidence, peace, comfort and hope in songs such as "Yes, There is Comfort," "He Whispered, Peace Be Still," "It is Well With My Soul," "Peace To Those Who Believe," "Security," "When God is Near," "Under His Wings," "Saviour, Again To Thy Dear Name," "Sweet Peace, the Gift of God's Love," "If We Could See Beyond Today," and "All That Thrills My Soul is Jesus." Production by Brad McCuen and Norman Leyden orchestration augmented the uplifting theme with strong, confident and majestic musical backups balanced with gentle almost placid variations at times. Many listeners gave testimony to the spiritual therapy that Bev's works offered in times of political stress and tensions. For the album, once again, Bev called upon the song writing skills of Fanny Crosby, Norman Clayton, Ira Sankey, Alfred Ackley and Horatio Spafford.

Bev is inspired whenever he recounts the story of how Horatio Spafford wrote "It is Well With My Soul." He says that in the dark winter days of November 1873, Horatio, a dedicated Chicago Presbyterian layman sent his dear wife and four young daughters across the Atlantic to England. He anticipated joining them when he concluded some pressing import business in his legal practice. Sadly in mid-Atlantic, the ship collided with another and sank in twelve minutes. Several days later when the survivors were finally counted in Cardiff, South Wales, his four daughters were not there. Mrs. Spafford tearfully cabled her husband back home with the words "saved alone." Taking the next available ship to join his grieving wife, passing over the place of the disaster, he penned these inspiring heartfelt lyrics of "It Is Well With My Soul" in his cabin.

When peace like a river attendeth my way,

When sorrows like sea billows roll,

Whatever my lot—Thou hast taught me to say,

It is well, it is well with my soul!'

—Horatio Spafford (1828-1888)

Autumn was spent in the beautiful Tennessee countryside with all its color. The prized venue was the RCA Victor Studio in Nashville for Bev's exciting, jolly and carefree session with the Jordanaires. "Okay, let's do 'Roll Jordan Roll' and 'Goodbye Pharaoh.'"

Steve Sholes spoke while taking control. He glanced through the studio glass at Bev and Elvis' famed backup group for a nod of reassurance that he was not out of step with their thinking.

"That's a good idea, Steve!" came the reassuring, laughing voice of Gordon Stoker, the Jordanaires' spokesman. Looking over the mike at Bev, he smiled and said, "You know Bev, I've noticed our audiences love our hand-clapping, spiritual songs! They even stir the most conservative church folk! They inevitably melt and if they don't clap their hands, they secretly tap their toes under the pews!"

Bev laughed and responded by returning Gordon's smile with a friendly nod. Behind the glass, as Steve Sholes listened back with great pleasure to the resultant recordings of the two peppy spirituals. He laughingly remarked to his engineer, "Ya know, Buddy that's the nearest George Beverly Shea's going to get to rock 'n roll!"

He was right. When the rhythmic tracks appeared on the RCA Camden album, Bev was also surrounded by his more comfortable hymnal moods. Songs minted included "The Holy City," "Stand By Me," and Alfred Ackley's "At the End of the Road." Also, there were several songs on the subject of prayer: "Now I Lay Me Down to Sleep," featuring his very young son, Ronnie; "If I Could Pray Like a Child Again;" and "Command and I'll Pray." The Christmas Seal Foundation charity selected Bev's version of "If I Can Help Somebody" from the album as its theme song. Last but not least, recorded that day, was a fun song originally popularized by the Cowboy Church Sunday School Kids, Stuart Hamblen's "Open Up Your Heart and Let the Sunshine In." A hearty vocal backdrop for the kids' song was provided by Atlanta's favorite gospel quartet, Hovie Lister's Statesmen as Bev sang lead.

So successful was the budget release of the RCA Camden album, another followed quickly entitled *Tenderly He Watches*. The song "Tenderly He Watches" met and empathized with the public's sense of insecurity at the height of the Cold War tensions. It was written by the country music husband and wife duo Lulu Belle and Scotty Wiseman from Billy Graham's home state, North Carolina. The

duo are better remembered as the writers of the big hit "Have I
Told You Lately That I Love You?" Two Sunday school favorites
on the RCA Camden album were "Jesus Loves Me" and "I'll Be a
Sunbeam." The most plaintive, sad song in the collection was "Take
My Mother Home" taken from Christ's words on the cross to the
disciple John at Calvary. Suitably, John Newton and Edwin Excell's
"He Died For Me" followed plus "Sunrise" written by Poole-Ackley.
Out of place seemed the Christmas song "There's a Song in the
Air." Bringing up the rear was another Stuart Hamblen song. This
time "The Army of the Lord" was a stirring march from Big Stu.

Painful Separations

By now Erma and Bev were busy parents of two fast growing
children, Ronnie and Elaine. The down-to-earth realities of
marriage and the burden of parenthood were suddenly upon
them after many years of being on their own. Life was now
hectic. "We made our home just outside Chicago," declared
Bev in jest. "It was just a stone's throw from Chicago's O'Hare
Airport which was my second home!" He added more seriously,
"We were really in love and looking back now we were very glad
we'd made Christ the head of our home!"

Bev was, however, delighted when his family was able to stay
with him for lengthy periods such as London, in 1954, and
Australia for three months in 1959.

Forgotten Words

Clearly, no singer of sacred songs captured the hearts of
gospel music lovers more completely in the fifties than the Billy

Graham soloist. Bev Shea's stardom rose steadily in the decade and by 1958 his music was loved and respected wherever the faithful congregated. The album simply titled *George Beverly Shea* featured many Shea favorites of the day including Walt Disney star Jimmie Dodd's "He Was There," Stuart Hamblen's "Known Only To Him," Doy W. Ott's "Mercy, Lord," Fannie E. Stafford and Homer A. Rodeheaver's "Somebody Cares," Ida L. Reed and BD Ackley's "Only A Touch," John W. Peterson's "No One Understands Like Jesus," and Norman J. Clayton's "Now I Belong To Jesus." Bev's orchestrator, Charles Grean co-penned "There's a Time." To complete the set were the Gene Autry favorite, "Somebody Bigger Than You and I," Basel Androzzo's "If I Can Help Somebody," Warren Roberts "Somewhere Along the Way," and Bev's co-penned "Sing Me a Song of Sharon's Rose."

A nightmare for any performer is a time when his or her mind goes unexplainably blank and the lyrics to a song just cannot be brought to mind. Unquestionably, it happened to Bev on more than one occasion through the years. What made such situations worse for him was they happened in front of tens of thousands of people! "I'll never forget," says Bev, "the night in 1958 at San Francisco's Cow Palace—the Giants' baseball stadium—when I forgot the words before a full house!"

Often pianist Tedd Smith and organist Loren Whitney were unaware what Bev's chosen-song would be until he started singing. That evening, Bev moved positively to the rostrum, secretly signaling to Tedd that the song would be in two flats. He then launched into the opening lyrics. "Holy, holy is what the angels sing and I expect to help them make the courts of heaven ring…"

While Tedd continued faithfully into the next verse on the piano, the next lines failed to come to the vocalist's mind. Bev turned to Cliff Barrows and smiled. Over the sound system he spoke jokingly, "My mother warned me that this would happen one day, Cliff! Why did it have to happen at the Cow Palace?"

Cliff and Billy and others on the platform broke out in laughter at Bev's embarrassing predicament while the vast audience erupted into heartfelt applause. Grinning broadly, Bev picked up the song at the chorus point, then Cliff gently reminded him of the elusive words so that he could complete the song to the crowd's delight. The song over, the quick-thinking Cliff led the crowd into a further round of laughter with some appropriate jovial quip.

"From that time on," said an unfazed, elderly Bev years later, "I knew that I couldn't absolutely rely on my mortal memory, so I started to tote a little pocket-sized black notebook that had the lyrics to my solos—just in case!"

Also Bev recalls a special moment of paternal joy that occurred at the same place a few days later. "In the Cow Palace during the San Francisco Crusade, our daughter, Elaine came forward. She had on a little rust-colored coat and a flat straw hat. I can still see her coming up the aisle. Mr. Graham looked around and said, 'Bev, Elaine is coming forward!' I was so touched by that." The seven weeks of San Francisco crusading drew three quarters of a million people and registered 25,000 decisions.

ROCK 'N ROLL YEARS

By 1958 changes in society, politics and art were happening fast and furiously. Television by now was quickly superseding the cinema as the public's number one source of entertainment.

Experienced Christian singer, Ann Downing remembered that while in high school she heard Billy on television. "I'll never forget how powerfully he preached and how beautifully George Beverly Shea sang 'I'd Rather Have Jesus.' That was when I really understood God's message to me that Jesus had to be first in my life if anything else was going to happen."

Never one to hog the limelight, Bev modestly and philosophically asserted, "Before television came along in 1957, I used to sing three songs a night during the crusades. After the crusades started being televised and the big name guests came along, I sang one simple song just before Billy Graham would speak. I tried always to sing a song appropriate to the subject of Dr. Graham's preaching. I didn't sing to thrill anybody—just a brief solo, two verses and a couple of choruses to quiet the audience before Dr. Graham began to speak. I just loved the old hymns that glorify God."

During the summer and autumn of 1960 exciting meetings were held across Europe, steadily recovering from the devastation of World War II. Bev remembered that after Switzerland, the team held crusades in Germany, including one in Berlin by the Brandenburg Gate. The event was less than a year before the feared and despised Berlin Wall was hurriedly erected. Without the wall, he recalls how the East Germans streamed across the divide despite menacing Soviet tank movements, police persecution, and the official Communist government media.

Hundreds of miles further east of Berlin was Israel, a land with its own political troubles at the time. Nevertheless that year, the Holy Land provided Bev with some favorite repertoire material. *The Holy Land* recording was a milestone concept album from

RCA outlining many events in the Biblical history of Israel. It was produced again by Brad McCuen and orchestrated magnificently by Norman Leyden. Majestic anthems and strident marches such as "Zion Stands With Hills Surrounded," "We're Marching To Zion," and "On Jordan's Stormy Banks" blended well with gentle devotional travelogues such as "Beautiful Garden of Eden," "Calvary," and "Memories of Galilee." Also well represented were hymns such as "The Lord is My Shepherd," "O Come, O Come Emmanuel," "Break Thou the Bread of Life" and "Christ The Lord Is Risen Today." The evident popularity of these old hymns prompted the record company to ask Mr. Shea for more.

UNSEARCHABLE PROVIDENCE

More recordings came only a year later. *Hymns That Have Lived 100 Years* was a nostalgically conceived keepsake album of established church favorites, not necessarily of American origin. It had a definite British flavor and devotional highlights were plentiful. Bev was always convinced of the value of sacred music in Christian worship, believing that music could sometimes do what preaching could not. "Christian song lifts the soul of man. I like to think that music reaches the heart in a hurry. When the message of Jesus is lifted up in the soul of the singer who is redeemed by Christ, then hearts are made ready for the Word. Who could fail to be moved when the soloist, choir or congregation sings before a message: 'Breathe on me, Breath of God, fill me with life anew! That I may love what Thou dost love and do what Thou wouldst do?'"

The timeless album started with George Duffield's rousing call to arms "Stand Up, Stand Up For Jesus" and was followed by the truly inspired and inspiring "Rock Of Ages," written by England's renowned eighteenth century reformationist, Augustus Toplady. It was said that it was written after he was caught in a fearful thunderstorm. His rugged shelter was in a cleft of a huge rock in Cheddar Gorge near Bristol. Other outstanding classics included were Reginald Heber's "Holy, Holy Holy," Henry Francis Lyte's "Abide With Me," Bernard of Clairvaux's "O Sacred Head Now Wounded," Joseph Addison's "The Spacious Firmament," Sarah Adams' "Nearer My God To Thee," Ray Palmer's "My Faith Looks Up To Thee," John Keble's "Sun of My Soul," "Fairest Lord Jesus," and William Cowper's "God Moves in a Mysterious Way."

Bev was aware that for those who moved in the circles of classic English literature, the name William Cowper (pronounced Cooper) was highly honored as a poet. Born in Berkhamsted in England in 1731, he was physically frail, mentally fragile and emotionally sensitive. Family tragedies and bereavements added to his severe melancholia. Despite this handicap, God endowed him during his sixty-nine years as a literary genius who enriched Christians ever since. Few lyrics ever capture the subject of the unsearchable nature of God's providence the way his poem *God Moves In a Mysterious Way* does. Clearly, RCA and Mr. Shea were on a winning streak. But surprisingly, production control of the Shea recordings was fated to change again that year. By the time the next recording sessions rolled around, the game of musical chairs was being played out at RCA.

Social Alarm and Anxiety

Taking over from Brad McCuen, Hollywood's Darol Rice was now firmly in the Shea production seat. For nearly the next couple of decades, he oversaw several very popular Shea album recordings. Darol perceived shrewdly that if the Cold War fifties were conceived as times of public fear, then the dawn of the sixties would bring an even greater growth of social alarm and anxiety. It seemed world affairs were going from bad to worse. Bev always expressed to his producer that he felt that faith was the best antidote to fear. Therefore for his next few album projects, he returned to inspirational repertoire that conveyed calmness, confidence and comfort plus the challenge of commitment to Christ.

Crossroads of Life and *In Times Like These* were both concept albums to meet the public mood and the perceived needs of the hour. Thus at the peak of public dread about nuclear conflict, Bev's faith-inspiring songs spoke of peace, optimism, protection and hope in Christ. Recorded in RCA Victor's Music Center of the World studios in Los Angeles and produced by Darol Rice, the albums included contributions from Fanny Crosby, Ira Sankey and Stuart Hamblen.

Addressing the public quest for something to believe in in current times of insecurity, Bev's new album in 1961 *Crossroads of Life* encountered the mood. Opportune songs such "The Wayside Cross," "He'll Carry You Through," "Lead Me, Saviour," "In the Hour of Trial," "Let Jesus Come Into Your Heart," "In the Shadow of His Wings," "Lead Me Gently Home, Father," "Jesus Saviour, Pilot Me," "You May Have the Joy Bells," and "Count Your Blessings."

Always a brass band fan, Bev was told by his father how the Victorians would love to hear "Count Your Blessings" from a traditional brass band although it was popularized most by Ira

Sankey's vocals. Few knew the connection between Nashville's Grand Ole Opry and this beautiful hymn. The cheery tune was written by Edwin Excell who was born in 1851 in Stark County, Ohio. He hit the road at the age of twenty to become a singing teacher establishing singing schools wherever he went. Later he became associated with Sam Jones, a well-known Southern revivalist, who in 1892 built the Union Gospel Tabernacle (Ryman Auditorium) in downtown Nashville, Tennessee. The building became a long time home to the *Grand Ole Opry* radio show. The lyrics to "Count Your Blessings" were penned by the Reverend Johnson Oatman. He was born in Medford, New Jersey in 1856 and later licensed as a Methodist lay preacher. He wrote 5,000 hymns as a hobby while working for many years, like Bev, in the insurance business. When Johnson Oatman died in 1922, he left his inspiring poetic gem.

In 1962, a year after *Crossroads of Life,* came yet another new album entitled *In Times Like These.* It was a powerful musical statement of faith produced again by Darol but in the more simpler setting of the Whitney Studios of Glendale, California. Highlights of the dozen songs of hope for *In Times Like These* were Ira Sankey's "A Shelter in the Time of Storm," and Eddy Arnold's "Who At My Door is Standing." The album was an evident outlet for Bev's passion for pipe organ sounds on sacred material such as "My Prayer," "Nearer, Still Nearer," "I Walked Today Where Jesus Walked," "How Firm a Foundation," "Songs in the Night," "For the Beauty of the Earth," "Green Pastures," "From Every Stormy Wind That Blows," "The Christ of Every Road," and the engaging title song, "In Times Like These."

The powerfully emotive song, "In Times Like These" was written during the days of World War II by Ruth Caye Jones who said that she had the prophetic words of the Apostle Paul in mind, "that in the last days perilous times shall come" (II Timothy 3:1). Written in the family home located in the Dormont area of Pittsburgh, Pennsylvania, the lyrics and melody of "In Times Like These" came to her in the middle of her ironing. Pulling a pad of paper from her apron, she jotted down the inspired work. When her son Bert returned from school that day, she declared, "The Lord's given me a new song today, Bert! I can't wait to sing it to you!"

Later after their meal, gathering the interested family around the piano, movingly she sang and played the song through for the first time. Before it concluded the mist in her eyes turned to tears. The family all sensed that special divine anointing but little they knew how God would use her song in years to come. Many years later, Ruth said one of the thrills her life was when she was invited by Bev to sit on the Billy Graham Crusade platform in Columbus, Ohio. Then in typical style before singing her song, he introduced her to the vast crowd who applauded her accordingly. She modestly blushed at the legitimate acclaim but, as Bev said, it was well deserved.

Bev's friend, Don Hustad, the organist on the *In Times Like These* project was a former professor of the Southern Baptist Seminary in Louisiana. An accomplished arranger prior to joining the Graham team, he was also chairman of the Department of Sacred Music at the Moody Bible Institute and received wide acclaim as the conductor of the Institute's famed *Moody Chorale*. He played organ for many years with the Graham team.

Following in his footsteps with the team came John Innes, a talented Christian musician from Scotland. At the age of sixteen, south of the land of his birth, he initially heard Bev in 1954. Broadcasting from the Harringay Crusade via the old World War II telephone land lines, Bev impressed the teenager. At eighteen, he moved to the US to study. He graduated from Wheaton College and received a masters at Northwestern University. At this time, he became associated with Don Hustad who introduced him to work with the Graham team. Down the years, he often played the organ at the crusades and accompanied Bev in sacred music concerts.

FICKLE MUSICAL TASTES

During the years of the Cold War, the Graham team took many a community hostage with their engaging evangelistic message. Old and young became deeply challenged! The team contributed greatly to the revitalization of faith among hundreds of thousands, and to the continuation of gospel music ministry into a new generation. However, by this time musical tastes were again changing radically. Many were caught up in the hype and the excitement. But neither Bev, Cliff nor the others in the team allowed themselves to be blown about by every change in the direction of the public's musical tastes. Like many established structures of society, the focus of some Christian music began to dramatically change during the period towards more overtly pop sounds. Society's previously accepted values and norms were under tremendous attack in morality, fashion and art forms. Bev resolutely ensured that the Shea music repertoire and production remained conservatively true to the message.

Bev always enjoyed mission excursions whether in the US or abroad. Nevertheless, it was also refreshing to return to the warm and familiar environment of Music Center Studios in Hollywood for more RCA recordings. As he entered, he was met by John Norman, a skillful engineer who would be at the controls. The scriptural truths of the Old Testament were the menu of the day. Earlier in the year, Bev received a call from his producer, Darol Rice. "Bev, we've got us a great new, unusual blend of song and spoken words that we'd like you to record called 'A Man Called Moses!' It's an album that we want you to record retelling the immortal saga of the Exodus in dramatic story form and songs backed by Nathan Scott's fine orchestra. The material for 'A Man Named Moses' is drawn exclusively from Jewish sources and is due for release in 1962. The musical's Jewish text and lyrics have been provided by Lenny Adelson and the music by Jerry Livingston. I reckon that the album should be very popular in the wake of that Hollywood movie blockbuster *The Ten Commandments* starring Charlton Heston."

Singer, Doug Oldham confesses that he started out as "a kid with a lot of dreams, destined for greatness especially when invited to lead one song for a crusade ministers' prayer breakfast." He said it led to a humbling experience. "On the way I dropped my car keys in the mud of the cinder parking lot." Struggling to keep his trousers clean, grumbling under his breath, and crawling on all fours in the mud, he searched for his keys under his car. From behind came a deep voice, "Hey, let me reach that for you! I've got longer arms."

To Doug's surprise the voice was from Bev Shea.

"No, Mr. Shea!," Doug insisted. "I can't let you do that. Look, you'll be getting ready to go on the platform and now your knees are the ones getting covered in dirt!"

Bev was, however, even more insistent. "I can do it. I'm just helping out a friend!"

Doug says that the event was his first introduction to Bev. "I learned that day that Bev's got a servant's heart."

Chapter 8

In Times Like These
1963-1967

"The first time that I ever heard George Beverly Shea sing was in the sixties at a Billy Graham crusade. I was really amazed and, if I'm really honest, slightly envious. He stood there and this voice came out that sounded so confident, rich and resonant. What also really amazed me was it didn't matter whether he sang something ancient or modern. With the passage of time, things haven't changed. He still sounds confident, rich, and resonant today."
—Sir Cliff Richard, Surrey, England

RURAL AND FOLKSY

Critics throughout the years compared George Beverly Shea's voice to the musical movie legend of the thirties and forties, Paul Robeson. For depth, power and tone there was an obvious association particularly when their repertoire crossed. Although spirituals had occupied a major portion of Bev's concert repertoire, not until 1963 did he decide to devote almost an entire album to the genre. Indeed, of the dozen tracks on *George Beverly Shea Sings His Favorite Songs and Spirituals*, half were devoted to songs that survived the slave culture of the early south.

He was serenaded by the lush background of the Nathan Scott Orchestra—again in RCA Victor's Hollywood studio. Selections included "Deep River," "Steal Away," "I Got A Home In-A Dat Rock," "My Lord, What a Mornin'," "The Wayfaring Stranger," and "Goin' Home." The latter, of course, was adapted classically by the famed composer Dvorak in his *New World Symphony*. Also on the album, the more modern country and western material associated at the time with Stuart Hamblen, "How Big is God," and Eddy Arnold, "May the Good Lord Bless and Keep You," dovetailed well with the spirituals. To complete the set, with studio engineers John Norman and Ivan Fisher at the controls, Bev interpreted "The Christ of Every Crisis," penned by his friend Lee Fisher; "He is No Stranger (To Our House)," "Just For Today," and "The Blind Ploughman."

The album sleeve of *George Beverly Shea Sings His Favorite Songs and Spirituals* was engagingly rural and folksy showing Bev with his beautiful one-year-old dog called Laddie who could quite easily be mistaken for Hollywood's canine star, Lassie. The album was a huge success. RCA's self-effacing sacred music soloist was on a roll and in high demand. What was emerging was a definite move towards concept albums where all the songs followed a skillfully woven theme from start to finish. It was obvious, too that studio compatibility for Mr. Shea unusually stretched with ease from Los Angeles to Chicago to New York and to Nashville. RCA's normal practice was to concentrate their recording stars in one specific area. Such switches in studio venues were rare for RCA artists but for Bev they brought with them great diversity in arrangements and production.

HOMESICK EVENT

Outstandingly, the Los Angeles Crusade of September 1963 at the Los Angeles Memorial Coliseum boasted a choir of 5,000 singers who joined Bev in spirituals and sacred song favorites such as "I Would Be Like Jesus" and "Until Then." He noted with great satisfaction that in the final service there was an attendance of 135,000! That same year still in LA for the production of *The Earth is the Lord's*, producer Darol Rice again indulged Bev's passion for the big church organ sound. He engaged not only the Nathan Scott Orchestra but also an Artisan Organ, courtesy of their depot in Altadena, California. Organist Donald Hustad, commenting on the album at the time, said that the album presented songs about man's experiences of communion and fellowship with God. His conclusion was that they spoke of the joy and comfort found in a house of God whether it be an old fashioned prayer meeting or a majestic cathedral. He remarked, "Who but the most callous cynic is not moved by the theme of Bev's song, 'When Children Pray?' It is their simple trust, expressed in a table grace or at bedtime, of which Jesus spoke, 'Whosoever shall not receive the kingdom of God as a little child shall in no wise enter therein.'"

Bev felt that the song, "When God Speaks" was a reminder that prayer is not mere monologue, but dialogue. God sometimes speaks through cataclysmic acts of nature or dramatic events of history, but also sometimes in the still, small voice that only a single heart can hear. *The Earth is the Lord's* was described as an art song of dignity and praise based on Psalm 24. "O Lord Most Holy," with music by Cesar Franck, offered the listener an opportunity to worship the eternal God who is most holy, most mighty and yet our loving Father. Prayer gives a man or woman courage to face life's challenges each day. Don Hustad pointed out that not all praying takes place in the chapel or the cathedral. Much of it is like the simple conversation of two friends walking in a garden illustrated by "The Garden of My Heart." Don quoted the psalmist who said of our heavenly Father, "He shall cover thee with his feathers, and under His wings shalt thou trust; His truth shall be thy shield and buckler." Don continued, "Our forefathers, armed with quality of faith, conquered the North American wilderness. 'All Is Well' was often sung around the evening campfires as they pushed their wagon trains across the lonely plains in the early nineteenth century. The words of 'All My life Long' were written by Clara Williams expressing the soul's longings in terms of hunger, thirst and poverty. The refrain exults in Christ who is the 'Bread Of Life,' 'A Well Of Water' and 'Untold Wealth that Never Faileth' to those who believe in Him."

Bev remembered nostalgically his boyhood meeting with Mrs. Clara Williams. It was his own idea to sing "All My life Long" to the familiar tune of "Redeemer" by James McGranahan. To Bev, the album session was a wonderfully homesick event for him. "Come Unto Me When Shadows Darkly Gather" was a favorite in the Wesleyan Methodist church circuit where he grew up and where his father had faithfully served as the minister. The hymn was no doubt derived from the words in Matthew's Gospel Chapter 11. Each stanza ends with the same promise, "Come unto me and I will give you rest."

Bev knew that Philip Paul Bliss' "Let the Lower Lights Be Burning" was a song born out of a near tragic experience. One turbulent night when a thick fog obscured the essential lighthouse of a rocky harbor in the Eastern Great Lakes, a passenger boat was steered to the dock by the assistance of emergency lower lights placed along the shore. Don said, "It is a challenge to each of us to keep one's small light burning in order to guide some other soul to safety. It is heartening to know that we are not alone in the stormy pilgrimage of life. There are many who stand in faith beside us; there are also many who have gone on before, from whose examples we still gather strength and help. Some of them gave their lives in order to be true to themselves and to God. 'Faith of Our Fathers, holy faith; we will be true to Thee til death!'"

Interestingly, *The Earth is The Lord's* and *O Lord Most Holy* allowed Bev to display his semi-classical recital skills. "Faith of Our Fathers" was a Victorian sacred song of Roman Catholic origin, well known and beloved in the US by all traditions. Apart from this and a few other occasions Bev never usually drifted far from his Protestant roots and culture for sacred repertoire.

PLUCKED FROM DIVERSE CULTURES

For the American government, 1964 was a fearful year of social unrest and occasional violence as the issue of human rights continually took center stage across every state, but particularly in the South. It was championed by Martin Luther King. Bev remembers the anxious apprehension of some when it was announced that the Graham team would hold racially unsegregated meetings in Birmingham, Alabama. Because the team had always taken a progressive attitude towards change, threats on their lives by white and black militants abounded. Much overdue in the sixties, tolerant legislation and determined municipal application was needed to redress the regressive human rights and social conditions of the South. With 300 police officers on duty, the successful Graham meeting on Easter Sunday drew a friendly crowd of 30,000 composed evenly of whites and blacks. Billy's message and Bev's songs majored on Christian love, acceptance and reconciliation echoing the words of the Apostle Paul in Ephesians 2:19-22.

"Now therefore ye are no more strangers and foreigners, but fellow citizens with the saints, and of the household of God; And are built upon the foundation of the apostles and prophets, Jesus Christ himself being the chief corner stone; In whom all the building fitly framed together groweth unto an holy temple in the Lord: In whom ye also are builded together for an habitation of God through the Spirit."

By this time, the adolescent musical taste of rock 'n roll was certainly in vogue popularizing the rhythm and blues music of the South. Bev's assorted song repertoire always plucked from diverse cultures. Comfortably, he started with Negro spirituals and steadily progressed to Thomas Dorsey's "Peace In the Valley" and then to Andrae Crouch's "The Blood Will Never Lose Its Power" and such.

Filled to the Capacity

In the UK in 1964 from September 24 to October 10, Bev and his talented pianist, Tedd Smith had the privilege of doing special evenings of sacred music and song. They were held in many parts of the British Isles including England, Scotland, Wales, and Ireland, North and South. Bev recalls, "I'll never forget being in the YMCA in Dublin with an auditorium packed with 500 wonderful people."

The tour included the prestigious Royal Albert Hall in London, ten years after the Harringay meetings. "As we stood outside that great hall on the previous afternoon and viewed the billboard signs, we saw that Sir Adrian Bolt's orchestral evening was coming up. Next to it was our sign! We looked in amazement and said almost simultaneously—'Oh, if only we'd remembered, we have no camera!' We were overjoyed, however, to see the hall filled to the capacity of 5,000, 800 were standing. As Tedd and I went out onto the stage my heart jumped, a man in uniform parted the stage curtain for us. He commented, 'People say that you never amount to anything in this world until you have filled the Royal Albert Hall.' I could be forgiven for being a little apprehensive after those rather inappropriate words, intended to be complimentary and given in a spirit of kindness. Yet, we both knew the truth of why the friends came in such numbers that evening in London. After my first song, which was the old sacred classic 'The Earth is the Lord's,' I greeted the audience saying, 'Thank you for coming. Tedd and I know why you're here—because you remember Harringay!' Yes, that memory is what brought the people to the Royal Albert Hall."

Sacred songs paraded on the UK tour by the Shea-Smith team were plentiful including several Ralph Carmichael compositions interpreted by Bev such as "All My Life," "He's Everything To Me," and "The Saviour is Waiting." Tedd's piano medley of spirituals was well received particularly at the Royal Albert Hall. A departure from the norm came when he decided to perform a musical called "The Running Man." It told the tale of a man's search for reality and his fulfillment ultimately in faith in Christ, illustrated by Tedd's powerful rendition of "I Know That My

Redeemer Liveth." Included in the program too was the West Indian favored "Tobago Interlude" written by Tedd during the visit of the Graham team to the Caribbean. Tobago made a lasting impression and when he returned to the US, he wrote a suite of descriptive music telling the beauties of the island.

Now a well known, influential Anglican minister in Central London, Richard Bewes was thrilled by the event. "When Bev Shea presented his Albert Hall concert, my wife Liz and I saw it as a must; he had such an influence upon us. The hall was packed. We sat right up in 'the gods,' in the very top section of the hall, where there were no seats at all; so we sat on the floor to listen to the singing. It was a marvelously memorable evening."

SUNRISE AND SUNSET

Back in the US that year, movie director Dick Ross remarked, "Anyone who has ever attended a Billy Graham Crusade will remember that special moment just before Dr. Graham gets ready to preach the message. For it is then that America's Beloved Gospel Singer causes heaven to bend a little lower with his consecrated artistry. Little wonder that Dr. Graham often steps to the pulpit reflecting on the ease with which an invitation for spiritual commitment could be given at that very moment, so hushed is the atmosphere, so eloquent the impact of the message in song."

Dick Ross commented on the *Hymns of Sunrise and Sunset* album, "In the Tabernacle of Israel stood an altar of incense against the veil that hid the Ark of the Covenant. Upon it, each morning and evening, the priests burned an offering of sweet incense, its delicate fragrance filling the holy place with a symbol of prayerful praise to the Lord God, Jehovah. These songs lead us in a contemporary observance of that ancient and moving ceremony of worship. The background for this musical tapestry is sheer delight. Mixed voices are interwoven with the glory and majesty of the pipe organ, with here and there a thread of added color by tasteful brass. To the discerning, sunrise and sunset are more than times of the day; they are meaningful designations for times of life as well. Who can deny that man's twilight years are made more rich by the fragrance of formative years spent in the Master's presence. There is a song [by Ralph Cushman] expressing the discovery of this wondrous truth:

I met God in the morning when the day was at its best;
And His Presence came like sunrise like a glory in my breast.
All day long the presence lingered, all day long He stayed with me;
And we sailed in perfect calmness o'er a very troubled sea.
So, I think I know the secret learned from many a troubled way.
You must meet God in the morning if you want Him through the day."

To the majestic backdrop of Nathan Scott's orchestrations, the Ira Sankey era of repertoire was again heavily in view via hymns such as "Day is Dying in the West" and "I Need Thee Every Hour." On the morning theme were "I Met God in the Morning," "Lord, in the Morning," "Take God By the Hand," and "Did You Think to Pray This Morning?" Taking up the themes of peace, strength and comfort for each day, Bev articulated such gems as "What God Hath Promised," "The Peace that My Saviour Has Given," and "Wonderful Peace." The sunset theme was to the fore in "An Evening Prayer" and "Rocked In the Cradle of the Deep" that was a departure from Bev's usual style of sacred material. Undoubtedly, the highlight track was "Great Is Thy Faithfulness," a gem of a song that Bev helped to make a classic.

High on the Shea ratings was the now classic song "Great Is Thy Faithfulness," co-written by Thomas Chisholm and William Runyan, now one of the Christian church's most beloved hymns. Runyan was a tall, delightful man that Bev recalled meeting in 1939 at the Chicago radio station WMBI. William penned the music to the poem *Great Is Thy Faithfulness* that was authored by Thomas.

As was often customary in those days, Thomas became a school teacher working in the same small country school where he himself was educated. At age of 21, he became the editor of the *Franklin Favorite* the local newspaper. He became a born again Christian at the age of 27 during a revival meeting held by Dr. HC Morrison in his hometown. Dr. Morrison later invited Thomas to become office editor and business manager of his *Pentecostal Herald* newspaper in Louisville, Kentucky. The first call on his life was as a Methodist minister, but due to ill health he was forced to leave the ministry. Instead, Thomas took up a position in the insurance business as an agent. It was during this time that Thomas began writing sacred poems, finishing more than 1200 in his lifetime. Hundreds of his poems were published in religious publications and some were also used as hymn texts. "Great Is Thy Faithfulness" was one such, and was based on verses from Lamentations 3:22-24, in which the prophet Isaiah extols the goodness and faithfulness of God even in the midst of tragedy.

In 1923 Thomas sent the poem to the Methodist evangelist, Rev. William Marion Runyan in Baldwin, Kansas. He was so moved by the theme of "Great Is Thy Faithfulness" that he resolved to compose music that would perfectly reflect the message. The resulting tune was entitled "Faithfulness." The song's popularity came into prominence after being used extensively by Bev's friend, the president of the Moody Bible Institute, Dr. Houghton. The Moody students took the song to their hearts and it soon became the unofficial theme song of the institute. The song's popularity, of course, was later enhanced by Cliff who used it extensively in the Billy Graham Crusades. In Thomas' later years, Bev and Cliff Barrows would visit the poet. Together they would recount God's faithfulness and on the popularity of Thomas' great hymn.

BILLY GRAHAM'S FAVORITES

By 1965, Bev had reached his twentieth anniversary with the Billy Graham team and therefore, an album entitled *George Beverly Shea Sings Billy Graham's Favorites* was clearly long overdue. Dr. Graham himself commented favorably about the venture. Bev states, "Billy is very much a traditionalist when it comes to music, although he tries to appreciate everything."

The grand *Billy Graham's Favorites* session was recorded in Chicago at the RCA studios nearest to Bev's home with recording engineer, Ron Steele at the controls. Chosen to back the Canadian soloist on this wonderful collection of devotional favorites were pianist Tedd Smith and organist Don Hustad. The organ chosen by Bev was an Allen TC4 model. Among Rev. Graham's favorites were some jewels by some of hymnology's greatest hymn-writers, ancient and modern including "And Can It Be?" by Charles Wesley, "But This One Thing I Know" by C. Austin Miles, "To God Be the Glory" by Fanny Crosby, "Standing on the Promises" by James

Rowe, and "The King of All Kings" by Stuart Hamblen. Most of the selections were on the subject of discipleship and reveal much of Rev. Graham's deep convictions. His ancient Scottish roots were displayed with "The Lord's My Shepherd" and perhaps his hillbilly roots came through with a song often associated with the Grand Ole Opry's comedian, Grandpa Jones, "When I Get to the End of the Way."

Billy was overjoyed with *Billy Graham's Favorites* and furnished his comments. "The name George Beverly Shea has become familiar to millions on every continent as America's beloved gospel singer. Bev was already well known when we joined forces. It is true that thousands have come to great auditoriums and stadiums all over the world just to hear Bev sing and to listen to the splendid choirs led by Cliff Barrows. Bev's voice is familiar to television and radio audiences throughout the world and his RCA Victor recordings have sold in the hundreds of thousands. The thing that makes Bev the outstanding singer of gospel song in his generation is not only his magnificent singing but his Christian living. He is one of the most devoted Christians I have ever known. More than any other singer in modern times, Bev literally sings the message of Jesus Christ to the hearts of people everywhere. We hear over and over thrilling stories of lives changed through his singing. I chose the songs I love the most and he sang them as only Bev can sing them, most ably accompanied by his talented team members, Tedd Smith and Don Hustad."

NASHVILLE SOUND RAZZMATAZZ

Through the years, Bev recorded much country gospel material but his roots were not of the typical country boy. The Shea family houses were not fancy and expensive but by the standards of the day, they were spacious, adequate and comfortable small town accommodation. They were certainly not country shacks or farmhouses. Nevertheless, Bev came to record-making prominence at a crucially historic time for Nashville's music industry.

Historically, one of the greatest, trendsetting styles to affect the world's notoriously popular music culture was the genre known generically as the Nashville sound. Already documented as far as being a recording artist was concerned, Bev bent over backwards to deliberately downplay the celebrity aspect of it all. In 1965, however, he was awarded the coveted Grammy Award in the sacred category by the National Academy of Recording Arts and Sciences for his notable album *Southland Favorites* with the Anita Kerr Singers. During the years, he achieved no less than ten nominations for Grammy Awards. He remembered with joy another unexpected recording industry presentation by RCA. "I remember once when I flew into Hollywood from Hawaii, the man from RCA phoned me and asked me to stay in town overnight. He insisted. Next morning at the hotel, I came down to the smart conference room where there were about fifty men drinking coffee. I saw a table there covered by a nice, plush cloth. When they pulled it off they revealed a special award for me as I had gone over the million mark in sales. It's been a great joy to know the message is getting out that way."

Not surprising after the success of his album *Southland Favorites*, Bev found himself musically in the middle of the Nashville sound. Although, never directly a member of the country music clan, he liked the excitement of the Music City. Recalled with great affection and nostalgia, those classic recordings always had a lofty air of distinction that dictated respect. As RCA head honcho Chet Atkins once said, "Bev always knew exactly what he wanted, making him proficient and painstaking in his disposition, in turn producing great artistry."

Bev's rich, deep voice became a major RCA seller. The bass-baritone artist had very comparable musical attributes as TV country host Tennessee Ernie Ford and his repertoire included much crossover. In the decades that followed, even in sophisticated Chicago, New York and Los Angeles studios, Bev's Nashville influences were now in his repertoire, making use of the Southern gospel songbooks. He never excluded other sacred music genres.

Predictably, often he would return to Nashville for RCA, most proficiently using quality studios and musicians. His masterful albums of the sixties displayed his Nashville sound to abundance. His indisputable personalized Nashville sound, however, came of age in the seventies. Cleverly, Bev nurtured his deep, mellow bass-baritone voice avoiding the theatrics of many of his contemporaries. For a while, he was joined by the talented Anita Kerr Singers. The group acted as backup singers for scores of big-selling names such as Jim Reeves, Perry Como, Hank Snow, Red Foley, Pat Boone, Hank Locklin, George Hamilton IV, Connie Smith, Skeeter Davis, Bobby Bare and Eddy Arnold.

Anita Kerr was a professional pianist since her teens who came to Nashville from Memphis in the late 1940s. The vocal group that she pulled together was the envy of many seeking regular work in the studios of Music City. When Chet Atkins started organizing sessions for Steve Sholes in 1950, Anita's phone number was often first on his list to call. Her vocal group could be relied upon to deliver soft, sweet, gentle harmony with a laissez-faire touch of informality. Produced by Darol Rice and arranged and vocally aided by Anita Kerr, the masterful *Southland Favorites* album opened with "Peace In the Valley." It was penned by the renowned Chicago pastor, Thomas Dorsey and was gaining a classic reputation. Originally published by Ben Speer of the Speer Family, in error he thought that it was a folk song in the public domain. In the mid-fifites, Ben innocently gave it to the Blackwood Brothers Quartet to record. They gave it evergreen status. The Blackwoods' version was beloved by an impressionable, truck driving teenager from Tupelo, Elvis Presley. Years later as a superstar, Elvis recorded the song himself using the Blackwoods' arrangement with the Jordanaires. Bev Shea then followed with his recording. Since then, the limelight that these versions gave the song projected it so widely it circled the globe! Another interesting inclusion on the album was "The Eastern Gate" inspired by the death of Ira Sankey.

Other memorable songs on *Southland Favorites* were Cindy Walker's "Child of the King," Ira Stanphill's "Room At the Cross for You," and Southern Gospel's "Prayer is the Key to Heaven." "Ship Ahoy," "The Last Mile of the Way," and "Sunshine In My Soul" rounded off a milestone project for Bev—his first recording in Music City.

A Prodigious Watershed

Elvis' recording base was also Nashville, Tennessee and like Bev, he recorded for RCA Victor. Although they never met, Bev would have liked for him to know that his Canadian grandmother was a Presley. Friends told him they personally found Elvis very likable, friendly, and sympathetic to Christian matters while the sensational media displayed distrust about his so-called outrageous charisma. Elvis was a great lover of Christian music, yet many considered him and his music to be a threat to the morals of young America. It was noted that he had a wild magnetism in his stage act, yet he revered his parents, was respectful of women, called older people sir and ma'am, and even served his time in the Army without attempting to shirk his responsibilities. There was no denying musically, he revolutionized his generation, a prodigious watershed in the history of popular music. His background and musical aspirations had clearly been deeply influenced by the Blackwood Brothers Quartet.

As a young boy, Elvis' home church was the First Assembly of God in Memphis, the same church the Blackwood Brothers attended. He regularly attended the teen Sunday school with a fellow classmate Cecil Blackwood resulting in a great friendship. The teenage friends gained a deep appreciation of gospel songs including the songs of George Beverly Shea. Elvis desperately wanted to join a gospel group but initially no opening was available. It seems likely that the Blackwood Brothers were probably Elvis' first specific contact in the performing arts, an influence greater than any other. No one could imagine back then the heights of stardom he would achieve. Bev's friend, George Hamilton IV stated, "Elvis never surrendered his enthusiasm for Christian music including George Beverly Shea's songs. It's rational to presume that Elvis always loved Christian music even when sadly blown by other forces. Gospel music remained a musical priority throughout his life, a love he never left. Christian groups that worked with him as backup singers included the Imperials, the Stamps Quartet, the Jordanaires and the Sweet Inspirations."

The only Grammy awards Elvis would ever receive would be for his gospel recordings. Elvis dramatically destroyed the show business establishment of the day unleashing a torrent of fresh talent from young Southerners who picked guitar and sang. This new sensation, initially called rockabilly in the late fifties rocked the security of the entire music establishment and industry, gospel music included. But it never threatened George Beverly Shea and the bedrock foundation that his timeless sacred music was built upon.

MILLION SALES

In the midst of musical revolution, the ongoing popularity of Christian music was evidenced by Bev's record sales volumes. They continued to rise throughout the decade. As mentioned, in 1965 he received the Plaque award from RCA representing album sales topping one million, the first Christian soloist to ever achieve that industry status. Three years earlier, Frank Sheffield reported that the largest crowd that New York's Yankee Stadium had ever seen—over 100,000 people—erupted into a roar of approval when they heard the announcer's loud exclamation. "And now here he is—America's beloved gospel singer, George Beverly Shea!!!"

Then followed in the months after, an interesting compilation album entitled *The Lord is My Shepherd* released on the budget RCA Camden label. Recorded in Australia in 1959, the title song "The Lord Is My Shepherd," with Tedd Smith at the piano, was of course, the old Scottish setting of the 23rd Psalm. Bev had often heard it sung so movingly at the Billy Graham Mission meetings in Scotland just a few years before. Also on the album, "I Found the Answer" and "I Asked the Lord" were penned by Johnny

Lange a successful writer of Tin Pan Alley fame. He wrote several hits for the likes of Bing Crosby, Gene Autry, Frank Sinatra, Perry Como and others of that era. Johnny successfully adapted his creativity to the inspirational music genre on these two songs. The Shea original "I'd Rather Have Jesus" was included once again along with "Leaning On the Everlasting Arms" from the Sankey catalog. The current success at the time of Hovie Lister's Statesmen Quartet prompted the use of "How Long Has It Been?" which was one of Mosie Lister's most successful creations. Bev commented at the time, "'How Long has it Been?' is one of the best new gospel songs around!"

From the west coast, from his friend Hal Spencer Bev received and recorded for the album "I Heard God Today" penned by Audrey Mieir. Born on May 12, 1916 in Leechburg, Pennsylvania, Audrey Mae Mieir was a quick learner, educated at LIFE Bible College. She was ordained into the gospel ministry of the International Church of the Foursquare Gospel. From 1937 to 1945 she was an evangelistic pianist on the radio and on personal appearances. From 1946-58 she conducted and organized several spirited choirs and the following year founded the Mieir Choir Clinic in Hollywood. By now a successful composer, pianist and choir clinician, she became very well known. She caught the eye of Hal Spencer of California's Manna Music Publications. Hal regularly passed her songs to Bev for his perusal. Her most famous offering was "His Name is Wonderful."

BEATLES' ZONE

In 1966 and 1967, the Beatles were making a musical impact firstly in the UK and then worldwide. National zeal was already high as England's soccer team had won the coveted World Cup at Wembley Stadium in 1966. At the same time in England, the Greater London Crusade in London's Earls Court and Wembley Stadium was said by Billy Graham to have "made the deepest penetration of any crusade we have ever conducted. It may take a generation to analyze the full impact!" High in attendance were mini-skirted girls and leather-jacketed boys with long hair. Amazingly, sixty percent of each night's audience, Billy was told, were under twenty-five years of age.

At the event, one of his favorite new songs was "Surely Goodness and Mercy" written in 1958 by Bev's friends, Alfred B. Smith and John W. Peterson. Based on Psalm 23:6, Bev says, "Our Good Shepherd's abiding goodness and mercy has remained with me throughout my life's pilgrimage and the promise of David's Psalm is that we shall dwell in the house of the Lord forever!"

John Peterson traversed the Atlantic to hear Bev passionately sing the song with the white-shirted Crusade Choir on a warm summer evening in 1966. John recounted to Bev how the song was written. One morning, while John was tinkering on the piano improvising, waiting for a melody to take shape, his friend Alfred came in the room. Soon together, they fashioned the great song from David's Shepherd Psalm. Eight years later, at the Greater London Crusade, choir director Cliff arranged it for Bev and the mass choir. Instantly "Surely Goodness and Mercy" became a crowd favorite. Throughout the second half of the twentieth century, Alfred B. Smith and John W. Peterson were prolific songwriters with many gospel songs published as well as many sacred cantatas. John's best known songs were the beloved "It Took A Miracle," "Shepherd of Love," "Heaven

Came Down and Glory Filled My Soul," and "Over the Sunset Mountains"—all recorded by Bev on RCA Victor.

Born on November 1, 1921 in Lindsborg, Kansas, John was the youngest of seven children in a Swedish-American family. Sadly, his father died when he was four-years-old. Becoming a Christian at the age of twelve, he was greatly influenced by his grandfather who was the first to realize the outstanding creative gift that God had given his grandson. With the onslaught of World War II hostilities, John was drafted, serving as a United States Army Air Force pilot on dangerous lonely missions over the Himalayas. During his Air Force days, his forthright Christian testimony earned him the nickname of "Deacon." Every morning at his bunk bed, he would be mocked but secretly admired by his service buddies for reading the New Testament.

His co-writer, Alfred Barnerd Smith was born in Wortendyke, New Jersey on November 8, 1916. A protégée on the violin, he guested as a soloist with the New York Symphony Orchestra under the baton of Walter Damrosch. Alfred studied at the Juilliard School of Music, the Moody Bible Institute, and Wheaton College gaining a bachelor's degree in 1943. The young evangelist used Alfred as his first song leader before Cliff Barrows. In 1941 Alfred began his first music publishing enterprise under the title of *Singspiration*. It was Bev Shea's first record label also. Sacred song compilation music books followed and in 1954, Alfred employed John Peterson as the music editor.

At the time of the London Crusades, it was observed in the media how amid all the social unrest emerged a radically new, musical pop sound. It came from the dour, dirty streets of the downtown port of Liverpool in the north of England. Collectively known as the Beatles, the revolutionary foursome of John Lennon, Paul McCartney, George Harrison and Ringo Starr met the reforming spirit of the age. Artistically, the Beatles turned the music industry's norms upside down. Theirs was a new kind of music. The group's unwise announcement at a highly covered press conference that they were "more popular than Jesus Christ" met with despair and shock. It became a matter for intense prayer on the part of many.

None could deny the earth-shaking effect of the Beatles' cultural invasion of the popular music scene. It adversely affected many indigenous pop music artists both sides of the Atlantic. The phenomenal publicity through *Billboard* magazine that had preceded the Beatles' first release in the US via Capitol Records caught the imagination of music enthusiasts in their teens and twenties. More crucial was the fact that the so-called Fab Four met the uneasy cultural mood of the times. With all the surrounding hype, the Beatles' first audio release in the US was certainly guaranteed to become a smash hit and in its wake came wave after wave of similar British rock acts.

CELEBRITY CHRISTIANS

As an American, however, Bev was more impressed by Englishman, Cliff Richard than by the Beatles. He heard his Christian testimony firsthand when he met him at Earls Court in London. An indisputable worldwide superstar, Sir Cliff, or Cliff as he was then, publicly apologized to an audience of twenty thousand for his nervousness and for not having a voice as "big as George Beverly Shea." But then publicly, he stated to the hushed crowd that he was now a born again Christian. Then to the accompaniment of Tedd Smith and Don Hustad, he sang Stuart Hamblen's "It Is No Secret" that he said that he learned from an Elvis recording. With those few nervous words of testimony and his song, Sir Cliff witnessed to his faith. The next day in British and European newspapers, Sir Cliff was hitting the headlines. Meanwhile, Sir Cliff was quietly assessing his new friends in the Graham team for himself. He was impressed by the team and especially the crusade's resident singer. "It was the first time that I ever heard George Beverly Shea and I was really amazed—and if I'm really honest—slightly envious. He stood there and this voice came out that sounded so confident, rich and resonant. What also really amazed me too was it didn't matter whether he sang something ancient or modern, he still sounded confident, rich, and resonant."

Years later in the musical movie about the Holy Land produced for the Billy Graham Evangelistic Association by Worldwide Pictures, Bev was delighted to see Sir Cliff on the silver screen with Cliff Barrows in *His Land*. Sir Cliff Richard continues to come through in triumph in the new millennium. For his achievements her Majesty Queen Elizabeth II honored him with a knighthood in the 1990s.

VIETNAM CHRISTMAS

As 1966 neared its troublesome end, an unforgettable Christmas season was ahead. Billy Graham, Cliff Barrows and Bev were invited to visit the American troops in war-torn Vietnam. That year at home in the US, the government was under severe public pressure. Seemingly, as a result of the Vietnam War, social unrest and outright rebellion against the establishment fearfully reared their ugly heads. The country's youth was not used to a lack of money or freedom as had been imposed on their parents during the Great Depression and World War II. Instead, a sense of moral freedom and carefree philosophy reigned. Thousands were concerned about the anarchy, the rebellious burning of draft cards and the other insults being heaped upon America's leaders.

It was tough, with Christmas fast approaching, saying goodbye to Erma and the children but he felt that duty called in Vietnam. Naturally, Erma was worried about such a dangerous trip but they knew that they could safely lean on the Lord. As he recalled, "None of the troops liked being in Vietnam. A visit from home brought seasonal cheer!"

On Christmas Eve in An Khe, Cliff, Bev and Billy were caught in a very wet, boisterous rainstorm that seemed unlikely to stop in time for the service. However, through the miracle of prayer, the sky cleared in time for Billy's sermon and Bev's solo, "I Heard the Bells On Christmas Day." Many GIs were moved to tears that day. Being Christmas, the lonely GIs requested that Cliff lead Bev and them in singing "How Great Thou Art" and "Silent Night." Bev says, "Christmas hymns remind us of Christ's First Advent and project our attention to His Second Coming. Expectation must necessarily be a part of the Christian's life. The real home of the believer is with Christ in heaven: here on earth he is, in a sense, an exile. One day, like a glorious sunrise, Christ will pierce the clouds and bring us final and total victory over death!"

Bev remembers that, as the soldiers sang, it was a moving and beautiful sight to behold. Thanks to a chaplain, the soldiers each lit an individual small candle sheltered from the wind by paper cups.

Sadly, for many years, the war in Vietnam continued to tragically and adversely affect America's national consciousness and stability. Many individual families and citizens became direct victims of the tragedies that every war brings. One such person was Mrs. Hollis who after losing her husband in the war wrote a responsive sacred song. In her grief, she wrote "One Day At a Time." Bev recorded Mrs. Hollis' song on his *These Are the Things That Matter* album.

So different from Vietnam's rain, trips to the California sunshine were delightful. Bev's visits to the Hollywood studios of RCA became pleasantly recurrent in the later sixties. It seemed the public was gaining a definite appetite during the war years for the George Beverly Shea sound. Sure enough, after a little tweaking and slight adjustments of microphones in Hollywood's Center of the World Studio by the engineer, John Norman, Bev recorded another set of classic sacred songs. *George Beverly Shea Sings Fireside Hymns* again boasted Nathan Scott as the orchestrator and Darol Rice as the producer. Dick Ross described the heart-warming album as "a circle of friends gathered around a family fireside where conversation and reminiscences are occasionally punctuated by the sharp crackle of logs." Reflections by firelight traditionally recall warm memories that are a reliving of the pleasant past and present. Dick considered that Bev's songs pointed to a wondrous future. It is an eternity where "there shall be no more death, neither sorrow, nor crying, neither shall there be any more pain: for the former things are passed away" (Revelation 21:4). Such words were great hope and comfort as the war raged on and on.

Bev's energetic first song on *Fireside Hymns* captured his carefree spirit, the sense of springtime and a taste of Pentecost. "Heaven Came Down and Glory Filled My Soul" was a lively

John Peterson testimony song. Contemporary writer, Ralph Carmichael composed the rhythmic "He's Everything To Me" that were featured in the movies, *The Restless Ones* and *His Land*. In the latter movie, it was a duet by the two Cliffs: Barrows and Richard.

The movie songs were followed predictably by older golden gems "Wonderful Words of Life" and "Hiding In Thee," written by favorites Philip Bliss and Ira Sankey. In contrast, Ira Stanphill wrote the tender "He Washed My Eyes With Tears," a moving song that stirred emotions even in the studio. "Beyond the Sunset," penned by Blanche and Virgil Brock, left a musical statement of hope to ponder as the studio session was ending. In quick succession came "I Believe In Miracles" co-written by John Peterson, "Beside Still Waters" penned by Ted Silva, and the beautiful invitation song "Come With Your Heartache" penned by cowboy Redd Harper and Canadian Oswald Smith.

Bev knew Dr. Oswald J. Smith as the beloved, world-renowned founder and pastor of The People's Church in Toronto, Canada. He then continued his ministry as the missionary pastor of this notable church. Acclaimed as the leading missionary church on the face of the globe, The People's Church regularly contributed millions of dollars to the cause of world evangelism. Recognized as a missionary statesman, Dr. Smith visited every continent to promote missionary endeavors and also conducted great evangelistic campaigns around the world. Homer Rodeheaver called Oswald "the greatest living hymn-writer in the world today." More than 600 poems, hymns and gospel songs come from his pen. Bev said that his songs were a comfort, inspiration, and blessing to many millions. For some of his songs, Oswald composed the tunes but for others the music was supplied by musicians such as Alfred H. Ackley, BD Ackley, Homer Rodeheaver and Redd Harper.

THE FLAGSHIP

By the end of the sixties, Bev was a highly respected member of the famed Chet Atkins' Nashville sound clan, yet he still never reveled in the pride, hype, or thrill of the status. His label, RCA Victor was the most prominent record label in the world and the flagship of the Nashville sound. In the new millennium, Bev still maintained a quiet interest in the continuing integrity of Nashville's music industry. Particularly, he tried to keep up to date with Christian music activity. Although he says that he's no expert, he likes to quietly monitor what's happening. Back then in the sixties, some discerning music experts were saying that the *Southland Favorites* album was professionally, Bev's highest studio achievement. Today in the new century, Bev recalls those heady days with great affection and much nostalgia.

After the great success of the album *Southland Favorites*, another volume was predictable. In 1966 *Southland Songs that Lift the Heart* was laid down in RCA's Nashville studios. The inspired session again featured the winning team of Anita Kerr and Darol Rice. As the bosses, they persuaded Bev to return to his musical roots with some emotional revival favorites such as Charles E. Moody's "Kneel at the Cross," Mrs. CH Morris' "The Stranger of Galilee," and Fanny J. Crosby's "Jesus Will Give You Rest."

Bev recalled to his musicians how "Beautiful Isle of Somewhere" was written by Jessie Brown Pounds in 1867 in the aftermath of the American Civil War. Her husband was the pastor of the Central Christian Church of Indianapolis. The songs "The Wonder of

It All" and "Adoration" came from the Shea household, penned by Bev and his mother respectively. He particularly chose his mother's song for the album, remembering how she said that she wrote it at the tender age of sixteen. "The Night Watch" and "Oh, Gentle Shepherd" were written by Bev's friend from Texas, Cindy Walker. Bev took great delight in recording "God Is Still On The Throne," a song written by Mrs. FW Suffield, a friend from his childhood in Canada.

Love's Entwining Fingers

A year later, Darol Rice again presided as the director of the album session held in Hollywood's RCA Studios. Bev's twenty-fifth album project was entitled *Take My Hand* with Darol and recording engineer John Norman. They included the highly respected arranger and conductor Basil Adlam. Busy days were ahead as Bev had twelve songs on *Take My Hand* including John W. Peterson's "Shepherd of Love" and "Over the Sunset Mountains"; and Ralph Carmichael's "I Found What I Wanted When I Found the Lord."

Interestingly, on hearing the completed *Take My Hand* album and surveying the sleeve's illustration of a child's hand touching an adult's hand, Dick Ross commented, "In the tenuous cycle of mortal existence, the human hand is a most eloquent symbol: the trusting hand of childlike dependence, young love's entwining fingers, the firm grip of mature fulfillment, and the fervent clasp of the sunset years, again groping in trust as at the beginning of life's journey. In choosing his repertoire, Bev reminds us of the ready response to the prayer to God to 'take my hand.' Whether voiced in the lisping petition of a little child, the faltering speech of old age, or in any of life's intervening years, the heavenly Father replies with the only genuine security provided for this earthly scene. In the words of the Lord, 'No man is able to pluck them out of my Father's hand.'"

ELECTRICITY-CHARGED

At some time or another RCA was bound to arrange an audio encounter between its gospel music artists, Bev and the high flying Blackwood Brothers Quartet. As expected, the Southern gospel genre was highly in view for this next extra-special album session with the Blackwoods. RCA's Nashville studio was the rallying point.

In the world of gospel music, the quartet was unique, a legend among peers, successors, and fans alike. No other Christian performers advanced the gospel music cause so daringly in their heyday. Also the thriving Christian music industry, the gospel concert circuit, and the Gospel Music Association were by then living legacies of their enthusiastic, ground-breaking vision, persevering hard work, and success!

Before they even met, in all their formative years, the trio of Graham, Barrows and Shea were close students of the methods, motives and fruit of all the evangelistic pioneers immediately gone before. Enthusiastically the trio tasked themselves with seeking to find the right way forward for their future evangelistic work.

In 1934 the renowned Blackwood Brothers gospel group started out in Alabama. In the decades that followed, the Brothers spread popular Christian music across North America. Before World War II, they put books in the hands of the public filled with gospel songs from James D. Vaughan, RE Winsett, Hartford Music, Stamps

Baxter Music and Gospel Quartet Music. These prized publications contained three major classifications of sacred songs—sweet solemn hymns, repetitive spirituals, and the happy gospel songs. The spirit of these numbers inspired multitudes including Beverly Shea. Back then, he could not have guessed that he, three decades later, would team up with the Blackwood Brothers to make sacred recordings on the world's foremost secular record label.

With James Blackwood still in charge, the Blackwood Brothers regrouped after two members, RW Blackwood and Bill Lyles, died in a tragic airplane crash in 1954. Now thirteen years later, there was a great sense of anticipation when the Memphis-based, Southern gospel singers, James Blackwood, Cecil Blackwood, John Hall and Bill Shaw, traveled the long miles to Nashville in their touring bus, looking forward to recording with Bev. Several months earlier on the phone, producer Darol Rice explained to James exactly what he wanted, "James, RCA wants to capture your Blackwoods in full flight with Bev. As you know, he has a great deep voice so it will be a special album release with your quartet's harmony! Jim Malloy will be at the dials and switches so you'll be in good hands. It will be both a blessed occasion and a fun time. I want you and Bev to help choose the songs. Let's go for a great album of well known oldies and also some newer songs."

This pairing allowed the Southern gospel quartet and the Canadian soloist to experiment with their vocal acrobatics. The title track, John Peterson's "Surely Goodness and Mercy," was new to the Blackwoods. Bev explained, "It's suggested by the words of King David's beautiful Shepherd's psalm."

The soloist and the quartet harmonized beautifully as the audio tapes in the studio rolled. Predictably, the exciting session incorporated the best of the Southern gospel songbooks. Included were "Where the Roses Never Fade," "Bringing in the Sheaves," "Just a Wayward Lamb," "Jesus Walks Among Us," "With Christ As My Pilot," "Heavenly Sunlight," and "Thanks To God." "Tell It Again" reminded Bev of the legendary Gypsy Smith. Classic lyrics were wonderfully augmented that day by the vocal blending of the Blackwoods' quartet with Bev's solos, and knowledgeable music buffs have praised the special harmony ever since. Afterwards, Hugh Cherry rightly described this electricity-charged meeting of the free-spirited Blackwoods with the conservative Mr. Shea as a milestone in the chronicles of gospel music.

James Blackwood philosophically believed in recognizing it as a devotional milestone. "Milestones were always important," he said, "to the ancient nation of Israel. Therefore 'Stones of Help' (or Ebenezers) were erected throughout the land as testimonies to the times God helped His people. The Bible says: 'then Samuel took a stone, and set it between Mizpeh and Shen, and called the name of it Eben-ezer, saying, "Hitherto hath the LORD helped us!' (1 Samuel 7:12). Simple as they were, stone Ebenezers served a useful national and personal purpose!"

James saw the meeting of Bev and the Blackwoods on *Surely Goodness and Mercy* LP in the context outlining of an Ebenezer. "How soon we forget that Christ Jesus is the same—yesterday, today, and forevermore! Looking back over Bev's lengthy career, like us he is grateful for the times when God helped him. Often, we human beings have diminutive memories when it comes to recalling times when God was there for us! That's why God motivated the Old Testament people to take time to raise their Ebenezers of Praise, palpable mementos of God's interventions!

We should take time to remember! As the old hymn declares, every time we raise by Ebenezer, it's a public keepsake of the specific occasion when God met us with blessings of relief, consolation and love!"

In 2001, Bev was reunited with James Blackwood and other old friends, including Cliff Barrows, for a nostalgic session at The Cove in North Carolina. It was a happy reunion under the auspices of the Gaither *Homecoming Friends* video session. It was a delightful, uplifting time for the old friends to wander freely together down memory lane.

Indeed as the old hymn said, by God's good pleasure, James Blackwood safely arrived at home at last a year later. He succumbed finally to pneumonia passing away on Sunday, February 2, 2002 in his hometown, just two days after Bev celebrated his 93rd birthday. James was 82-years-old. Until his death, he lived in Memphis with Miriam, his dear wife of 63 years, and continued an active concert schedule both as a soloist and as the featured artist of the James Blackwood Quartet. His two sons, Jimmy and Billy remain in Christian ministry. However, after his nephew, Cecil Blackwood's death the previous year, James decided to retire the name Blackwood Brothers. James death was the closure of the final page of an era.

Chapter 9

The Shadow of a Cross

1967-1972

"George Beverly Shea is the best friend that I have in this world. We have done so many things together like fishing, praying for specific causes, and travelling in concerts… all the kind of things that two men who love each other in Christ do together. I am so grateful that Bev has recorded so many of the songs that I have written. Oh, I thrill as Bev, with all modesty, prepares congregations to hear the gospel."
—Arthur Smith, Charlotte, North Carolina

BE STILL MY SOUL

In the Shea household of Western Springs, Illinois, there was an efficient workable routine in the affairs of most days in 1967. Erma busied herself with the chores of the home while Ronnie and Elaine knuckled down to their studies in high school. Meanwhile, between the Billy Graham missions and his calls back to RCA's Hollywood studios in sweet succession, George Beverly Shea once again lovingly worked on two new albums.

The first album entitled *Be Still My Soul* featured the classic "Finlandia" tune by Sibelius. The second album majored on the favorite "How Great Thou Art." This time he shared the studio with the mighty, soaring Ralph Carmichael orchestra, backing up everybody it seemed from Peggy Lee to Nat King Cole to Jimmy Durante to Jack Jones to Tex Ritter to Dean Martin. Now it was the turn of America's beloved gospel Singer.

"Hey, Ralph!" said Bev speaking jokingly through the microphone as he addressed his conductor and friend, "Did you know that this song 'Singing I Go' is a song that as a lad in Canada would awaken our house each morning? It's a song that still thrills me! In memory, I can still hear my mother singing as she accompanied herself at our family piano. It became a kind of musical alarm clock! So I guess that I've kept the tradition going by awakening listeners to what you could call the joy of Christian living with this great old song!"

As he smiled through the glass of the inner studio to his friend, Bev started to vocalize: "Singing I go along life's road, praising the Lord, praising the Lord. Singing I go along life's road for Jesus has lifted my load." The impromptu rendition finished on a very low bass note. Bev often said, "Mother never taught me that low note."

On a more serious note, Ralph later commented to Bev about the title song of the album. "Bev, 'Be Still My Soul' is especially pertinent in these troubled days. It seems that there's so much unrest and turmoil in the daily headlines! Praise God for the reminder, through the lyrics and melody of this selection, that for every man, everywhere, there is security and stability if only we will quiet our souls before God and give Him His rightful place in our lives."

Bev nodded in perfect agreement as he gazed over the morning's running order. It ranged from the pastoral Celtic quiet of "Be Thou My Vision," to the familiar simplicity of the sing along "In the Sweet By and By," to the rollicking rhythms of "O My Lovin' Brother," to the stately dignity of "Guide Me, O Thou Great Jehovah" from Wales.

Bev knew from his UK visits that the tiny land of Wales was long renowned for its love of song. It also is a land of revivals. From the early eighteenth century until the early twentieth century, Wales experienced a consistent series of Christian revivals as the Spirit of God moved upon its peoples. Singing Welsh evangelist William Williams was born in 1717. He served his generation with an enthusiasm for the proclamation of the gospel. For forty-three years, until he died in 1791, he traveled 100,000 miles on horse back preaching and singing the gospel in his native tongue. Known as the sweet singer of Wales, he penned "Guide Me, O Thou Great Jehovah," a classic poetic prayer that always reminded Bev of the Christian's pilgrim journey through life pre-shadowed by the Old Testament Exodus.

Bev's choice of songs for the albums provided ample opportunity for him to express his many musical moods. Ralph brought with him several great newer songs for Bev to record: "He'll Never Let You Fall," "All My Life," "The Saviour is Waiting." Performed with verve, the "Battle Hymn of the Republic" made a rousing, patriotic episode in the proceedings. Quickly following was Rodgers-Hammerstein II's "You'll Never Walk Alone" from the movie musical *Carousel* that featured tenor Gordon MacRae and pretty Shirley Jones. Musically speaking, returning down south, Bev did Mosie Lister's "The Day of Miracles" and "Where No

One Stands Alone," "O My Lovin' Brother," and the spiritual "Roll Jordan Roll." The latter was said to be Billy Graham's most requested spiritual. Bev's "I'd Rather Have Jesus" was again minted but this time, for the first time, in stereo sound.

For international appeal, Darol Rice wanted the hymns "Guide Me, O Thou Great Jehovah" from Wales, "Be Thou My Vision" from Ireland, and "Unto The Hills" from Scotland to be included. The sessions were completed with Norman Clayton's "If We Could See Beyond Today," Francis Havergal's "Like a River Glorious," Alice Pollard's "Have Thine Own Way, Lord," and Fanny Crosby's "Safe in the Arms of Jesus."

"Bev's descriptive reading of 'Safe In the Arms of Jesus' is one that holds very special memories for me," recalls Ralph as he looks back. "Also," he adds, " you can't imagine how grateful and excited I was to find that Bev included two of my own compositions in his album—'He'll Never Let You Fall' and 'All of My Life' from the Billy Graham film *For Pete's Sake* and an old song that means a great deal to me entitled 'The Saviour is Waiting.'"

In 1967 Bev was pleased to be booked at the legendary Cobo Hall in Detroit for a sacred music concert. Being so close, he decided to drive out to Birmingham, Michigan to see his old composer friend from his New York days, Thurston Noe. The Noes, Thurston and Mabel, had moved to be near to their son Dick who was working in engineering and design at the Ford Motor Company. With the help of a few songs and Thurston's Steinway grand piano, the happy gathering went down memory lane, somewhat lifting the family depression that started a year previously when Dick died at the age of forty-two. Sadly, a few months after his visit, Bev heard from Mabel of the death of

Thurston. She also added that his last wish was that the Steinway be passed on to his dear friend, Bev Shea. Soon, the grand piano was given a position of pride in the Shea home.

A GLAD RETURN

The smooth Nashville sound album, *Whispering Hope* marked a glad return to Tennessee's Music City in 1967 for Bev. Again, he was under the eye of skilled producer Darol Rice, engineer Chuck Seitz and the unruffled session conductor Bill Walker. Bill, an Australian, often worked with successful crooner Jim Reeves and was aware that the old song "Whispering Hope" was enjoying a new lease of life via a hit recording by Jim. It was written by Septimus Winner who strangely went under the female pseudonym of Alice Hawthorn. Despite the name, Alice was a male music publisher and teacher from Philadelphia who wrote many musical instruction books and songs such as the well-loved "Listen To the Mocking Bird."

The *Whispering Hope* session kicked off with one of Bev's early compositions entitled "Blue Galilee" and "Thank You" a simple worshipful song of thanksgiving. The session minted several hits, too from the Southern gospel genre of Christian music including "The Unclouded Day," "Where Could I Go?," and "He Touched Me" written by Bill Gaither. Bill's classic received renewed interest in the twenty-first century via the Gaither Vocal Band. Probably, however, the first version heard by Bev was by the Bill Gaither Trio composed of Bill, his wife Gloria and his brother Danny at a Billy Graham crusade meeting.

Other songs that followed included "What A Day That Will Be" which was penned by the Statesmen Quartet's Jim Hill.

"Without Him" and "Follow Me" were strong numbers from aspiring rocker Mylon LeFevre and Ira Stanphill respectively.

Born on Valentine's Day in 1914 in Bellview, New Mexico, Ira Stanphill's parents homesteaded in the area. Before settling there, the Stanphills survived a harrowing journey by covered wagon from rural Arkansas. When Ira reached the age of eight, the adventurous family moved on again, this time to Coffeyville, Kansas. Later after attending junior college from 1930 to 1934, Ira sang on a daily radio program at KGGF. Two years later, he became an evangelist and then pastored churches in West Palm Beach, Florida and Lancaster, Pennsylvania. In 1966 he moved on to pastor the Rockwood Park Assembly of God Church in Fort Worth, Texas. He wrote several country gospel classics including "Mansion Over the Hilltop," recorded by Elvis Presley; "Room At The Cross," recorded by Tennessee Ernie Ford; "Suppertime," recorded by Ricky Van Shelton; and "He Washed My Eyes With Tears," recorded by Bev Shea. It is likely that these artists learned many of their Stanphill songs from Blackwood Brothers recordings. The quartet were the first major Christian performers to recognize the value of the Stanphill pen. Sadly, Bev recalled that white-haired Ira suffered a heart attack in the late nineties and died. Shortly after, Ira's wife Gloria sang a moving duet with James Blackwood on a Gaither *Homecoming Friends* video as a tribute. At James' suggestion to Bill Gaither, several of Ira's great songs were performed for video that day. James also recounted how several years ago during a tent revival meeting in Germany conducted by the Assemblies of God evangelist Willard Cantelon and soloist Al Garr, one of Ira's songs was sung in the German language. It was disquieting when a depressed man entered the gospel meeting secretly toting a gun, planning apparently to commit suicide that evening. Instead, convicted, captivated and challenged by Ira's song and the sermon, the man went forward to the altar at the preacher's invitation surrendering to the claims of Christ on his life and was converted. Later the man became a minister of the gospel, crediting Ira's song as being the catalyst that brought him to faith.

CRAMMED ECONOMY SEATS

Britain's Harvey Thomas remembered very warmly trips he took with Bev Shea about this time. Harvey worked full-time with the Billy Graham team initially as a trainee and then as a Crusade Director from December 1960 to early 1976, working in over a hundred countries. He stated, "The impact of Bev Shea's singing everywhere has been enormous. The fact that it so obviously comes from the heart, is the hidden power to that wonderful voice. In around 1968 we were traveling around Australia and New Zealand in pre-crusade rallies prior to the crusades in 1969. In those days, one traveled around New Zealand in a little aeroplane called a Fokker Friendship which was a two-propeller-engined, wing-across-the-top-of-the-fuselage plane. There were just two crammed economy seats on either side in this little cabin and Bev and I were inevitably jammed together in them! Both Bev and I are about six feet three inches and in those days we both weighed around 250 lbs—so it was definitely what you might call close fellowship! Flying was also much bumpier in those days, particularly over mountainous areas of New Zealand and passengers were regularly thrown around the plane quite extensively. On one occasion, over the New Zealand Alps, Bev turned to Harvey between bumps and with his typical quiet, dry humor spoke with a straight face, 'If you could just lose a little weight, Harvey, the pilot could get this thing higher and we could avoid this weather!'"

THREE FEET OFF THE GROUND

So successful were the Nashville recordings that within a year Bev was back in the studio for the *I Believe* album project. As usual, Darol Rice presided as the A & R director of the session held in Nashville with the Nashville Sounds group, Bill Walker and engineer Chuck Seitz in attendance. As the session started, Bev was reminded by Darol that the popular "I Believe" song came from the pop field, popularized nearly two decades earlier by Frankie Laine. Familiar hymn-writing giants were again featured including Fanny Crosby's "Close To Thee" and "All the Way My Saviour Leads Me," Mrs. CH Morris' "Sweeter As the Years Go By," Philip Bliss' "Almost Persuaded," Charles Gabriel's "My Saviour's Love," and the Sunday school evergreen "Jesus Bids Us Shine."

Nationally renowned ABC network news commentator Paul Harvey was a celebrity who took a particular fancy to the *I Believe* album. "Of all the albums George Beverly Shea recorded for RCA, *I Believe* is one that will especially lead the listener by the ear to the thrilling awareness of what faith is all about. George Beverly Shea is for real! What he is becomes more beautiful than what he sings. This is soul music coming from a soul so brimming with love for Christ that it has flooded the world with songs. After spending a while with the Billy Graham team, any man walks three feet off the ground for weeks thereafter. Much of the blessing imparted by these inspired and inspiring young men is derived from their fellowship with Bev Shea."

In between busy crusades and concert dates of 1970, the RCA management persuaded a busier-than-ever George Beverly Shea back to their Hollywood Studios for more recordings with Darol Rice in charge. This time the Jimmy Owens' Orchestra and Singers were in attendance. In his LA hotel room, after the new day had dawned, Bev with the Bible and a cup of coffee settled down for his morning's devotional quiet time. In all the business and bustle of activity, he was disciplined to ensure that daily he touched base with the Lord. Opening the scriptures, he happened upon the Apostle Paul's challenging words in Ephesians 4:3. It said, "Walk worthy of the vocation wherewith ye are called, with all lowliness and meekness, with long-suffering, forbearing one another in love; endeavoring to keep the unity of the Spirit in the bond of peace."

Reaching the studio, there to greet him with a hearty handshake was Jimmy Owens. Bev knew of Jimmy's growing reputation as an experienced contemporary choir conductor and music arranger for movies, TV and audio recordings. He had been advised too that new songs were to be the flavor of the session. Such were "One Day At a Time" and "Will You Keep That Vow?" penned by Lollis and Anthony respectively. Jimmy himself had written and supplied the plaintive "Forgive Me, My Friend." Two years later, Jimmy and his wife Carol saw a special innovation in gospel music led by Pat Boone on both sides of the Atlantic. It notably altered the sedate traditional UK image of churches' use of contemporary Christian music in worship. The musical *Come Together* by Jimmy and Carol

Owens absorbed new songs and practices into the mainstream of hymnody that are still in use today. Jimmy says, "The seeds of *Come Together* were divinely sown in our lives."

At the time of Bev's recording, Jimmy and Carol with their two teenage children, daughter Jamie and son Buddy, started attending The Church on the Way pastored by Jack Hayford. Jimmy was also producing and arranging Pat Boone's *Jesus People* albums. It was while working on these that Jimmy invited Pat and his family to their church. One Sunday evening after services while the Owens were eating together at Jack Hayford's house, Pastor Jack dropped a casual suggestion into the chat. "Jimmy, why don't you and Carol write a musical about our church. The musical could set forth the principles of ministry to be shared with other churches?"

The suggestion struck a positive chord with the Owens. Gradually, the *Come Together* musical crystallized. Presentations spread across the US and abroad. It was a pivotal time in the church—the early days of the Jesus Movement, the Charismatic Movement, the House Church Movement and the Modern Praise and Worship Movement. Jimmy said that *Come Together* became a vehicle to help spread them all. Many attendees found a new freedom in their style of worship that still carries on today in local churches. The contemporary musical also promoted the use of up-to-date songs as well as older hymns like "Blest Be the Tie That Binds" in church services.

That day in the Hollywood studio with Jimmy's modern sounds, Bev felt a good sense of informality and freedom of worship without the production becoming frivolous or sacrilegious, retaining a strong emphasis on keeping discipline. "You know, Jimmy, I like these new songs."

Evidently pleased with how the session was going and pleased to hear Bev's words of approval, Jimmy smiled in reply. "Well Bev, King David in Jerusalem—an even more ancient psalm-singer than you—had a song that said 'He hath put a *new* song in my mouth, even praise unto our God: many shall see it, and fear, and shall trust in the Lord!"

This association with Jimmy happened at a most opportune time. Jimmy pulled out modern songs for the session from diverse sources. Ralph Carmichael supplied him with "The New 23rd." Southerner Arthur Smith supplied "These Are the Things That Matter" that became the title track for Bev's Jesus People Movement-inspired album. Arthur also wrote "Let Not Your Heart Be Troubled."

As the newer songs in the *Let Not Your Heart Be Troubled* session came alive in the studio, Bev felt more and more comfortable even though there was barely a conservative hymn in sight! Country-styled pop singer, Glen Campbell supplied his big hit "Less of Me" and RCA had great plans for the Shea version. "The Broken Vessel" was a new song penned by Los Angeles-based newcomer, Andrae Crouch. "You know Bev," said Jimmy, "Andrae Crouch is a rising talent. He tells me that he received the divine call into the gospel music ministry at the tender age of eleven!"

The Canadian's attention was seized so Jimmy continued the story. "Andrae's father, Reverend Benjamin Crouch was managing an East Los Angeles family cleaning business whilst also preaching on the streets of the city at weekends. Subsequently, Benjamin was called to take on full time pastorship of a small church. It seems, Bev, that initially he was somewhat reluctant to take the position partly because the church did not have an available pianist. Then

Andrae was called up in front of the surprised congregation. His father asked him publicly that if God gave him the gift of music, would he use it for the rest of his life to His glory? Andrae said 'Yes!' He was prayed for and within a week a miracle had taken place. Young Andrae was playing the piano under his father's new pastorship. In 1965 his group *The Disciples* was formed and doors started to open. Andrae's unique song-writing ability is becoming popular from shore to shore."

From that time, Andrae's God-given ability to marry a heartwarming melody with theological lyrics was recognized. From the Crouch songbook, Bev recorded several hit songs and Andrae was welcomed at many crusade meetings and Gaither video sessions. To complete the busy but enjoyable Hollywood session that day with Jimmy Owens, the peppy spiritual "Yes, He Did" was a lot of fun to record. But no track gave Bev as much satisfaction as the old evergreen hymn "He Will Hold Me Fast" penned by the Habershon and Harkness team.

PRESIDENT NIXON

"He Will Hold Me Fast" will be indelibly linked in Bev's mind with President Nixon's invitation for him to sing at the White House in January of 1969. Newly inaugurated, Billy and Bev along with Tedd Smith and Grady Wilson's brother, TW Wilson, were asked to conduct the President's first Sunday service in the White House's East Room. Bev sang "How Great Thou Art" accompanied by Tedd before Billy preached. Earlier that day in the President's private quarters, they ate breakfast with the first family. He remembers nostalgically and proudly, "Mrs. Nixon was seated on my left and daughter Tricia was on my right, with

Billy and Ruth Graham, Tedd, TW and the President. The atmosphere and conversation were informal, good-natured and warm. After the meal, the President surprised all present when he sat down at the grand piano and started to play the hymn, 'He Will Hold Me Fast'."

With Bev at his side, the President turned and asked, "Do you know this Mr. Shea?"

Bev nodded and gently sang along. "Yes, Mr. President. That's a beautiful hymn I used to sing when I was a boy in Canada!"

Bev says that for years he wondered how and when the President had learned such a devotional hymn. Then he was informed that, as a youngster, Richard Nixon attended the Los Angeles Church of the Open Door. There he attended a series of meetings conducted by preacher Paul Rader where "He Will Hold Me Fast" was the theme song. When the RCA Victor album *These Are the Things that Matter* was finally released in 1970, Bev dispatched a first copy to President Nixon with a note of greeting and thanks for drawing Bev's attention to "He Will Hold Me Fast."

Quickly following in 1970 came yet another album, the title track coming from Ralph Carmichael "There Is More To Life." As Bev explained at the time, he encountered these new sessions of more contemporary music cautiously as he knew that they were gospel songs for what RCA described as the NOW generation. "It was with some apprehension that I approached the spirited tempos. My musical associates listened to the playbacks and suggested to me that there will be many a young person who will hear and take to heart the message songs, who without the dynamic rhythms might not harken to the meaning. I certainly hope so!"

"He Has Time" was a little-known Mosie Lister gem. "Acres of Diamonds" was certainly a standard, a challenging testimony from Arthur Smith destined to be sung by Bev in many concerts. Hitting the charts at the time was Edwin Hawkin's revamped Los Angeles arrangement of Philip Doddridge's "Oh Happy Day" hymn from the UK. However, as was his desire, Bev stayed true to the tried and tested traditional version on the session that day despite some pressure from his producer to update things. Nevertheless, Bev was persuaded to put in a performance of "Standing in the Need of Prayer." Clearly, he was more comfortable in the classic hymnal territory of Augustus M. Toplady's "Rock of Ages," Frank E. Graeff and J. Lincoln Hall's moving "Does Jesus Care," and Fanny Crosby's "Jesus Will Give You Rest."

MAYFLOWER

A few weeks before Christmas 1970, Billy and Bev were invited to participate in the 350th anniversary celebration of the landing of the Pilgrims. In advance, Bev noticed that the choir that day was to be conducted by Bev's friend Norman Clayton, composer of "If We Could See Beyond Today," "Now I Belong To Jesus," and many other wonderful sacred songs. They had met first in 1943 while Bev was working with Jack Wyrtzen. When the day came, Bev was amazed when he discovered that the choir conductor was Norman Clayton *junior*, not Norman Clayton *senior*! It made Bev question, "How did all the years go by so quickly?"

February 1971 was still early in the new year, but musicians and vocalists in the Nashville studios no longer struggled with their resolutions. "Auld Lang Syne" was all forgotten in the February days that required new licks and lyrics for the *Amazing*

Grace album session. As usual, Bev chose his new songs with meticulous care, putting them on tape, and then repeatedly going over the demo tapings in advance of the sessions. He recalled how he worked with Cindy Walker and her dear mother on "Tender Farewell" before the actual recording.

Lyrics of older songs too needed to be called to mind! Previously, he recorded "In The Garden" and the title song "Amazing Grace" in his *Singspiration* and early RCA days. A few years earlier, folk star Judy Collins had an international hit with "Amazing Grace" followed by an instrumental hit of the tune with Royal Scots Dragoon Guards band. Bev's version this time had an outstanding narration proceeding it. In those days it seemed that Bev recorded almost everything that his friends Ralph Carmichael, Stuart Hamblen and Cindy Walker submitted to him. "One Day Nearer Home" and "Tender Farewell" were two lesser known Hamblen and Walker songs but Carmichael's "Reach Out To Jesus" has since gained evergreen status. Likewise "Wings of a Dove" penned by the late RCA producer Bob Ferguson and popularized by country star Ferlin Husky, became a major hit worldwide. It sat well alongside "Ezekiel's Wheel" and the catchy Barbara Bernier arrangement of "Do Lord, Do Remember Me." Barbara also contributed "Good Night, Sweet Jesus" while Paula Frances and Gary Romero provided "I Will Pray."

"Brother Bev," remarked producer Danny Davis, "you sure sang like a bird today!"

His gentle response was delivered in typically self-effacing mannerism. "I am in my seventies—thank you, Danny!"

On the day of the making of the *Amazing Grace* album, Tennessee newspaper editor and columnist Jesse Burt remembered how the Shea master recordings stirred interest. Many of the RCA office people came to listen. Writing to Bev later Jesse declared, "I'm confident Chet Atkins didn't mind this spontaneous pause for inspiration in the RCA office. It was an extraordinary tribute to your ministry of music. Your fellow professionals regard you so highly."

With the years, Bev became more and more impressed with the talents and professionalism of younger Christian artists. One bright spark, known simply as Evie, was a pretty, American songstress with a Scandinavian heritage. Appearing with the Billy Graham team, she truly became an international performer of highest note. She recalls, "Everything that I observed of the Billy Graham team including Bev just blew me away! I'll never forget the examples I saw in them of integrity, genuine humility and servanthood. They were so careful that they leave no room for anything inappropriate."

She told Bev that she was born of Norwegian parents who settled in the US. Even at school her vocal talents drew attention on both sides of the Atlantic. Eventually, she recorded in several languages including Norwegian and Swedish as well as English. With her husband, Pelle Karlsson, a native of Sweden and a successful recording artist in his own right, she made her home in Florida actively taking part in various forms of Christian ministry. Pelle worked on a Christian television project. The Karlssons had two children, Kris and his younger sister Jenny. They both united with their parents as a traveling music troupe. Evie says with some satisfaction, "There is no greater thrill than being able to share the Christian message in music and word with the family."

THE HEART OF JESUS

Bev does not think that there are many times when the tune detracts from the words that he sings although he feels that sometimes another tune might be better suited to the lyrics. "I felt this was true in writing the more familiar melody to 'I'd Rather Have Jesus.' Rhea F. Miller originally had other music to her beautiful words. When her written permission was granted to use the new music, she was so kind in saying that it might be more easily sung by the people. By the way, you can imagine the thrill I had during our time in Japan to learn that folks there were singing it from memory in their churches."

I'd Rather Have Jesus was a natural album release project in 1971. It was, of course, a Shea original written in his early twenties from Rhea F. Miller's beautiful words. First done as a single 78, but the new 1971 version had a more modern touch due to the Bill Walker arrangement. Many Christian entertainers say that they identify with the verse that says, *I'd rather have Jesus than men's applause.* It is still included in recording schedules, a gospel hymn classic that many artists have usefully performed such as Roy Rogers and Dale Evans, Wanda Jackson, Don Gibson, Loretta Lynn, Jim Reeves and Clint Miller. Clint said that he gladly made "I'd Rather Have Jesus" the title song of his 2001 gospel album. He said, "I was much inspired by Mr. Shea's clear Christian stand and I admire both him and his beautiful song."

In the studio that day, out of Bev's earshot a comment was made by Danny Davis to Bill Walker. "You know Bill, I wish everyone who records here is as well-prepared as Bev."

"I agree, Danny. Recording with this man is a very wonderful musical experience. He's a warm, sincere person!"

After the rousing foot tapper "I Want To Be Ready," soon Bev was back in his beloved hymnal mood with "Just As I Am," this time with a moving recitation inserted. "Ivory Palaces," "Sweet Hour of Prayer," and "Will the Circle Be Unbroken" also received his solemn comforting touch. Highlight of the session was Cindy Walker's moving "There Were Only a Few At the Cross" and "I Will Praise Him" penned by Bev and his now married daughter, Elaine.

Years later, "I Will Praise Him" was recorded again by the singing preacher from Wewahitchka, Florida Jerry Arhelger. Jerry was very impressed by listening to some of Bev's recordings while working with the music of Explo 72, one of the largest Christian gatherings of its day in Dallas, Texas. Jerry says, "Among all the Jesus Rock and Contemporary Christian performers, such as Larry Norman, Andrae Crouch, Lovesong, Chuck Girard, Danny Lee, the Children of Truth and others, was the evergreen George Beverly Shea. In his recordings I heard the heart of Jesus. Of course, I'd heard Mr. Shea before on television but I was stirred in spirit to renewal when I heard him again. His vocal abilities spoke volumes of his love for Jesus!"

Concluding the successful day's studio work on the *I'd Rather Have Jesus* project was "Reach For the Hand of the Lord" and "Oh Lord, I Am Not Worthy." Back at his hotel, he relaxed and contemplated the last song that spoke of mankind's unworthiness before God. He was reminded of the words of Psalm 69:29-30, "I am poor, let thy salvation, O God, set me up on high. I will praise the name of God with a song, and will magnify him with thanksgiving!"

Observing the session with the astute critical eye of a seasoned journalist, Red O'Donnell of the respected *Nashville*

Banner reported accordingly. "Personally, I feel listening to Bev's selections is like attending a church service, inspirational in effect, a real pro at work!"

EMPTY GARDEN TOMB

In the spring of 1971 along with his spouse Erma, Bev joined his friend Roy Gustafson and a group of eighty-nine people in an unforgettable tour of the Holy Land sites. All the important Biblical sites were visited including the Sea of Galilee, Bethlehem, Nazareth and Jerusalem. Boarding a small ship on the Sea of Galilee, they traveled from the small town of Tiberias to a community on one of the far banks of the sea, which is really a fresh water lake. Midway across the water, the ship engines were hushed by the Captain MA Ezekiel and Bev was invited to sing his "Blue Galilee" to the few assembled folk on board. It was a moment of great meaning.

Bev, however, treasures most the prized opportunity to sing at Easter time the moving spiritual "Were You There When They Crucified My Lord?" before the empty tomb in Jerusalem. "In 'When They Crucified My Lord?', I always include the verse about the resurrection," says Bev. "It asks the question, 'Were you there when He rose up from the tomb?' Some times I feel like shouting Glory! Glory! Glory!"

Incidentally, as an unending enthusiast, Bev was always happy and thrilled to hear conversion stories particularly when they related to the ministry of the Graham team. While in Jerusalem at that heartwarming event in the garden, he discovered that the keeper of the tomb was brought to repentance and faith in Christ in the Graham Amsterdam Crusade of years before!

A few months later in the summer of 1971, Bev received the devastating news that his elderly mother had fallen seriously ill. He rushed to lovingly pay her a visit in the hospital in Syracuse. She had survived her surgery remarkably well considering that she was in her nineties. Sadly, complications arose and the doctor informed the concerned family that her final departure was nearing. They gathered affectionately around her bedside, Bev's brother Alton absent because he was on missionary duty in Africa. The final goodbye was said on September 1. Bev reminded himself of the empty tomb in Jerusalem that he had viewed in the previous Easter. Amid all the grief and pain of parting there was absolute hope in Christ. The parting was temporary in the words of the old communion hymn, it was only until He comes.

'Til He come! Oh let the words linger on the trembling chords;
Let the little while between in their golden light be seen;
Let us think how heaven and home lie beyond that 'Til He come'!
When the weary ones we love enter on their rest above—
Seems the earth so poor and vast? All our life- joy overcast?
Hush be every murmur dumb it is only 'Til He come'!

That blessed hope—the Second Advent theme—was taken up again in the seventies by Bev in the new anthem, "The King Is Coming," a new Gaither song. By 1972 Bev was a very familiar face in the RCA studios in downtown Nashville. In the corridors of the studios, he would greet many artists including country stars, George Hamilton IV and Billy Walker. The regular Music City recordings that the gospel soloist did were welcome respites in the heavy Billy Graham team schedule. Among all the album projects, however, he sensed in advance that *The King is Coming* album project was another special Ebenezer milestone in his long career, augmented by Decision Magazine's outstanding cover photo by Bud Meyer.

Before going into the studio that day, Bev spent a long period of meditation pondering his Bible reading of that day. As he read the ancient passage, the Psalmist David's words of Psalm 92:1-4 seemed to confirm the rightness of the avocation to which he was long committed. "It is a good thing to give thanks unto the Lord, and to sing praises unto thy name, O most High: To show forth thy loving kindness in the morning, and thy faithfulness every night, Upon an instrument of ten strings, and upon the psaltery; upon the harp with a solemn sound. For thou, Lord, hast made me glad through thy work: I will triumph in the works of Thy hands."

Armed for a few days of dedicated session work, instruments in train, paraded Bill Harris, Farrell Morris, Jerry Shook, James Capps, John Williams, David Briggs, Weldon Wyrick, Byron Bach, Martha McCrory, Marvin Chantry, Gary VanOsdale, Stephanie Woolf, Steve Smith, Zina Smith, Samuel Terranova, Sheldon Kurland, Carl Gorodetzky and George Nowlan into the shadows of the studio. These famous musicians were closely followed by producer, Danny Davis. There were greetings, hugs and handshakes all around as the old friends marshaled themselves around the microphones for a day of musical memories.

"The King is Coming," penned by Bill and Gloria Gaither about the coming of the Lord Jesus back to earth, was a fitting opener to the session's hard toil! Later, Ruth Graham expressed her love of the song. "'The King is Coming' is one of my favorite songs. When my dear mother was dying that's the only hymn she requested when we asked her what songs we could put on tape for her to listen to. I love the song's great lyrics and poetry."

With arranger Bill Walker and engineers Roy Shockley and Tom Pick in attendance, the spirited, toe tapping numbers "Something A-Burnin' in My Soul," "Jacob's Ladder," and Ira Stanphill's "Happiness is the Lord" were fun for the experienced musicians to do. An added treat on the latter song was when Mrs. Jeanine Walker joined Bev on a children's chorus favorite. To follow came Dottie Rambo's new use of the melody entitled "He Looked Beyond My Fault (And Saw My Need)." Then in quick succession came Lee Fisher's "Hope in God," Kurt Kaiser's "Pass It On," Cindy Walker's "A Child of the King," and Fanny Crosby's "Will Jesus Find Us Watching?" The session was closed on a happy note and looking back Bev remembers *The King is Coming* as days of pure nostalgia.

Witness to the session, fellow RCA Victor star, Connie Smith exclaimed in the words of Psalm 34:3: "Oh, magnify the Lord with me, and let us exalt His Name together!" She continued, "In essence, Psalm 34:3 is the purpose of Bev's album. Being a great admirer of Bev for many years and having talked with him personally during this album, leaves me in no doubt in my mind that Psalm 34:3 is his prayer for the project. His full, rich deeply-dedicated voice is filled with the precious love of Jesus Christ. I sense it when I'm around him. It was a joy and privilege to meet Mr. Shea and to watch his album come forth from the hearts of the people involved. Behind the scenes, but equally important, is the participation of the whole Shea family. Along with the concern and urgency in the heart of George Beverly Shea to exalt his Lord and reach the souls of men for Christ, is the ever faithful support of his wife Erma, his son Ron and his daughter Elaine Anderson."

FEEL THE SPIRIT

Later that year, RCA's Music City studio resounded to a reunion of the now classic trio of Bill Walker, Danny Davis and George Beverly Shea plus their musical retinue for the *Every Time I Feel The Spirit* album. With the studio technical wizards, Leslie Ladd, Tom Pick and Ray Butts working their audio magic, recording began. First that day was "I May Never Pass This Way Again" that had high sales for Perry Como. In the mid-fifties Perry's television show was hitting the highest ratings. He was born in Canonsburg, Pennsylvania in 1912, and started work as a self-employed barber who had a driving aspiration to sing his way to the top. Many remember him as a deep thinker of sorts, he would often philosophize. What people appreciated most about the great song-stylist was his humble insight, even-tempered disposition, relaxed style and manly modesty. Perry explained, "I now have what money can buy. But what money cannot buy, I have always had!"

Next on the *Every Time I Feel the Spirit* album session came two well-known spirituals, "Every Time I Feel the Spirit" and "By and By" always added a change of pace. These were paraded alongside the traditional evangel-hymnology of Robert Lowry's "Shall We Gather at the River" and Fanny Crosby's "Close to Thee." Modern country music was also displayed as per "Time Out for Jesus" and "Jesus Was a Carpenter" just previously recorded by Charley Pride and Johnny Cash respectively. Sampling the Southern gospel songbooks, Bev gave warm versions of "Life is Like a Mountain Railroad,"

Charles Tindley's "Leave It There," and Doris Akers' "Sweet, Sweet Spirit." Throughout the years the song "Sweet, Sweet Spirit" received hundreds of interpretations ranging from Elvis Presley to Pat Boone to the Imperials to Bev. Doris Akers said that her original melody and lyrics were written many years before following a moving experience during a pre-service prayer meeting with her choir on a Sunday morning. She recalled, "The Holy Spirit came down on me and my choir in a sweet gentle sense of powerful presence. I could see Him displayed on the choir members' warm expressions!"

From the experience was born the classic song, first published in solo sheet music form by Bev's friend Tim Spencer in 1965. Later that year it appeared in choral octavo form arranged by another of Bev's close friends Kurt Kaiser, which became the accepted popular version of Doris' song. The melody was christened "Manna" (after the publishers Manna Music Inc. who were located in Burbank, California) by Hal Spencer (Tim's son) who was manager at the time following the death of his father.

Chapter 10

Through It All
1973-1979

As a youth pastor and Youth With A Mission worker, I have had the pleasure of seeing scores of young people dedicate themselves to Jesus. One of the greatest tools that God has used in these young people's lives is music. I am grateful to you Mr. Shea for your years of integrity and commitment as you have used your talents to help millions make a life-changing decision to follow Jesus."
—Ed McGirr Denver, Colorado & Dudley, England

BEFORE HE SPEAKS

George Beverly Shea said that, from the earliest years, Billy Graham was gracious enough not to arrange too many daytime activities. "The reason is that we are to prepare ourselves physically and spiritually for the evening meeting. In the afternoon, Cliff Barrows and I will discuss the subject of the message and the song that will precede the sermon. Mr. Graham likes songs familiar at this point and it is our privilege to sing them. What a responsibility this is!"

By 1973, Bev was at the height of his successful Nashville adventure with RCA Victor. Yielded afresh to his evangelistic task, he appropriately recorded the *Hallelujah* album project that came again from the Bill Walker and Danny Davis partnership. Producer Danny, of Nashville Brass fame, was a seasoned professional who originally headed a band in New York before going to MGM where he enjoyed success with the production of Herman's Hermits, Connie Francis, and Johnny Tillotson.

Danny held Bev in high esteem, "I'm privileged to call Bev my friend. He has so much tenderness and warmth that once in a while I have to remind myself what a great artist he is! It is most important to him that his singing is his best and that the recording shall be an extension of what he tries to convey in his personal consciousness."

As Danny took control of proceedings in the studio behind the glass, his mind drifted back to the previous summer when Danny and his Nashville Brass were appearing at the massive Ohio State Fair. He remembered being approached by a lovely elderly lady. She nervously asked, "Are you the Danny Davis whose name appears on the back of Mr. Shea's albums?" He replied with a smile. "Yes, Ma'am, that's me—yours truly, Danny Davis!"

"Wow!" The elderly lady exclaimed as her eyes widened and her voice level rose. "What is Mr. Shea like, Mr. Davis?"

Danny raised his eyebrows in surprise at the personal directness of the lady's question. Usually guarded in such circumstances, he was not used to having a member of the public pin him down so directly about an artist that he produced. Quickly he concluded that he had only good things to say about George Beverly Shea anyway! "Ma'am, I can tell ya' Bev's a great guy—a great fella!"

Sitting in the dimmed studio, Danny recalled the look on her face —almost shock, surprised that Danny would call the man she knew as Mr. Shea by the name "Bev," his affectionate Christian name. He remembered his final words to the elderly lady before duty called him away. Smiling at her, he said, "Ma'am, somehow I think that if you ever get the chance to meet and say hello to Bev in person, you would from then on always refer to him as Bev, too!"

Back to the immediate, seeing that all was ready to roll with engineers Al Pachucki and Ray Butts, Danny announced with playful authority in a rawhide, cowboy accent, "Okay, boys! Head 'em up and move 'em out! Let's go!"

The spirituals, "Little David, Play on Your Harp" and "I Have Decided To Follow Jesus" bounced along that day with a happy lilt backed-up by famous session musicians in the RCA studio basking in the fresh Tennessee sunshine. The most unusual Shea offering that afternoon was "To My Mother" by Robert MacGimsey. To spiritually challenge everyone that day was the formidable question "Who Moved?" penned by Richard Blanchard and Lee Turner. That was followed by Albert Hay Malotte's classic version of "The Lord's Prayer" that had been featured so powerfully two decades earlier in a Mario Lanza Hollywood movie.

To complete the *Hallelujah* album project were two of Bill and Gloria Gaither's greatest songs "There's Something About That Name" and "Because He Lives." Bev recalls that Bill and Gloria were married in the early sixties, at the height of the paranoia of H-bomb fear caused by the Cold War standoff between the Western allies and the Soviets. Soon they were facing the birth of their first child. At breakfast time, peering over the morning newspaper with a look of anguish, Gloria read aloud the headlines to her spouse. She spoke of Moscow's latest frightening announcement of yet a further escalation of atomic weaponry between the super powers. "How can we face bringing a child into a world like this, Bill?"

It was a time for him to be strong and firm. It was clear from the slight tremble in her voice that Gloria was fearful. "Because He lives, Honey! Life is still worth the living!" Bill's response was measured and calm. He was in the process of recovering from a debilitating bout of mononucleosis but his faith was built on the promises of God and not his subjective feelings.

"It's at times like these, Gloria, that we can testify that our new life in Jesus provides trusting believers with a wonderfully fulfilling life, now and for eternity!"

Gloria's expression changed from a frown to a smile. "You're right, Bill! The scripture promises that our times are in His hands! Yes, because He lives, we can face tomorrow! What an exciting theme for an Easter song!" Indeed very soon, the first two verses of "Because He lives" took shape. The song lay unfinished at the parlour piano until Gloria's dear father died. In that tragedy, the song was completed with the emotional but triumphal third verse about *seeing the lights of Glory*.

GUIDING GENIUS

Danny Davis and Chet Atkins, manager of the Nashville RCA Studios, listened to the Shea recordings of the Gaither songs on the *Hallelujah* album. Chet leaned back in the office chair with misty eyes sensing an unexplainable divine anointing on what he heard. Chet was born in 1924 in Luttrell, Tennessee and rose to be one of the true myth makers of Music City. Firstly, he gained success as a backing guitarist and then as a guitar virtuoso of international fame. It is believed that Chet's greatest legacy, however, is the Nashville sound. Promoted by RCA to their top job in Nashville, he headed up the world's greatest stable of popular, country and Christian recording artists ever assembled. Interestingly, Bev was the only one of the group signed by RCA under the classical artist category. Chet Atkin's RCA Victor clan, of which Bev was privileged to be an integral part, was an elite group of fine performers destined to set the pace. For Bev, even years later, those times spent with other great artists under Chet Atkins' RCA wings conjure heartwarming nostalgia. Those glorious times were never duplicated before or since. There was a host of international stars such as Perry Como, Roger Whittaker, and even Liverpool's Paul McCartney of the Beatles queuing to record under Chet Atkins' guiding genius.

Chet's professional assessment of Bev is interesting: "George Beverly Shea is possibly the most popular gospel singer in the world today. He has recorded for RCA since 1951 and during that time he has done all types of religious material for the label. It's a good cross-section that includes current favorites, songs from the country field, spirituals and all-time popular hymns. One of the most complimentary things I can say about George Beverly Shea or any other artist is that they are hard to please. Many weeks of thought go into his careful selection of songs for an album, and deciding on interpretation preceded that. I know no one who has tried harder to attain perfection in his work and all facets of his life. To my way of thinking, he has come close! I'm proud to be his friend."

Chet's popular protégé, Grand Ole Opry star, George Hamilton IV also remembered Bev in those days. "George Beverly Shea was known in Nashville as the quality songwriter of 'I'd Rather Have Jesus,' 'I Will Praise Him,' and 'The Wonder of It All.' By the early sixties his rich, baritone voice was already known worldwide. I remember he often visited Nashville to record. Like me, he was a member of Chet Atkins' clan with numerous sacred albums on RCA Victor. He was usually ably produced by Darol Rice or Danny Davis with great arrangers like Anita Kerr and Billy Walker in attendance. Bob Ferguson, one of my producers gave Bev his song, 'The Wings of a Dove' to record. The resultant recording is wonderful. Previously, the song was a hit for Ferlin Husky. Much hype was made about the Nashville sound! But in my view, my associates—Chet Atkins, Bill Walker and Danny Davis—were essentially sensitive musicians who loved their art. Thankfully, the Nashville that Bev and I knew in those days was not built by the accountants, lawyers, sales persons or computer programmers of today. Sadly, conversation nowadays spins more on unit sales, merchandising, and markets than the arts of music and songwriting!"

GONE, YET SINGETH

At the time, Bev was particularly drawn to the sacred music of the late Texas native Jim Reeves. When Bev first recorded for RCA, Jim's deep velvet voice was still to fully mature. He was still struggling to get pop recognition while Bev was already known. Bev remembers how Jim's father had died when he was only ten months old, leaving his poor mother to fend for nine children on the family farm. Life was tough for Jim. Eventually, via radio announcing work, he made it to the heights of stardom as a vocalist. Initially, he hit with novelty songs like "Bimbo" and "Mexican Joe."

Life itself toughened the character of Jim Reeves. Under the auspices of Chet Atkins, he reached his greatest success with the smooth, deep velvet sounds of *He'll Have To Go* and the beautiful albums of sacred songs that included Jim's heartfelt version of Bev's "I'd Rather Have Jesus," an interpretation Bev thought was impressive! When Jim tragically died in a plane crash, Bev sadly mourned his premature passing. He recalled his RCA comrade with respect and affection. "Jim Reeves was a country singer in the highest tradition. Sensitive to good tone, he never forgot the secret to fine country singing is feeling. Interestingly, Jim's popularity never waned since his untimely passing in 1964. One might say, to paraphrase the Bible, 'he being gone, yet singeth.' Like many great country artists, Jim loved the old hymns and gospel songs and sang them with a reverential nostalgia from the heart. The sacred numbers by this warm, intimate artist brought a new dimension of Jim Reeves to his many admirers. His rendition of the favorites come through more like a prayer than a song. I am uplifted hearing Jim Reeves' gospel songs."

Bev's Nashville orchestral arranger, Bill Walker caught the attention of Jim during the filming of his *Kimberly Jim* movie in South Africa. Trained at the Sydney Conservatory of Music, Bill was the musical expert secured by Jim for work in the US. Arriving in New York City, Steve Shoals showed Bill the ropes at the 24th Street studio during an Eddy Arnold session before Bill headed for Nashville for the first time. On July 31, 1964, Steve gave Bill two tickets for the Broadway show *Oliver*. As Bill exited the theater after the show, he was met in the lobby by a somber Steve who informed him that Jim Reeves' plane was missing and that he should quickly head for Nashville. When

Bill arrived, he was informed of the tragic death of his friend. Suddenly, as well as losing a good friend, he was now out of work in a foreign land. Chet Atkins swiftly stepped in and hired him for RCA recording sessions, securing Bill a work permit green card via some lobbying of the Tennessee congressional delegation. Bill's skills were soon put to good use in the studio and on TV series including the *Johnny Cash Show*. Bill Walker was to add a richness of orchestration to the existing Nashville sound that suited and benefited Bev Shea for more than a decade.

SUITS AND TIES

Bev's longtime friend, Eddy Arnold was one of the most patriarchal of the RCA team, along with Hank Snow. Another Chet Atkins' family member, Tennessee native Eddy, continued as one of Bev's long term confidants. In the early fifties when Hank Williams' gutsy honky-tonk style ruled the roost, Eddy wore suits and ties, resolute in upgrading country music. With an easy-going disposition, Eddy evolved into classy crooner, a worthy inductee into the coveted Country Music Hall of Fame. Bev recorded three of Eddy's hit favorites: "Who At My Door is Standing?," "C.H.R.I.S.T.M.A.S," and "May The Good Lord Bless and Keep You." Bev felt that Eddy—his affable Tennessee friend—brought elegance, sophistication and millions of fans to country gospel music selling more than 85 million records. Bev was sad to hear the news that Eddy died on Thursday, May 8, 2008 at the age of 89. Bev held his country-crooning RCA partner from Dixie in high esteem. He appreciated that his colleagues in the RCA brigade were major celebrities and were helping to spread the Good News in song.

Another major Nashville-raised celebrity that Bev admired and respected was Pat Boone. Bev enjoyed that special velvet-smooth sound of the Los Angeles-based, evergreen Christian entertainer. Pat's golden voice graced songs embracing almost every conceivable human sentiment. No believer like Bev could fail to be stirred by the fervent high spirits of his gospel hit, "A Wonderful Time Up There." Taking the pop charts by storm, Pat's early reign of success brought him thirteen gold records and a fervent following equaled only by Elvis. Pat's prized recording successes were all the more remarkable because of his Christian commitment and artistic diversity. Against all the dour critics' predictions and media's annoyance, he commendably scored million sellers, notching up a steady, chart domination in many parts of the globe.

Amazingly, Pat set for himself increasingly high standards in diverse pursuits that included music, book-writing and acting. Many aspiring performers that followed tried to copycat his success. None succeeded with such flair and versatility in all three fields remaining a lifelong ardent supporter of the Christian faith and charitable enterprises. But what did Pat say about Bev? "George Beverly Shea is my hero! If there was a Mount Rushmore for gospel singers George Beverly Shea should be right in the middle of it! For virtually Billy Graham's whole public ministry, this incredible and stalwart singer has been on the front lines, praising the Lord and inviting millions to enter into relationship with Him. I'll never hear 'How Great Thou Art' without thinking of, and thanking God for, Bev Shea. I've only participated in two Graham crusades, one in Los Angeles and the other in Washington DC, and always felt a little 'unnecessary' with this great singer on the stage already. Fortunately for me, I've always sung my songs *before* Bev Shea, since he generally sings the last song before Billy preaches. I just hope I can stand somewhere near him in that heavenly chorus."

In 2008 Bev recounted with a grin, "Pat visited us recently in North Carolina wearing his white buck suede shoes. Upon Karlene's compliment to him, Pat answered, 'Those shoes paid a lot of bills!'"

IMPOSING PERSONALITY

Fellow Canadian, Hank Snow, born in 1914, was an RCA Victor vocalist of arresting quality who enjoyed a very lengthy career on the same label as Bev. With his high-heeled, western boots and sequined cowboy suits, The Singing Ranger was an imposing personality. Hank's parents bitterly divorced when he was only eight-years-old. Four unhappy years later, while living with his elderly, stifling grandmother, he ran away from home at the tender age of twelve. The sea life beckoned and he spent four years on the wild Atlantic doing exhausting dirty work in the fishing fleet.

During the tough days of economic depression, he somehow managed to scrape a living out of a musical career that rose to great acclaim. Later, he started the Hank Snow Child Abuse Foundation. A country music legend for more than fifty years who left a historic legacy, he was a member of the Chet Atkins clan. He died just ten days before the dawn of the third millennium at eighty-five years of age. Hank's son, Reverend Jimmy Rodgers Snow, pastored the Evangel Temple Church in Nashville, hosting the *Grand Ole Gospel Time* radio show that followed the *Grand Ole Opry* broadcast each week. He was helped greatly by his attractive, sweet-natured wife, Dottie. Jimmy's choir, the Evangel Temple Choir provided the backup vocals to the well beloved, Johnny Cash million-selling Jerry Reed song, "A Thing Called Love." It was Jimmy Snow who led Connie Smith to faith.

Connie, who guested many times on the Billy Graham Missions, was born in Elkhart, Indiana in 1941. Raised in Ohio as one of fourteen children, she was discovered by songwriter Bill Anderson and moved to Nashville to achieve great fame. However, this did not bring the fulfillment she desired. After appearing on a TV broadcast, she was led into a deeper Christian experience by the Reverend Jimmy Snow. From that time on, she became a very vocal and articulate advocate of the faith in Music City. Later, she married the talented Marty Stuart. Bev understands from his buddy, George Hamilton IV that the Grand Ole Opry members consider Connie Smith their unofficial chaplain. She often sang gospel songs on the Opry when not many other artists were doing so. Bev is proud of the way she sings "How Great Thou Art" especially on Dr. Billy Graham's Missions.

GRACE, CHARM AND HUMILITY

While on the subject of Grand Ole Opry country music performers, Bev considered his dear friend Johnny Cash to be a diamond in the rough. Honed into a beautiful jewel of God's grace, Billy Graham said, "I have never met a man who combined spiritual depth, musical ability and international fame with such grace, charm and humility as Johnny!"

Born in 1932 in Kingsland, Arkansas, Johnny told Bev how he knew severe hardship from the start as the Great Depression swept across America. Yet from the depths of despair, faith arose in the hearts of those who looked heavenward! Johnny's poor, sharecropper-parents, Ray and Carrie Cash, adventurously decided in the bitter winter of 1935 to take up President Roosevelt's New Deal offer of twenty acres of scrub land, a house, a barn, and a mule. Johnny's family set off for the Dyess Colony of Arkansas. There young Johnny learned the real meaning of hard work followed by the sad loss of his dear older brother, Jack. At the young age of twelve, Johnny opened his tender heart to Christ, experiencing an abiding refuge and strength to last throughout life. Bev recalls Johnny telling him that music was the joy of his rough life, thrilling to country sounds of the Opry. He said that nothing, however, touched his heart as much as gospel music, surrounded with sounds of the Blackwood Brothers, the Chuck Wagon Gang, Jimmy Davis, Sister Rosetta Tharpe and the Golden Gate Quartet.

At eighteen, at the height of the Cold War, Johnny was drafted into the Air Force and sent to Germany. Always a leader, he rose to the rank of staff sergeant. Service life broadened his horizons as he saw the harsh life of Europe recovering from years of conflict. Leaving the Air Force in 1955, stimulated by Pat Boone's Christian example, Johnny auditioned in Memphis as a gospel singer. He was asked instead to sing some country songs as well as his self-penned gospel song "Belshazzar." Eventually, he secured a prized record contract on the now legendary Sun Records label along with other all time greats from the same era: Elvis Presley, Roy Orbison, Jerry Lee Lewis, Charlie Rich, Conway Twitty, and Carl Perkins. Carl later turned to Christ and appeared with Johnny and Bev in many crusade meetings. In reminder of his biggest rock 'n' roll hit "Don't Step On My

Blue Suede Shoes," Carl described himself in later life as a disciple in blue suede shoes.

Bev says that even in the Graham meetings, Johnny's stage attire was predominantly black, indicative of the social causes that his songs crusaded for. Bev says that Johnny was truly inspired to pen many great gospel songs, some autobiographical. He loved to sing Johnny's "When He Comes" that Johnny was inspired to write as he viewed the sun-kissed Eastern gate of Jerusalem at dawn from the Mount of Olives. Full of prophetic significance, the gate is believed to be the gate that the Messiah enters immediately after His Second Advent.

Bev believed that folks loved Cash songs because of his ballads that mirrored true human emotion. The Cash pilgrimage in life was not always easy, full of personal conflicts with the temptations of the world. But he unearthed the truth that Christ's grace converts trials into triumphs. His boyhood faith, despite the meandering roads he followed, was always a spiritual rock.

Bev contributed to Word Records' wonderful twenty-track CD tribute to celebrate Johnny's Golden Anniversary. The CD featured other fascinating tributes to the Man in Black from the likes of Glen Campbell, Pat Boone, James Blackwood, Arthur "Guitar Boogie" Smith, Cliff Barrows, Jerry Arhelger, Bud Tutmarc, Wes Davis, Paul Wheater, Terry Smith, Bill Clifton, Jimmy Payne, Garth Hewitt and many more. Bev was happy to comment accordingly, "My country music friend Johnny Cash's wonderful song, 'When He Comes' reminds me of Christ's soon return for His loved ones. As the old scripture says 'They shall be mine,' saith the

Lord of Hosts, 'in that day when I make up my jewels. I'm thankful to Johnny for this gem of a song."

THUMBS UP SIGN!

In 1954, Houghton College in New York State conferred on Bev an honorary degree. In the seventies, Bev was also honored by two very different awards. In 1972 he received a Doctorate of Sacred Music from Trinity College of Deerfield, Illinois. Then in 1978, he was elected to the Gospel Music Association Hall of Fame in Nashville.

As a result of his Nashville connection, he has known many of the greats of country music throughout the years. Many have recorded their own versions of Bev's compositions.

An RCA colleague of note, of whom Bev is very fond and speaks kindly of is North Carolina native, George Hamilton IV. George IV paid tribute to Bev on a compact disc with a moving narration tribute backed by music entitled *A Lifetime In Gospel Song*. Bev in turn says that no one during the last fifty years deserves a more enviable reputation in international music than George IV. As Pat Boone also said, "George is an accomplished modern-day troubadour who travels the world sowing music seeds of good will."

After fifty years, George IV is uniquely dubbed as the International Ambassador of Country Music. In July 2000, he was elected to the North Carolina Hall of Fame receiving warm family congratulations from his close royal friends, the United Kingdom's Duke and Duchess of Hamilton. Bev says that he always found George IV to be intellectual, modest and courteous both on and off stage and fully devoted to his spouse, family and Divine Master. Known for his Southern courtesy, he represented Music City's interests with great distinction and worked with Dr. Leighton Ford and Rev. Billy Graham on several evangelistic missions.

George IV says that from a distance, he always admired, respected and was in awe of Rev. Graham and his team including George Beverly Shea. He had never worked with Dr. Graham until he was invited by musical director, Cliff Barrows to be a guest soloist in the Billy Graham Crusade held in Anchorage, Alaska. George recalled, "I always remember how nervous I was but George Beverly Shea took me kindly under his wing. When I first arrived at the hotel, he invited me down to the hotel's coffee shop for refreshment and fellowship, and throughout the crusade meetings often gave me the thumbs up sign! I will never forget the sincerity of his encouragement!"

Later, after Alaska, Cliff asked George IV to join the Graham team as a guest soloist for the series of meetings under the banner of Mission England. George IV says that he remained in awe of Bev. He said that Bev made a deep impression that has become a great blessing to him. "What is of great importance is that, as I listened to Bev, I learned so much. The experience helped me grow as a Christian. I learned that my witness as a Christian was a very personal thing, nothing to do with my career. Because of Bev, I try to ensure that I kept the career issues as separate as possible from my witness opportunities. Bev, in my humble view, is God's singer for our generation!"

MUSICAL CHAIRS

In the mid-seventies, many changes were afoot in the music industry. It was a time of musical chairs for many artists and executives as major record companies revolutionized their policies in favor of new policies and strategies that involved younger performers and higher profits. Astutely, Word Records signed up the mature George Beverly Shea after he'd spent a quarter of a century with RCA Victor.

Word's first Shea release in 1975 was aptly entitled *The Longer I Serve Him*. This Bill and Gloria Gaither song matched the performer's motivation perfectly. Co-produced by Arthur Smith and Kurt Kaiser, the album featured choral backgrounds by Charles F. Brown and arrangements by Kurt and Bill Pursell, a stalwart pianist from Nashville. Several friends supplied their prize compositions for Bev to record including "Bring Back the Springtime," "My Song for You," and "Oh, How He Loves You and Me," all penned by Kurt Kaiser. Newer songs included "Until That Time" from Charles Brown, "Would You" from Grace Hawthorne and Buryl Red, and "The Shadow of the Cross" from Arthur Smith.

At the conclusion of the session Bev expressed his thanks to Kurt and the team. "Kurt, let me say that it's been a pleasure to work with you and Word in making this recording. I'm most grateful to you for your beautiful arrangements and for your newest song, 'My Song for You' that you completed just in time for the first down beat. Also, it's been a joy to have Arthur Smith and his guitar and rhythm section with us plus his song—ever a favorite of mine—'The Shadow Of A Cross.' I'm delighted, too with Bill Pursell's piano work and his orchestral arrangements and Charlie Brown's help in the artistry of the backing singers: Bonnie Herman, Kitty Haywood, Don Shelton and Lee Dresslar. I pray that the messages of these songs will fill hearts with hope and joy as they have mine."

Bev was not looking for a response but Kurt beamed a satisfied smile and retorted in kind. "Bev, I've enjoyed immensely working with you on this beautiful album. You've contributed greatly to the musical enjoyment of millions of people around the world with your rich bass voice and spirit of humility. In my view, your unparalleled career marks you out as the premier gospel singer of the twentieth century!"

Those in the studio within earshot nodded in agreement as mumbled "amens" resounded around.

ANGEL MINISTRY

The following year, the US was strangely awash with general cultural interest in angels. The shops had no shortage of angel plaques, statuettes and books, not all scripturally-based. In response, Billy Graham wrote a very balanced, unhyped and inspiring book on the subject while Word Records invited Bev to record an album on angels. When Cliff Barrows heard about it, he jested with his friend. "You know, Bev, angels are difficult to describe but you certainly don't fit the regular conception we have of angels. You're far too masculine, hearty and rugged! But seriously, I do concede that you have a God-given ability to minister with warmth and majesty—that's truly the ministry angels possess."

This time the recording venues were split between Arthur Smith's Charlotte studio and the Paragon Studios in Chicago. In charge of production was Ashley Huey with Bill Pursell and John Innes in attendance. Highlight tracks were two story songs, penned by the Crossroads Quartet's Maggie Griffin, "Guardian Angels" and "You Sent an Angel."

In 1978 Bev expressed his gratitude to Jarrell McCracken, president of Word Records, for his suggestion to include well-known favorites in the *The Old Rugged Cross* album collection. He thanked also Vice President Kurt Kaiser for his guidance in production, arranging and conducting the excellent backup music. There was warm appreciation too for organist John Innes and the top notch musicians from Chicago's finest orchestras who were on hand.

Interestingly, Bev commented on the repertoire. "The song 'I Have Come From the Darkness' says, 'I have come from the darkness to the Light of the Lord. I have come from the night to the day.' It is an expression of joyous relief! Listeners will find themselves singing this lilting song. Truly, our days on earth are more blessed in every way by the hourly presence of the One whose very name dispels the darkness! Andrae Crouch caught the inspiration of a well known camp meeting song and he gave us a new one—'His Blood Will Never Lose Its Power,' no less inspiring. Old truths meet new needs every time. 'Leaning on the Everlasting Arms' is known so well. God's arms of love are strong. I hope listeners feel His arms around them always."

After Billy and Ruth Graham visited the parish church and the grave side in Olney, England of the composer of 'Amazing Grace,' I wanted to have this experience too. So that we could copy the words on the weather worn stone, my friend Don Hustad pulled aside the tall grass. There we saw the meaningful message that John Newton wanted the world to see. I was so touched by it that in the next few hours I committed to memory 'Glory' by Dick Baker, a new song will reach hearts as we walk through the events of our day, good or bad. 'What Am I Worth?' is Arthur Smith's new song. It is a thrilling thought that no matter where we are or what we are doing, the Lord Jesus loves us with an eternal love and we can win that battle of life in partnership with God.

'Learning To Lean, I'm Learning To Lean On Jesus' by John Stallings has words and a melody that seems to ride along with me as I go downtown for the groceries, or head out for O'Hare Airport to take another long journey. 'The Old Rugged Cross' is truly a song to be remembered. I appreciate so much the beautiful accompaniment by our colleague John Innes at the majestic Episcopal Cathedral organ. The church is in the downtown area of Chicago, a few blocks from the recording studio, and so we had to run lines down the main aisle and in the streets. It didn't seem to matter that a few buses and taxis ran over the wires. The organ recorded beautifully and came over clearly on the headphones in the studio. My soul was lifted as I sang! We've cleared translations thus far in many tongues for 'I'd Rather Have Jesus.' In my work with Billy Graham, I've learned it in some of these languages. 'Let Us Break Bread Together' is called an American folk hymn. There is no fellowship so enjoyable and uplifting than to visit, pray and sing with church friends who understand life's joys and sorrows. We share as we assemble together around the Bible, the hymn book and the old gospel story!"

CONTEMPORARY SEVENTIES

Gospel music until the seventies, whether from the likes of George Beverly Shea or Mahalia Jackson or Pat Boone or Tennessee Ernie Ford or the Blackwood Brothers, was aimed primarily at the older church members. In the new decade of long hair, mini-skirts and flared trousers, the younger generation wanted Christian music to attract all ages but especially the young. Suddenly, innovative sounds arose from artists like Elvis Presley, Cliff Richard, Andrae Crouch, Second Chapter Of Acts, Jessy Dixon, Barry McGuire, Larry Norman and many more! Contemporary composers, arrangers, and producers started writing more modern material potentially much wider in taste and scope.

On the Californian coast in particular, thousands of teenagers and twenty-somethings were turning to Christ as winds of revival, reformation and renewal blew worldwide inspired by the likes of Chuck Smith, Jack Hayford, Jimmy Owens and Pat Boone. Not everyone in the old guard, however, initially approved but the younger generation warmly embraced the changes as repertoires and arrangements illustrated.

Later decades continued to push back the established cultural horizons in Christian music as a whole. Large and noteworthy music gatherings started to take place such as England's Greenbelt Arts Festival and the Spring Harvest conventions. Christian Artists' Conventions were hosted in different parts of the world by pioneers like Cam Floria and Leen La Riviere of Continental Ministries. The Billy Graham team pioneered youth events like Spree 73 in London, England and Explo 74 in Dallas, Texas. Youth-inspired means of evangelism and discipleship prospered too in those days via organizations such as George Verwer's Operation Mobilization, Bill Bright's Campus Crusade For Christ, and Loren Cunningham's Youth With A Mission.

Fueled by the new trends, musical professionalism was now found throughout the growing Christian music genres. Many of the audio recording projects were now made in studios in

London, Chicago, New York, Los Angeles, and in particular, Nashville. Thousands of new recordings followed from a galaxy of many new Christian artists with substantial God-given talent such as Michael W. Smith, Amy Grant, Sandy Patti, Karen Lafferty and Keith Green. By the end of the century, it seemed that professional diversity was complete as Christian artists foraged into the whole spectrum of styles ranging from rap, dance, jazz, soul, rock, country, folk as well as praise and worship. Diverse types of Christian artists, such as dc Talk, Steven Curtis Chapman, Delirious?, Matt Redman, Michael W. Smith, Avalon and Randy Travis, proliferated. In the UK and the US, new festivals and conventions that majored on contemporary expressions of music prospered profusely.

TRAGEDY

In 1976, tragedy struck the Shea household. Bev was to lose his closest and dearest. No one can overestimate the shattering impact made on him and his children, Ronnie and Elaine, with sudden death of his dear wife, Erma. The couple had happily observed their forty-second wedding anniversary on June 16th. But in the weeks that followed, Erma became increasingly weak and finally succumbed to cancer. A sad Billy Graham spoke at the Western Springs Baptist Church, Illinois at the September 8th memorial service. Reverend Arthur S. Brown paid a moving tribute to Erma. "This memorial service is a thanksgiving to our God for His great gift: a life, a precious life that lived among us and influenced so many of us. Erma worked with her husband in all of his recordings, helping to choose the numbers to be recorded, transposing the music for his organists and accompanists."

No one emerges from a family tragedy unaffected in some way or other. Bev was heart-broken and grief-stricken. His personal faith was not shattered. Bev said that he tried to remain close to the Lord and the promises of scripture. He took strength from the promise found in Isaiah 26:3-4. "Thou wilt keep him in perfect peace, whose mind is stayed on Thee: because he trusteth in Thee. Trust ye in the Lord for ever: for in the Lord Jehovah is everlasting strength!"

Years later looking back, Bev praises God for the strength, courage, hope and peace that God supplied in abundance through those days of grief. "As the song ['Farther Along'] says so well *Farther along we'll know all about it...* We don't always know the reasons on earth. Down here, we know only in part! But when we reach heaven, all will be revealed! I take comfort from Christ's words to His followers at the Last Supper. He said, 'I will not leave you comfortless: I will send to you the Comforter, which is the Holy Spirit, whom the Father will send in My name, He shall teach you all things, and bring all things to your remembrance, whatsoever I have said unto you. Peace I leave with you, my peace I give unto you: not as the world giveth, give I unto you. Let not your heart be troubled, neither let it be afraid.'"

Pained in heart, it was important that life still went on. No longer was there anyone to come home to. There was no one to discuss the day's events with or share plans for the future. Additionally, there were the necessities of daily living. Now everything from shirts and ties to bread and milk needed to be organized by him. It was a time of major adjustment. The depths of his Christian resources were restored. He personally claimed the promise that Christ gives to all believers: My grace is sufficient.

In his heart, despite the pain and loss, he felt that he still had a purpose to fulfill on earth. In those dark days of bereavement, he earnestly prayed that he could live in the truth of the old scripture that says that truly God gives a song in the night. As a Christian believer, these poetic words of Fanny Crosby were an encouragement for him to look beyond.

When thy cup is mixed with sorrow—look beyond, look beyond!
There will come a bright tomorrow—look beyond, look beyond!
O'er the darkest clouds of night hope still hangs her beacon light;
Through the glass that faith doth lend, ever trusting, look beyond!

When for higher pleasure pining—look beyond, look beyond!
In thy Saviour's arms reclining—look beyond, look beyond!
Only He can know thy fears, soothe thy heart and dry thy tears;
He, thy best and truest friend, bids thee, trusting, look beyond!

Though thy dearest ties may sever—look beyond, look beyond!
Parted here but not forever—look beyond, look beyond!
From their bright celestial dome heavenly voices call thee home
While thy Brother and thy Friend bids thee, trusting, look beyond!
—Fanny Crosby (1820-1915)

Chapter 11

Great Is Thy Faithfulness
1980-1989

As a contemporary Christian singer-songwriter, my lasting impression to this day of Mr. Shea was in 1984 at the Mission England Crusade. While attending this meeting as a teenager, and I guess as a baby Christian, I was greatly encouraged by his anointed and spirit-filled testimony in song. It was also a great privilege to meet him afterwards and be encouraged by Mr. Shea to pursue Christian music and more importantly to grow deeper in my personal 'walk with the Lord'. I praise God for Mr. Shea, one of many who follow in his 'musicianary' footsteps.
—Wes Davis, Bedfordshire, England

In Due Season

Despite his age, 1980 was turning out to be yet another prolific year for churning out quality recorded material. Indeed that year, George Beverly Shea reached seventy years of age, yet was still actively crusading with Billy Graham team. Some music critics were saying that he was singing better than ever. Bev's attitude to the ongoing work was an echo of the Apostle Paul's words recorded in Galatians 6:9-10 that he loved to quote. "And let us not be weary in well doing, for in due season we shall reap, if we faint not. As we have therefore opportunity, let us do good unto all men, especially unto them who are of the household of faith!"

Speaking of the first song of the day, the breezy voice of Kurt Kaiser came from behind the studio's glass partition with an air of authority. He was sitting with the engineer, Denny Purcell at his side. Disciplined as ever, Bev settled down to the familiar studio routine at Nashville's RCA Studio.

Sure enough, after a little tweaking and slight adjustments of microphones, the tall Canadian was ready again for the tapes to roll. His old Aussie friend from RCA days, Bill Walker had arranged and conducted several of Bev's sacred album sessions. He said that he felt sure, with the songs chosen, that this particular project would be one of the Mr. Shea's best. Sure enough, Bev gave much soul to the interpretations and was in excellent voice. Bill remembers, "Kurt and I and all twenty-five of us in the studio and control room were deeply moved by what we heard and felt."

Some older songs, "Have Thine Own Way Lord," "Yes, There is Comfort," "At Calvary," were familiar Shea territory. Bev himself co-penned "Blue Galilee." At the end of the session, turning to Bill, Kurt remarked, "You know Bill, when the name Bev Shea comes to mind many descriptive terms that come to me are integrity, genuineness, faithfulness, godliness, gentleness, and communication."

SECOND MARRIAGE

Inevitably, in everyone's life storms and tempests come during the course of the seasons through the years. In the summer of 1981, Billy Graham's mother died. At her memorial service in Charlotte, Bev sang the beloved Psalm "The Lord

Is My Shepherd." Like Billy, Bev admits that he had his share of storms and tempests. Asked how he was able to cope, he replied, "I have to go in prayer to the Lord, asking him to give me direction and to give me strength. He has been so good to me, and He has given me a desire to continue to serve Him. I am very unworthy."

Despite the Billy Graham team's busy schedule plus Bev's additional recording commitments life for him become increasingly lonely since the death of his spouse Erma. Sensitive friends became more aware and concerned about his solitary plight. Indeed, while in Korea, Billy one day mentioned to Bev that ten years as a widower was long enough! He was introduced to Karlene Aceto who was working for the Billy Graham Evangelistic Association in Billy's hometown office in Montreat, North Carolina. About this time, I asked Bev if he had any unfulfilled dreams. He answered with a twinkle in his eyes. "Well, Paul, my dear wife Erma passed away eight years ago. I find it very strange living without her. She was a woman of great humor who would invent things to make me laugh. I've a new home and I just wish she was there. I've been praying for the Lord to possibly let me meet somebody. I should say that I have met somebody but that person still hasn't said yes... yet!"

Finally, she did say yes and after a brief courtship, Karlene and Bev were married in the Graham's mountain home just before Christmas. Bev's friends directed him to the powerful wisdom of the book of Proverbs. "Who can find a virtuous woman? For her price is far above rubies. The heart of her husband doth safely trust in her, so that he shall have no need of spoil. She will do him good and not evil all the days of her life."

The marriage was a happy union. Five years later with great gratitude, Bev stated, "God has been so good in giving me a helpmate again, after Erma's death some thirteen years ago. I was seventy-six years old when I married again. I am sure that Karlene was a wonderful God-sent helpmate to me. The Lord was good to give me someone who had been working in our association for fourteen years, someone who knew everybody whom I have known. She has been traveling with me since our marriage; she is a beautiful person."

In view of Bev's experience of a second marriage, Cliff Barrows asked him what advice he would give to an eighty-year-old person who wonders if there is anything left for him to do in life. Cliff asked, "What about the future? Do you think much about it?"

There was no hesitation in Bev's spirited answer. "Oh yes, Cliff, I do think about it, and I think that as you reach eighty—just keep the smile on your face! Let other people know that you are okay, even if you have a pain somewhere. That smile radiates and touches others. Enjoy it... enjoy eighty. I like those words, 'fear not tomorrow, God is already there.' Someone asked me not too long ago, 'How do you want to be remembered?' I said, 'That I always stayed on key.'"

The newly married Sheas chose to purchase their RCA *Reader's Digest* house in the same beautiful small town as the Grahams live, near Asheville in the Blue Ridge Mountain range. Bev says that he praises God that the royalties from his Readers Digest box of CDs came out just at the opportune time when they needed a deposit to purchase a new home. Soon after their marriage, the happy couple were hitting the road together. Greatly enthused, Karlene said that the Crystal Cathedral in California was the first place that her husband took her after their wedding and honeymoon.

They had only been married for two weeks when Bev was asked to sing on the Robert Schuller's *Hour of Power* television broadcast seen worldwide.

SONG-STYLIST

Later Bev was delighted to be awarded the recording industry's prestigious Gold Angel statuette by Religion in Media of America as the All-Time Gospel Singer. Before a capacity audience in the Grand Ballroom of Hollywood's Sheraton Universal Hotel, the noted entertainer Carol Lawrence said, "I was thrilled when I was asked to present this award. I remember so well that the 100th Psalm begins with the admonition to enter the Lord's presence with singing and millions of worshipers around the world have been ushered into the very presence of God through the consecrated artistry of George Beverly Shea. His voice has been preparing the hearts of Billy Graham's audiences for the evangelist's spoken word. His ministries through records, radio and television broadcasts, on the concert platform and as a composer have given him a unique place in the realm of gospel music."

Affectionately George Beverly Shea was called "America's Beloved Gospel Singer." Equally at home singing in the simple service of a rescue mission or in a full length, sacred concert in London's Royal Albert Hall, New York's Carnegie Hall, or in a great stadium with Dr. Graham, he had evolved into a much beloved sacred song stylist. The tall Canadian bass-baritone was now recognizable in name and voice by millions around the globe through crusades, concerts, radio, television and recordings. His diverse albums presented him in programs that covered a wide spectrum of musical styles and spiritual contexts.

He was professionally competent and emotionally comfortable whether his song was a classic liturgical melody, a majestic British folk hymn, or a simple American folk spiritual. Each was carefully selected and prayerfully sung with selflessness, comeliness and earnestness.

From an insurance firm to showing people how to obtain heaven's blessed assurance, Bev said that every hymn, gospel song or spiritual he sang had to be a testimony to Almighty God. This deeply felt consecration accounts for his reverent treatment of older hymn favorites as well as the newer compositions. High on his personal priority was the non-negotiable condition that whatever song he sang had to be firstly, in harmony with the ancient Holy Scriptures and secondly, with the truths of the orthodox Christian message. By the eighties, he was heard and seen with the team on television and radio broadcasts galore around the globe.

LIKES AND DISLIKES

When it came to his subjective love of specific songs, Bev, unlike most vocal performers, was not opinionated but held strong convictions about his selection of songs. He wanted songs that touched the heart!

Concerning the past, looking back objectively, it is plain to see that Bev's lengthy music ministry has seen a pleasing parade of contrasting musical styles and assorted poetic songwriters. Yet in his time, he left others to pioneer or perpetuate the changes in musical fashions. On the song writing side, the authors and composers he most often called upon ranged from Charles Wesley to Stuart Hamblen to Bill Gaither to Fanny Crosby to

Ira Sankey to Philip Bliss to Andrae Crouch to Cindy Walker to Arthur Smith and many others.

Bev says that he is delighted that these classic songwriters advanced beyond trite and banal sentimentality to include strong theology. He said that he always tried to encourage lyrical poets and tune smiths whose material was true to the testimony of the scriptures. He is very pleased to have observed Christian music's developing maturity. Asked whether he approved and was happy with the modernization of Christian music, he replied, "Oh, I can't be an expert. I try to appreciate that most of these kids really love the Lord and are trying to spread the message, instead of singing the secular songs of the hour."

Always on the lookout for worthy material, his lengthy music ministry watched the growth of new generations of contemporary and aesthetically-rich Christian artists. He speaks well of those stalwart and talented artists. "I'm gratified to state that in the present there are still invigorating and innovative Christian performers, deserving of their heavenly calling!"

As a professional singer, Bev's songs were always rich in spiritual teaching and imagery. His ministry motivation was centered in his fundamental understanding of the central message of the Great Commission found in the words of the Apostle John.

For God sent not His Son into the world to condemn the world; but that the world through Him might be saved. He that believeth on Him is not condemned: but he that believeth not is condemned already, because he hath not believed in the name of the only begotten Son of God. And this is the condemnation, that light is come

into the world, and men loved darkness rather than light, because their deeds were evil
(John 3:17-19).

Bev's traditional style never faced the necessity to negotiate the deceptive transformations in musical territories that fads and fashions normally bring. Yet, there was always cohesion in his musical works. His remarkable capability that stands out over time was to pick quality sacred songs that reflected his knowledge of the scriptures.

Last but not least his sacred songs always reflected his best qualities as a singing Christian minister. As a noteworthy composer of classy melodies and the author of meaningful lyrics, the sacred songs he wrote incorporated the same quality, high integrity message as his repertoire choices. He composed the music at age twenty-three to one of his best-known solos, "I'd Rather Have Jesus," to words by Mrs. Rhea H. Miller on the family piano. He also wrote or co-wrote "The Wonder of It All," "I Will Praise Him," "Sing Me a Song of Sharon's Rose," "I Love Thy Presence, Lord" and "The Prodigal Son."

PRAISE AND WORSHIP

In the 1980's Bev was introduced to a brand new set of modern sacred songs recently penned in the British Isles. The occasion was Mission England, the opening week of which was in Bristol. He was really excited about the prospect as he joined a select group of outstanding guest soloists that included Sir Cliff Richard, George Hamilton IV, Sheila Walsh, Sandi Patty, Dennis Agajanian, Marilyn Baker, Larnelle Harris, Myrtle Hall, Andrew Culverwell,

Dave Pope and Graham Kendrick. Those colorful days made deep impressions on Bev. He explained that Mission England, and later Mission Scotland, became noteworthy blessings to him as he listened to its music. He said that he experienced so much. The UK events aided his appreciation of the more modern styles of praise and worship songs that became popular in the second half of the twentieth century. He said that he could never forget those wonderfully fresh, majestic melodies of praise such as Laurie Klein's "I Love You Lord."

Cliff Barrow's choir rendition of "Majesty" became a modern day Christian anthem, as his friend, crooner Pat Boone explained. "Jack's lyrics spoke of the Kingship of Christ, a most lofty theme. They declared so powerfully the truth of the sovereignty of Christ. They herald the day when, as the scripture declares, every knee shall bow before Him and acknowledge Him to be truly 'His Majesty, King of Kings and Lord of Lords!'"

As usual, in Mission England and Mission Scotland, Cliff Barrows' engaging smile and effervescent charm motivated the crowds of thousands to lift their voices in praise of God in song. Bev thought that the stately musical sounds of the massive choirs under his direction brought to contemplation an anticipation of what awaits the saints in heaven! Bev agreed with Cliff when he said, "Mission England will long be remembered in the history of the Christian church as a time of spiritual refreshment and awakening as the Holy Spirit moved in a unique way across the land. It was a time of new songs lifted in praise; marvelous things done by the right hand of God; and triumphant victory for the Lord who reigns over all. In those precious weeks, we met to celebrate our faith through the proclamation of God's word, through prayer, through praise, through fellowship. How can we ever forget the football stadiums filled to overflowing with joyful multitudes singing the praises of God as thousands responded to the preaching of his word through Billy Graham?"

During Mission England, Arthur Smith remembers Bev singing his song, "The Shadow of a Cross" in London's Earl's Court. "My wife, Dorothy and Bev's wife Karlene and I were sitting on the platform alongside Cliff Barrows, TW Wilson and a group of distinguished people. As the crowd was beginning to anticipate Bev's singing and Billy's preaching, Billy turned around, reached over and taking my arm said, "Arthur, please ask Bev to sing 'The Shadow of a Cross.'"

Arthur promptly whispered Billy's request to Bev. With a knowing smile, he consented accordingly. "Oh, I did thrill to Bev's rendition of 'The Shadow of a Cross' that night," said Arthur, "as with all modesty he prepared the congregation ready to hear the gospel. Thousands came to know Jesus that night because of Billy's strong preaching message."

Predictably, the weather at times all across the United Kingdom was inclement. Singer and TV host Sheila Walsh remembers the cold very well. "I remember sitting on a cold stage with Mr. Shea at a mission meeting. The wind and rain were beating down on us and he took the blanket off his knees and gave it to me. I thought to myself at the time, 'I'm sure at his age he feels the cold more than I do.' But the incident illustrates the measure of the man's character, a man with such a big heart. I also recall another incident. Again, I remember sitting on a platform with and listening to Bev singing that incredible hymn, 'Great Is Thy

Faithfulness' in that rich voice that seemed to ring through that whole sports stadium. Then Graham Kendrick leaned over to me and said, 'Sheila, when you're his age, do you think that you'll be able to sing like that?' I replied, 'No, Graham, I won't be able to sing like that at that age cause I can't sing like that now!'"

Sheila's friend, Graham Kendrick was a fairly new name to Bev but one that now epitomizes the best of the British contemporary Christian music scene. Graham and his band often opened up the Mission England meetings. Bev agreed with Sheila that there was no denying that Graham had a special way with words. Raised in Putney Baptist Church near southwest London's River Thames, he was well apprenticed by his father, the minister. Soaked in Biblical knowledge from an early age, Graham said it enabled him to musically retell many of the familiar scriptural incidents through the eyes of the people there. He told Bev that as a Christian poet, he adventurously used appropriate imagery and symbolism, but points out that the source of his inspiration is the living Jesus Christ in his experience. In his songs, Graham said that he felt the urgency to not only preach the gospel but to encourage other Christians, particularly the young, to do likewise.

MIDNIGHT TONIC

Peter Honour of England's Pocket Testament League remembered how Billy Graham and the team were always welcomed to Britain over many years, especially for his mission to London. "It was an outstanding time of evangelism. Hundreds of churches joined together to befriend folk outside of church life and bring them to hear the powerful preaching of the Good News, by Billy Graham and his team. Mission to London was centered on four different venues: West Ham Football Ground in East London; Crystal Palace Sports complex in Southeast London; Earls Court Arena in West London; with a grand finale at Wembley Stadium. I remember Billy remarked to the 85,000 present that every time he preached in Wembley Stadium it rained except on one occasion—then it snowed!"

Peter Honour was invited to lead the Follow Up Team that processed the thousands of cards completed by the mission counselors when people responded to Billy's nightly invitation to receive Christ. Leading a committed team of over 1200 trained volunteers from a huge variety of London churches was a challenge to Peter. But he says that his ten section managers did a marvelous job organizing people to sort cards, provide nightly statistics, research further information required, check details, type forms, collate materials, and by 6 a.m. the next day have letters ready in mail bags to post to church ministers and enquirers. He says, "The Follow Up Team's work was a tiring nightly operation. Many of these volunteers had already sung in the choir or helped as a steward and when everyone else went home they stayed—many from 10 p.m. until 6 a.m. the next day—or until they dropped. As the team leader, I had a responsibility to make sure the work was accomplished. I'm glad to say that the Follow Up Team workers didn't fall asleep on the job! A catering team made sure that everyone had plenty to eat and drink throughout the night. And Mission Chairman Rev. Richard Bewes agreed with me that certain personalities would drop in to bless and encourage the workers as midnight tonics. Around 11 p.m. the work stopped and the team listened to leaders such as George Hoffman, then with Samaritan's

Purse; Richard Bewes with his telling anecdotes; National Mission Director Gavin Reid; and singers such as George Hamilton IV, Cliff Richard, and George Beverly Shea. I recall vividly one memorable night. Bev came accompanied by Cliff Barrows. As soon as they set foot in the indoor football pitch at Crystal Palace where the Follow Up Team were working, a hush went around the room. People stopped their work and you could hear comments such as, 'Yes, it really is Bev Shea!' and 'Oooh, this will be a treat tonight!' I remember how I called the workers to attention, gave the usual announcements, and presented the statistics for that night. This was always a joy for me as it was always accompanied with loud applause. Then I said briefly, 'Brothers and sisters, we are delighted to welcome to our office tonight, two great champions of the faith. Two men who have worked tirelessly with Dr. Graham. Two men who love to sing God's praises. Let's welcome our brothers in Christ Cliff Barrows and Bev Shea!'"

Loud and prolonged applause followed the team leader's words. When the noise waned, Peter says that Cliff spoke for a while, encouraging and thanking the workers. He then suggested, "Why don't we sing together? Would you like that? What should we sing?"

Peter continues, "Several ideas came from the floor. But by far, the strongest request was for 'How Great Thou Art.' So then and there, right in the middle of the night, the 400 workers joined in the chorus as Bev personally sang them that beautiful song, conducted by the master of all choir leaders, Cliff. That night, after such inspiration from Mr. Shea and Mr. Barrows, the Follow Up department worked even harder and better than usual.

It seemed as if all the tiring jobs were accomplished quicker and easier than any other time!"

DIVINELY INSPIRED

Despite the weather, during gaps in the very busy schedule of Mission England, Bev, with Cliff Barrows and George Hamilton IV, thrilled at the prospect of visiting two historic sites important to the chronicle of gospel music. Bev remembers the experiences with warm nostalgia. "It was an immense and unforgettable thrill to sing along in harmony with Cliff and George as George strummed on his old Grand Ole Opry guitar near the sites where the magnificent hymns 'Rock of Ages' and 'Amazing Grace' were penned!"

Rock of Ages, cleft for me,
Let me hide myself in Thee;
Let the water and the blood,
From Thy wounded side that flowed,
Be of sin the double cure,
Cleanse me from its guilt and power.

Nothing in my hand I bring,
Simply to Thy Cross I cling;
Naked, come to Thee for dress;
Helpless, look to Thee for grace;
Foul, I to the fountain fly:
Wash me, Saviour, or I die.
—Augustus M. Toplady (1740-1778)

It was a hymn known and loved by all, a favorite throughout the years from Bev's childhood to old age. He lost count of the number of times that he had recorded it. Emotional feelings flowed deeply as the trio articulated the unchanging truths of the timeless classic. The hymn was written by the eighteenth century Calvinist, Reverend Augustus Toplady. It was understood that Augustus was divinely inspired while taking urgent refuge from a violent storm in the cleft of a huge rock in Burrington Combe, near Cheddar, England.

A week later, the trio next visited a site that Bev initially remembered was related to him by Billy and Ruth Graham. The loving couple had some prized time to themselves and were motoring in England when they came to Olney in Buckinghamshire. It was there that John Newton, composer of "Amazing Grace," rests today. Greatly moved by what they read on his memorial stone there in the Anglican churchyard, they could hardly wait to get back to the hotel and tell Bev, Cliff and George IV. Thus the trio set off fifty miles north of London in pilgrimage.

Olney was a quaint, historical country village. Sure enough, just as the Grahams had said, there in the corner of the parish graveyard they viewed the stone in memory of Church of England cleric, Reverend John Newton. To Bev, his story is as exciting as fiction. John was born in 1725 and entered the Royal Navy at the age of eleven. He eventually deserted becoming a slave trader. After a dramatic conversion in a sea storm, he became the faithful minister of Olney and wrote "Amazing Grace" in 1779 as an autobiographical poem. Having seen the place where John Newton rests at first hand, Bev wrote this narration. "They were meaningful words... the ones I read in the small church yard at Olney, England where the composer of this great hymn of faith was laid to rest. Inside the church—his pulpit. Outside on his stone, this inscription: *John Newton, clerk, once an infidel and libertine, a servant of slaves in Africa, was by the rich mercy of our Lord and Saviour Jesus Christ preserved, restored, pardoned and appointed to preach the faith he had long labored to destroy.* There is great strength in the hymns that are inspired by the Scriptures. I love Psalm 71:23 that says, 'My (lips) shall greatly rejoice when I sing unto Thee; and my soul, which thou hast redeemed.'"

Surely the John Newton saga is an astonishing chronicle of how the Christ of Calvary can change even the most evil and desperate of lives. From a blaspheming, cruel, hell-bound slave trader to a great preacher and hymn writer—that's amazing grace, indeed!

Bev says that he will never forget the thrill of singing 'Amazing Grace' together with Cliff and George in Newton's parish church. The American trio unequivocally voiced the plaintive testimony-in-song in the small country church, with spiritual emotion.

Throughout all his years in sacred music, Bev was highly familiar with "Amazing Grace" and had sung it hundreds of times. Yet that day, standing next to Cliff and George IV in the old Olney church, he was deeply moved again by the significance of the lyrics they were singing. Although, not human slave traders like the song's writer, they felt that they could identify intimately with the sentiments of the heart-felt, autobiographical lyrics.

> *Amazing Grace, how sweet the sound that saved a wretch like me;*
> *I once was lost, but now am found, was blind, but now I see.*
> *'Twas grace that taught my heart to fear, and grace my fears relieved;*
> *How precious did His grace appear, the hour I first believed!*
> *Through many dangers, toils and snares I have already come;*
> *'Tis grace that brought me safe thus far, His grace will lead me home.*
> —John Newton (1725-1807)

THUNDER CRACK

More than twenty years later, the London music columnist and songwriter Roger Hill was looking back to Mission England when he stated, "I heard my first Bev Shea album decades ago. He was and still is my number one sacred soloist. So it was a big thrill for me when I watched Bev singing at the Billy Graham Mission England meetings held in London during 1989. I will never forget the thunderstorm on the Saturday evening at Wembley Stadium. Dr. Graham preached with such great authority with torrents of rain pouring down the back of the stage's inadequate plastic canopy. But the icing on the cake was when a thunderbolt struck the VDU screen as Bev was singing the first line of 'How Great Thou Art,' *I hear the rolling thunder! Thy power throughout the universe displayed!* As the echo of the thunderbolt dramatically bounced back around the historic stadium, Bev emphasized the line, *I hear the rolling thunder!* Truly that special evening, Bev was impressed with his Creator's sound effects to 'How Great Thou Art.'"

In 1986 Word Records' A & R director, Kurt Kaiser embarked on the ambitious Ebenezer milestone project of *George Beverly Shea and Friends*, an album of duets with many well-known singers. Kurt set sail for many recording studios. The plush orchestra was recorded in London providing gorgeous backgrounds over which to sing. The background singers and the rhythm track for "Ezekiel's Wheel" were recorded in Nashville. In Chicago, Kurt recorded Cliff Barrows who found time to sing "Jesus Whispers Peace" just before he had to rush to the airport for a trip to Europe. Bev and Kurt stayed and recorded the remaining vocals and Bill Pearce added his creative trombone track. Kurt was joined by Evie Karlsson in Orange County, California before he and Bev drove north to Canyon County to spend an interesting three hours with one of the most colorful people they said that they had ever known, the elderly Stuart Hamblen. One of the greatest storytellers ever with his West Texas drawl, he kept them spellbound. The trips were completed with recordings with the Gaithers, Amy Grant and Sandi Patti in Nashville, Dallas and Alexandria, Indiana.

Billy Graham was overjoyed on hearing the new album. "It's special to have several of Bev's friends and my friends join him on an album. Bev's been an associate and friend for nearly forty years. His warm and gentle way of singing gospel songs has prepared the hearts of people over and over again during our crusades. Many beautiful songs are being written these days, and yet, I must admit that I find myself responding within my heart to the older melodies and lyrics that speak directly of God's forgiveness and of His love for everyone!"

Bev says that Billy admits to being a traditionalist although he tries to appreciate everything. Cliff recalls how for years, he and Bev in meetings would sing the spiritual, "This Little Light Of Mine" in two-part harmony. One night Cliff asked Billy to make it a trio. Now and then it became quite a feature with Billy joining in a loud "no" to the musical question of "Hide it under a bushel?" The crusade crowds loved hearing the trio's "This Little Light Of Mine" ever since.

LONGEVITY

In 1989 on the occasion of his eightieth birthday, Bev was asked the fundamental question of what gave him the greatest joy and satisfaction as he sings. "Well, first, I'm glad that the people are hearing the words. There is evidence of the message to sing. I can sing about the truth that I have experienced in my own heart."

The questioner probed further, "Did you ever dream you would be singing at the age of eighty, Bev? How do you account for your longevity?" It was not easy to get to the heart of what the Canadian really thought as he remained so modest and so keen not to draw attention to himself. Predictably, his answer pointed heavenward. "I just do the best that I can. I am so grateful to think that I have had the privilege, all these years, of singing a simple song on the subject Mr. Graham is going to speak about. It's a great privilege."

On the last day of January 1989, in Washington DC, the National Religious Broadcasters organization presented *A Salute To George Beverly Shea* in honor of his eightieth birthday. Al Sanders hosted a detailed *This Is Your Life* with many surprise guests and video appearances of prominent people in his life.

"We have had a marvelous time together in all these years." Billy spoke winsomely and with genuine affection for his longtime friend. "I remember the first time that I met Bev Shea when I was a pastor of a small church. We were going to have this radio program called *Songs In The Night* on a 50,000 watt radio station. When we decided to take the program, I went to see Bev at WMBI. Going in, I introduced myself to him saying, 'Mr. Shea, we're starting a radio program on Sunday nights, will you come and sing for us?' He replied, 'Yes, I'll come!' That was in 1943 and I'm glad to say that he's been singing with us ever since!"

The hugely respected evangelist enthusiastically joined the distinguished throng of seasoned broadcasters in a hearty round of applause. As his eyes moistened, Bev humbly accepted the gathering's praise in his usual self-effacing, shy manner. Eighty candlelit cakes appeared as a grand ending at the NRB.

Soon the Graham team was back on the international trail for a welcome return to the United Kingdom. Now the Anglican minister of All Souls Church in West London, Richard Bewes recalls the busy days with great pleasure and satisfaction. "Every time that Billy Graham and his team have come to the UK in recent years, I have had the opportunity of meeting Bev Shea. He is an utterly gracious and modest Christ-centred man. When I was chairman of Mission 89, here in the capital, for a month of meetings, naturally I would see (and meet) Bev many times. I remember seeing him on the platform, when the mission came to West Ham Football stadium and as the invitation was given by Billy and the enquirers were coming forward in immense numbers, Bev was weeping. I remember thinking, 'After all these years of evangelism in every part of the world, the wonder of the gospel still gets to him!' It was at the Crystal Palace meetings a week later that as Bev was finishing his solo I murmured to Billy that in many ways there was a new generation in Britain now, who would not have been too familiar with Bev. Billy took his cue, and as he got up to speak, he announced, 'That was George Beverly Shea. He has been with us from the beginning all these years. He has sung to more people than Frank Sinatra!'"

On the other side of London in 1989, RT Kendall was the successful minister of Westminster Chapel. RT, originally from the bluegrass state of Kentucky, invited Mission England team members, TW Wilson, George Hamilton IV and Bev Shea to witness on June 18, 1989 at Westminster Chapel which is adjacent to Buckingham Palace. RT stated that the night's meeting was most memorable as all three gentlemen participated. However, as Bev Shea sang "I'd Rather Have Jesus," RT said that he had to pinch himself to believe that it was true that America's beloved gospel singer was in his pulpit!

Chapter 12

Amazing Grace
1990-1999

"Without a doubt, George Beverly Shea has blessed more people by his singing than any other gospel singer, past or present. It doesn't matter who is in the audience—youth or adult, friendly or unfriendly—they can tell that Bev is 'the genuine article!' His focus is of such intensity that you just have to listen. His interpretation of gospel music is so moving that it seems each song is his last opportunity to sing to you!"
—Ralph Carmichael, Los Angeles, California

SOLID THEOLOGY

By the nineties George Beverly Shea was undoubtedly the best known gospel singer that the world had ever known. Yet amazingly, it did not seem to have gone to his head. Questioned why not, he humbly replied that from the beginning he did not "think of thrilling anybody." His humble desire was always to simply serve. He said that he just wanted the message of each song to be easily understood and come across as pleasing as possible. In regard to taking his style from anyone else, he admitted that he especially liked John Charles Thomas.

Bev said, "God can use anyone who is yielded to the idea of lifting Christ up to the individual or to the crowd. I began to feel that responsibility and just wanted to be a workman that needeth not to be ashamed. All too often I've had reason to be disappointed with myself, but the loving Lord knows my heart and has kept me going."

Bev was never more comfortable than when he was amid the solid theology of classic hymns. The UK's Word label issued a CD entitled *The Blessed Lights of Home* that featured twenty-eight timeless classics. Instrumentally and vocally arranged and recorded in Nashville by Robert Stirling, it featured the magnificent Victory Voices and Orchestra with Bev as the guest soloist. Highlights were "Amazing Grace," "God Will Take Care of You," and "Precious Lord Take My Hand."

ENCOURAGEMENT

Bev's interests were not solely in evergreen hymns, he was always an advocate of new artists in the Christian field. He was genuinely known by his associates and friends—those close and not so close—as always being an optimistic encourager of others. For example, Wes Davis, contemporary Christian singer and songwriter, recalls meeting him at London's Earls Court. Wes was a young teenager and—as he admits—a baby Christian. But he says that he was greatly moved and motivated by Bev's "anointed and spirit-filled testimony in song." More so, however, Wes remembers what a great privilege it was to meet Bev afterwards and be inspired by the experienced Mr. Shea to pursue Christian music as a calling, and more importantly, to grow deeper in his personal walk with the Lord. Wes says that he praises God for Mr. Shea and delights to be one of many who follow in Bev's footsteps by using music in ministry.

Such encouragement is a much repeated story on both sides of the Atlantic. Over many decades, despite lack of great experimentation, Bev went down new trails, including his 1994 duet with dc Talk member Michael Tait. The prized event was the *Inspirational Homecoming* CD project, a tribute to the Bill and Gloria Gaither as songwriters. Included in Gaither productions were luminaries such as Steve Green, Doug Oldham, Eddie De Garmo, Sandi Patti plus many more including the surprising ancient and modern mix of young Michael Tait and the elderly Mr. Shea on "Because He Lives."

As well as being the world's undisputed beloved singer of gospel music for over half a century, he has been classified in all sorts of other ways. He was never enamored with labels. He said that if he is to be categorized under anything then just file him the under "Christian singer" and he will be happy. That, he declares, is all that he ever wanted since he first heard the Ira Sankey and Fanny Crosby songs in his youth. Most popular singers meander via trends of the eras in which they live. Indeed, most if not all professional performers bend and adapt to fads and fashions. In contrast however, Bev, has never been much of an experimentalist, always remaining conservative and wanting to hold to the old established, tried and tested paths.

STRIKING THE RIGHT CHORDS

Whether the happy-go-lucky youth of the nineties approved or not of his conservative style, Bev was still striking the right chords with the more conventional church audiences. Typical was the October 1996 visit to the First Baptist Church of Clinton packed to the rafters for the Sunday night concert visit of Bev and his pianist, Kurt Kaiser. Hugely experienced and influential in Christian music, Kurt was Bev's record producer and the Dove Award winning composer of "O How He Loves You and Me" and "Pass It On." Together Kurt and Bev were then doing about a half dozen live concerts a year in substantially-sized churches and auditoriums. Asked to comment on their teamwork, with a grin Kurt said, "I'd describe Bev's singing voice as a phenomenon. Everybody else that I know at that age is old and decrepit but not Bev!"

During the 90-minute sacred music concert, the two internationally-known Christian artists did not disappoint their capacity audience, saving 'How Great Thou Art' for the concert's ultimate number. The evening had its variety. Bev had interspersed some compact narrated prologues among the dozen or so songs that he sang. The concert did not require an introduction for "Oh Lord my God when I in awesome wonder."

He sang majestically with the skilled sound of Kurt's temperate piano melody aiding the familiar words. The church audience was composed of all ages but in particular silver, white and bald heads in the congregation nodded in time with the music. When Bev reached the chorus of "How Great Thou Art," he knew the delighted people could not resist joining in. Consequently, his voice diminished fleetingly in volume as he encouraged them to make a joyful noise unto the Lord with him. Despite resting frequently during the concert while Kurt played his keyboard solos, it was said that Bev, at eighty-seven years of age, exhibited no hint of indisposition or lack of enthusiasm. He cheerfully confessed, however, to the surprised congregation that he was fifteen percent deaf in one ear, and that he survived a frightening accident just a week earlier. "We were trying to put away an old boat in the garage," he said with a smile, "I hit the pavement, full face, resulting in 20 stitches to the forehead."

He laughed and chuckled showing no indication of the injury.

His wavy white hair was combed in its customary swept-back style. Standing straight and tall in front of the congregation in his smart dark suit and tie, his right hand firm around the microphone, his deep rich voice never wavered, cracked, or missed a high or low note. He joked that his only compromise with old age was the security of now having notes handwritten from memory. These, he said, he kept within his coat pocket to ensure that he always had the lyrics to his songs should memory fail. As he arrived at his first break in the evening concert, he smiled at his listeners and joked. "Well good folks, this pocket of notes doesn't have anything else in it right now, so I guess it's halftime and I shall just sit down!"

The amused audience erupted with warm laughter, applause and sincere appreciation. It was evident that they were very eager to hear the second half. Accompanist, Kurt confided that he is most grateful for his long association and friendship with Bev. "George Beverly Shea and I have been involved in concerts for many, many years. To have someone champion one's cause in music is important and I'm grateful. While I have written several pieces with Bev's voice in mind, it has been special indeed to have him perform this music in our concerts all over the USA and up in Canada. In particular, his singing of 'O How He Loves You and Me' has been the major reason that this piece has been so widely used all around the world. I am indebted to him."

FULLY PERSUADED

In Europe in 1995, Word Records released an outstanding special collection of Shea repertoire aptly titled *Fully Persuaded*. The 20 tracks included peppy spirituals, country gospel songs and old-time hymns such as "The Old Rugged Cross," "Early In the Morning," and "When He Comes." Bev was overjoyed to see many of his song gems appearing on CD for the first time. He wrote to me in England, "Paul, I want to thank you for bringing together those songs for the new *Fully Persuaded* CD. I know too that my beloved producer colleague, Kurt Kaiser will be pleased with the release, writing several of the songs. May all of this be used of the Lord to cause more to know Him, our Saviour. As the scripture declares, 'Therefore with joy we draw water out of the wells of salvation and say, praise the LORD, call upon His name, declare his doings among the people, make mention that His name is exalted." (Isaiah 12:3-4)

In the nineties Bev and Karlene continued to live a mere mile from the Graham house in Montreat, North Carolina. The Sheas still felt fully involved in the work of the Billy Graham Evangelistic Association. At times in the mid-nineties, he pondered whether he should leave the crusade team because of his age. "I thought that maybe I should just ease off," he said, "but Mr. Graham's son, Franklin Graham telephoned me and said he wanted me to stay as long as his dad was able to preach... There was no way I could say no to Franklin. I love his father, Mr. Graham. Billy has always been a very gracious Southern Christian gentleman who doesn't have a selfish bone in his body."

In return, Franklin was very complimentary about his father's long-time friends. "As we look back over the many years, I'm grateful when I think of Bev and Cliff. They faithfully prayed for Daddy and loyally backed him with their faithful friendship, always such an encouragement!"

The older he became, the more Bev realized how important heritage, relationships and roots were to him. More and more, he said that he cherished family, friends and faith. Karlene was privileged to travel with Bev to all missions and crusades, personal appearances and enjoyed the many visits of family and lifelong friends who came to Montreat. Without doubt, she was a distinctive person in her own right! Bev was often heard openly to say that he was genuinely most proud of her!

Hits In Every Way Except Name

For his significant contributions to Christian music, Bev was inducted into the Religious Broadcasting Hall of Fame in February of 1996. A year later, the University of North Carolina Center for Public Television produced a Bev Shea tribute hosted by George Hamilton IV. The TV show entitled *The Wonder Of It All* featured special guest appearances from Cliff Barrows, Paul Overstreet, Arthur Smith, Bill Pearce and the Moody Brothers.

Tributes are apt as for over three-quarters of a century there were many truly great inspirational songs like "How Great Thou Art," "Great Is Thy Faithfulness," and "I'd Rather Have Jesus," pioneered by Bev in many parts of the globe. They were and are hits in every way except by name. Of all people, of course, he is certainly not surprised how popular these classy songs ultimately became. He always believed quality sacred songs to be good art as well as good ministry. The success of "The Wonder of It All," "The Love of God," "It Is No Secret" and such confirms the fact that they are spiritually uplifting songs.

Eventually, songs of real merit given due exposure will establish themselves internationally as standards. Much of the Shea repertoire consists of admirable examples of songs that contradict the theory that gospel music is neither commercial nor viable in the secular market place. Bev himself asserts that throughout the decades, many people identified deeply and personally with his songs. Bev agrees that the psalmist, David, gave believers a formidable task when he announced, "O sing unto the Lord a new song!" This means that no Christian should be content solely with yesterday's spiritual encounters. Every individual new dawn should contain a surpassing understanding of God and a maturing association with Christ. Everyday's new spiritual conquests should be attested to with enthusiasm. This process produces up-to-date words of testimony and prayer, and also fresh songs of faith and worship! To base one's life and ministry on King David's words, in Bev's view is a commendable philosophy of life!

At the start of the new millennium, Bev was fast heading for his 75th anniversary in Christian music! Although he made his first gospel singing broadcasts pre-World War II, he ardently and genuinely said that, after all those years, singing is still enjoyable! In the sunset years of his life, he was the epitome of the classic gospel singer, an esteemed man who had fully paid his dues and knew his trade inside and out. Since he started, he said that it was difficult for him to think of his Christian music ministry as work. For to him it was truly a labor of love, a lifelong love affair ever since he first heard church hymns as an impressionable child at his mother's knee and in his father's church in Canada. He still approached every new day with an enthusiastic zeal. There was still an excitement about his future plans, hopes and desires.

Fast approaching a century of life, there was still no leisure time. Asked whether he ever got nervous when singing to crowds of tens-of-thousands, he raised his eyebrows and knowingly smiled as he replied. "Perhaps everyone needs to be a little nervous at such times. Somebody once asked the opera singer Gladys Swarthout when she was most nervous while singing. She answered, 'In a living room. I don't know what to do with my eyes.' So, in a small group you can be more shaky than when singing in a stadium. But always I try to remember that as the preacher gets his strength from the Lord, I must do the same. It is truly wonderful to feel God's presence while singing about the Lord Jesus whether I'm at the piano at home or in front of the large audiences at Mr. Graham's crusades!"

For all the memorable years of dedicated service, Bev was deeply grateful to have been able to make his profession and a living from something that was really an occupational joy. With no reservation, he said the long ministerial career in music had been a pleasure. But what he esteemed most was the close relationship with Christ Jesus, the Saviour and Lord. He adjudged that it had been an incomparable privilege to serve Him and His church.

In the Spring of 1997, Bev and Karlene were relaxing in their living room softly singing at the piano when the telephone rang. In the warmth of the greeting there was no mistaking the Carolina accent in the friendly voice of Arthur Smith. "Hello Bev, this is Arthur. How would you like to join your ole pal doing an album of old hymns and gospel songs over here in my studio in Charlotte? I was thinking it would be great for us to do favorites like 'Showers of Blessings,' 'Leaning On the Everlasting Arms,' 'Precious Memories,' 'Just a Closer Walk With Thee,' 'Power In the Blood,' and ' Kneel at the Cross'"

The Canadian smiled at the quick recognition of the beloved hymns. "How could I say no to you my brother? We've enjoyed a half century of warm family friendship!"

Arthur's barn in Sardis Road, now turned into a state-of-the-art recording studio, was the rallying point for the session. Instruments in hand, the Crossroads Quartet arrived: David Johnson on steel and electric guitar, Don Ange on piano, Don Schulyler on bass, Del Buchannan on drums, and Tommy Faile on acoustic guitar. Their arrangements allowed them as Southern gospel experts to blend with Bev's bass-baritone. It was a fun session. Arthur and Bev, familiar friends since 1947, genuinely enjoyed working with all.

As Bev bounced along with "Little David Play On Your Harp," Arthur cheerfully quipped, "Keep to the rhythm, Bev!"

CAPITOL ROTUNDA, WASHIINGTON D.C.

Bev was delighted to be asked to sing before a distinguished company of members of the House and Senate on the occasion of the presentation of the Congressional Medal of Honor to his dear friends, Billy and Ruth Graham. It was held in the Capitol's huge marble rotunda, decorated with paintings and statuary depicting America's history. Accompanied by pianist Tedd Smith, Bev sang "God Bless America." Such a rare and beautiful ceremony attended by what seemed like all of the government's notable leaders.

On September 11, 1999 in Dallas, Texas, Marketplace Ministries celebrated its fifteenth anniversary by giving its Integrity Award to Bev. The organization also honored one of its Baptist employees. Accordingly, Lane Park, a chaplain to four North Texas businesses was honored as the Chaplain of the

Year. Bev knew that the Marketplace Ministries organization, founded by Gil Stricklin in 1984, contracted with companies of all sizes to provide chaplains to meet the spiritual needs of their employees. The ministry's largest client was Pilgrim's Pride, with more than 11,000 employees. In fifteen years, Marketplace Ministries grew from one chaplain to 650 who worked in 165 cities. During the celebration at the Anatole Hotel in Dallas, Gil Stricken presented the Integrity Award to Bev, who was accompanied by Karlene and son, Ron. Bev then presented a mini-concert, accompanied by Kurt Kaiser at the piano. Although Dr. Graham could not be present, he sent a letter congratulating Bev, which Gil read. The letter said, "No one is more deserving of an award for integrity." A video presentation then told the story of the long Shea life and ministry.

INTO THE SUNSET

Living such a long life inevitably meant that Bev had to say goodbye to many dear friends. He knew Roy Rogers and Dale Evans since the exciting 1949 Los Angeles Crusade days. In July 1998 Bev heard with sadness that his friend Roy, age 86, died of congestive heart failure at his home in Apple Valley, California. Shortly afterwards, Dale too was called home. Roy's rise to world fame brought him the title "King of the Cowboys" through his feature length movies. They helped to brighten a saddened and war sick world in the decade that followed World War II. Later with his attractive wife Dale, he delighted millions more with his tremendously popular TV series. In the thirties, changing his original name from Len Slye to Dick Weston, he finally settled for Roy Rogers. He then helped form the famous cowboy singing group, The Sons Of the Pioneers who were often used in director John Ford's John Wayne Western movies. Originally a trio, the close-harmony group became famous for their yodeling in four-part harmony and songs such as "Cool Water," "Way Out There," and "Tumbling Tumbleweeds."

Roy's solo show business career began to blossom when in 1937 he signed for Hollywood's Republic Studios. The top singing cowboy of his day was Gene Autry but from Roy's first starring role in *Under Western Skies* it was obvious a bright star was rising. The action-filled musical extravaganzas set in the West showed Roy and his wife Dale, immaculately dressed in extremely ornate cowboy costumes. They also owned the famous animal movie star Trigger, the smartest horse in the movies. Throughout the world, toys, books, clothes and trinkets began to appear bearing the Roy Rogers brand tag. Numerous companies cashed in on this successful Hollywood image.

Bev knew well that the duo's strong Christian commitment was unashamedly shared with fans. At the height of their career in 1954, they accompanied the then relatively unknown Billy Graham and his team to London. Providentially, those exciting meetings in Harringay projected Billy to the worldwide pulpit that he was to fill for the rest of his life. Bev says that just the mention of the names Roy Rogers and Dale Evans makes nostalgia overflow from the hearts of millions who always preserved a special place for this husband and wife duo.

Through the years, Roy and Dale had more than their share of personal family tragedy. Their only natural child was born severely handicapped and died when she was only two years of age. They lost their teenage son Sandy who died in Germany serving in the

US Army. One of the adopted children, a little Korean girl named Debbie, was killed in a church bus accident when only eleven-years-old. Sadly, their fifty-two years of marriage were not without deep trials and tragedies. Yet despite such personal loss, Bev says that their optimistic faith, courage and enthusiasm inspired people everywhere. Privately, their home, family, and personalities reflected their steadfast faith and belief in their Saviour.

Publicly, it seemed that in every appearance that Roy and Dale ever made, they included at least one song of faith, sometimes Bev's composition "I'd Rather Have Jesus," and a spiritual message. The colorful duo heavily influenced a whole generation of youngsters pointing them to clean cut, wholesome Christian values.

Roy Rogers would have approved of Cliff and Bev's *Green Country Pastures* on Word UK's Timeless label. The CD serenaded their longtime unity by sharing some outstanding country and western material. Although not in duet, the prized album found the twosome featuring Cliff, with narration and quartet songs, and Bev, with solo songs. They were in top form. Highlights included a tribute to Stuart Hamblen with "It Is No Secret," "Known Only To Him," "Until Then," "Teach Me Lord To Wait," and the "Open Secret." The concluding track, "Day Is Dying In the West," was a reminder that the two saddle pals, although still in the saddle, were fast heading into the golden sunset where all good cowboys go at close of day.

Day is dying in the west,
Heaven is touching earth with rest,
Wait and worship while the night
Sets her evening lamps alight,
Through all the sky.

Holy Holy, Holy, Lord God of Hosts!
Heaven and earth are full of Thee;
Heaven and earth are praising Thee,
O Lord most high!
—Mary A. Lathbury (1878

Bev's Word album *The Blessed Lights Of Home* picked up strongly on the theme of heaven. Highlights among the twenty-five songs included the Gaithers' "The King Is Coming," the spiritual "My Lord What a Morning," and Rev. Isaiah G. Martin's "The Eastern Gate." At the recording in Nashville, Bev recalled years before standing in the sunshine on the summit of the Mount of Olives. The Mount overlooks the ancient wall of the old city of Jerusalem. There clearly before him in the wall stood the Eastern Gate, the anticipated entry point into the city for the Messiah, the soon-coming King Jesus. Who could not help but smile at the impertinence of the pagans who centuries before bricked up the entrance in a vain attempt to prevent the inevitable!

I will meet you in the morning just outside the Eastern Gate,
Then be ready, faithful pilgrim, Lest for you it be too late!
O, the joy of that great morning with the saints who for us wait,
What a blessed, happy morning, just inside the Eastern Gate!
—Words: Isaiah G. Martin

When Bev's friend, the late James Blackwood, was asked in 1998 what was the highlight of his lengthy career James reply was movingly surprising. "There have been several high spots like winning the national TV talent show with the Blackwoods; singing to thousands for Dr. Billy Graham; and recording with

George Beverly Shea. If I had to pick the best it would be one night in Greenville, South Carolina before six thousand folk. I was singing 'I Will Meet You In the Morning' and decided to leave the platform and shake hands with people in the audience as far as my microphone chord would allow. People started rising and coming down to meet me from high up in the auditorium. Then I saw a little grey-haired lady on crutches advancing down the aisle, tears flooding her face. Coming up close she embraced me with a hug and said, 'James, I will... I will meet you in the morning!' I still choke up when I picture that scene. She reminded me of my little old mother, four feet nine inches tall, who barely came up to my shoulder. She always remained faithful in prayer—a prayer warrior to the end. She called it praying through meaning until she felt her prayer had been heard in heaven. My dear mother went to be with the Lord in 1963 at the age of sixty-seven. That little lady in the aisle reminded me of her, which makes the memory sweet and special."

For Bev too "The Eastern Gate" held memories. Firstly, it was a highlight track on his Grammy award-winning *Southland Favourites*. Secondly, it was an emotional reminder of the songs of Fanny Crosby and Ira Sankey that he heard originally in his youth. In the year previous to Bev's birth, as Ira Sankey lay dying, Fanny Crosby wrote a final letter to her dear friend. Ira by that time also suffered Fanny's affliction of blindness. Being his senior by several years, she said she never expected him to cross death's river before her. "I will meet you in the morning just outside the Eastern Gate, over there!"

These words of hope in her beautiful, comforting letter touched the heart of the failing giant of sacred song. They were words of deep gospel music significance. Fanny Crosby and Ira Sankey, both faithful pilgrims, were ready for the joy of that "Great Hallelujah Morning!" Thus the theme of her letter became the theme of one of George Beverly Shea's most memorable and beloved songs.

Chapter 13

The King Is Coming
POST 2000

"The greatest gospel singer since David the Shepherd Boy is George Beverly Shea. He is a modest human being who does not blow his own horn. Like a Stradivarius violin, Bev's voice just seems to get richer and deeper with age. In my opinion, he's singing better than ever these days."
—George Hamilton IV, Nashville, Tennessee

TIMELESS QUALITY

To greet the new millennium, the famed EMI record label produced the impressive new Shea CD entitled *If That Isn't Love*. It came under the direction of New Zealander, Jeff McKenzie and the production auspices of Cliff Barrows, Belma Ruth Reimer and John Lenning. The CD paraded the musical talents of Bill Fasig and John Innes who assembled at the Max Trax Media studio in Fort Mill, South Carolina with David McCallister at the controls. Billy Graham made a typical and predictable announcement on the release of the twenty-track Ebenezer album. "Of all the gospel singers in the world today, the one that I would rather hear than any other would be George Beverly Shea."

This was offered as a gift to the Billy Graham Evangelistic Association listeners and thousands responded. Not bad for a ninety-one-year-old singer's latest release! The CD also received good solid reviews as Bev was at his best on new goodies such as Mylon Lefevre's "Without Him," Richard Blanchard's "Fill My Cup Lord," "Fanny Crosby's "My Saviour First Of All," among many others. Perhaps the best of the bunch was Dottie Rambo's title track, "If That Isn't Love."

At the age of 74, Dottie died in a bus crash near Springfield, Missouri. It was early Pentecost Sunday morning on May 11, 2008. According to a Missouri State Highway Patrol report, few details were available, but there were reports that overnight storms and high winds caused the 1997 Prevost bus to crash into a guard rail and an embankment at around 2:20 a.m. Dottie was a prolific writer and singer whose hits include "We Shall Behold Him," "Holy Spirit Thou Art Welcome (In The Place)," "I Go To the Rock," and "Sheltered In the Arms of God." Elvis Presley, Barbara Mandrell, Carol Channing, Whitney Houston and Dolly Parton were among those who recorded her songs.

Also on the *If That Isn't Love* CD was Vep Ellis' "Do You Know My Jesus?" It suited Bev perfectly. Alabama-born, singing-evangelist Vep was a Church of God minister based in Cleveland, Tennessee. Starting off, when barely fifteen, he wrote hundreds of inspired gospel songs of timeless quality. "'Do You Know My Jesus' was always a favorite," thus commented James Blackwood. He recalled, "We recently did Vep's songs on the top-selling Gaither music videos."

While attending the Lee College Bible School in Tennessee, Vep met and later married fellow student, Pat. They parented four boys and one girl. At the height of his song-writing career, he wrote for the Stamps Quartet and their associates. Every year in his heyday, his church publishing company issued a new song book that was enthusiastically received each year. Later in 1962 he became song leader and soloist for the renowned preacher Oral Roberts. Oral said of Vep, "His songs have real spiritual depth and meaning with a direct approach to the individual, directing him to find help and hope in Christ!" Later in life, Vep planted and pastored a church in Clearwater, Florida. After several heart attacks, he moved to Tulsa. There he spent his final years under the care of his son, the minister of a local church.

EAST TO WEST COAST

In the morning sunshine of a spring day in March of 2000, at the age of ninety-one, Bev sat down at his home's office desk somewhat more cluttered than usual. It seemed that he had recently had little time to catch up with his personal office administration because of travel. He and Karlene had just returned from California as a guest of Dr. Robert Schuller at his Crystal Cathedral. There Bev sang "I'd Rather Have Jesus," with a thirty-five piece orchestra, to an international television audience located in hundreds of countries. Pleased to be home, he reached for his desk diary to review the six months just passed as Karlene cheerfully delivered a welcome cup of coffee. "Would you believe, Karlene-honey, I've looked in my calendar and I've had forty-three evenings of activity since only last September? Praise the Lord for all His support and yours too, darling!"

Karlene smiled as she responded, "Yes, dear! Some of those forty-three bookings took you from the east coast to the west coast and back again! Florida, California, Canada and even Holland! Not bad without an agent."

One unusual appearance was a special dinner in the ballroom of the Beverly Hilton in California's Beverly Hills. Bev remembered the evening with great satisfaction. "It was a wonderful privilege for this old guy to sing as a witness for Christ at such an event with so many notable people at the tables such as Mrs. Joan Kroc, wife of the founder of the McDonald's restaurant chain. She's to be credited for giving millions of dollars away to the Salvation Army in honor of her husband, Ray Kroc. In his early days, he loved to take the bell from a Salvation Army lassie and ask people to drop dollars into the Christmas offering bucket."

Some of the other personal appearances were dinners sponsored by the Salvation Army as fund-raisers. Bev recalls, "Also honored at the Salvation Army was Jerry Jones, owner of the Dallas Cowboys, and country singer Reba McEntire."

Another personal appearance was the Gospel Music Association's induction of Billy Graham into the Gospel Music Hall of Fame. Bev recalls, "When I told Billy about the GMA award, Billy's jovial response was, 'Don't they know that I can't even carry a tune?'"

The Canadian returned to sing in Nashville once again in the new millennium in the June crusade meetings of 2001. Keen to remain true to the last, he enjoyed every minute of the highly attended event. It was Billy's first crusade of the third millennium held at the new Adelphia Coliseum in Nashville. The question on the lips of several music journalists was, "How long is George Beverly Shea going to continue to sing?" His sharp, swift answer was that he wanted to keep on singing until the age of 100! He was certainly well on the way—even in his mid-nineties—enjoying the privileges of retaining a powerful voice and youthful outlook.

IN FINE VOICE

These qualities were fully evident in his current CD of the time entitled *Echoes of My Soul* on yet another new label. This time it was Star Song, a label not usually associated with traditional Christian music. Bev was in fine voice with characteristic material. There were the ever present Ira Sankey and Fanny Crosby sing-a-longs that included "In Tenderness He Sought Me," "O Saviour Thou Art Mine," "Ninety and Nine," "Blessed Assurance," and "I Will Sing the Wondrous Story." Among the other offerings were Bev's big hits that included "The Wonder of It All" and "How Great Thou Art."

Harvey Thomas, founding president of the Fellowship of European Broadcasters, states that he has many happy memories of Bev Shea spanning over thirty years. "One memory of Bev is Bev's appearance with Cliff Barrows at the Amsterdam Evangelists Conference of July 2001. There were 10,000 evangelists present from nearly 200 countries of the world—a great majority of them quite young. On the opening night, Cliff Barrows was leading the singing and introduced Bev. The singer came to the microphone and said in that wonderful deep voice, "I'm going to sing a little song called 'I'd Rather Have Jesus' and I must say that when I wrote the music to this song at the age of twenty-three, I certainly didn't imagine that I would be singing it to you here tonight at the age of ninety-one!'"

Harvey continued, "Ten-thousand of us were absolutely silent as he sang as beautifully as ever and then, quite unrehearsed, Cliff Barrows came to the microphone behind him and said, 'You know, tonight Billy Graham is not well enough to be with us here in Amsterdam, but he is watching on a live satellite television feed to the hospital in Minnesota. I don't think we could let tonight pass without our 10,000 voices joining Bev Shea in singing, 'How Great Thou Art.'"

Hugely experienced and widely traveled, Harvey Thomas related this story to me with misty eyes. "I must say, Paul, that it was one of the most meaningful and emotional moments of my life. I had then been out of the Billy Graham team working with UK Prime Minister Margaret Thatcher for fifteen years, but the memories of crusades all over the world flooded back as Bev and Cliff led us in 'How Great Thou Art.'

Fortunately, I had my mobile phone with me and as Cliff announced it, I dialed my wife, Marlies, who was back home in London, and just held the mobile phone up so that she could hear Bev and all of us singing. When I hear of contemporary Christian music, I keep wishing that a lot more of it contained the spirituality, the genuineness, and the outreach that poured out of Bev Shea every time he sang."

Richard Bewes says he was also amazed how well Bev was still singing at the age of ninety-two. "I loved hearing him in Amsterdam 2000. The theme of the event came through the Apostle Paul's words, 'Giving thanks unto the Father, which hath made us meet to be partakers of the inheritance of the saints in light: Who hath delivered us from the power of darkness, and hath translated us into the kingdom of his dear Son: In whom we have redemption through his blood, even the forgiveness of sins!' When Bev stood up and sang 'How Great Thou Art,' he received a standing ovation from the 10,000 delegates. Again, he and Karlene and I were able to have some unhurried fellowship at the Europa Hotel where we were staying and I was greatly blessed by their fellowship."

After attending the BGEA's Amsterdam gathering of international evangelists in Holland, Bev suffered a very nasty attack of European flu, as did the majority of participants, followed by a painful bout of shingles. Nevertheless, he recovered and at the age of ninety-two facing surgery for cataracts on his eyes, he was back on the road still singing and sharing as strongly as ever. Still a draw, his reputation and wonderful voice were reason enough for many to turn out to his concerts. For instance, a full audience attended to hear him sing at a rally in Fresno, California. He blessed and entertained the vast crowd with many of his popular gospel songs including some that he wrote and co-wrote.

Participating in the Fresno meetings was a newer talented Christian artist from Laguna Beach, California named Fernando Ortega. Speaking of Bev, he expressed how amazed he was to see the veteran still performing so well at so great an age. "I wish I could, but I doubt if I'll be singing my same songs when or if I reach my nineties. George Beverly Shea is remarkable, a man to look up to!"

Dismissive of talk about old age, still saying that he was young at heart, Bev loved to crack jokes about himself. "Mark Twain said, 'Age is mind over matter, if you don't mind, it doesn't matter.'"

Despite the jokes, he unconditionally kept going as he said, "I have learned to look up and He's there. He loves us. He has given me more than I deserve. I've had moments, even when working for Mr. Graham when I've felt as if I wasn't effective enough and I've known discouragement. But I go to the Lord and He extends His grace. On many occasions, I go to the piano and play an old favorite. God always encourages through His Spirit and renews our strength."

Asked about his good health, he gives God the glory. "I continue to sing as the soloist for the Billy Graham crusades. It's a job I've held since 1947. Dr. Graham and I have been friends since 1943 when I was the announcer on a Chicago radio station and sang on a broadcast called *Hymns From the Chapel*."

Since the last crusade he has sung at four of Franklin Graham's Festivals and two of Will Graham's Celebrations.

Cliff Barrows says, "Some people ask me what it's like singing with Bev and I say that it's the frosting on the cake. Nothing can top it apart from perhaps singing a duet with the psalmist King David in heaven. I count it a great joy to have been able to sing with Bev on the few songs we do together such as 'Jesus Whispers Peace.' It is a reminder of the Bible promise that 'we know that all things work together for good to them that love God, to them who are the called according to his purpose.' 'Jesus Whispers Peace' is meaningful for Bev and me because we both lost our mates to illness. But in that time of grief and loss we experienced God's perfectly wonderful peace. Later God in His mercy and grace brought other partners into our lives, ones of His choosing who have filled that void. God has given us both great cause for rejoicing and cause to sing again!"

Cliff and Bev also serenaded their longtime unity by sharing a Christmas CD. Although The prized album on Word UK's *Timeless* label found the twosome featuring some outstanding First Advent material. Cliff, with narration and music, and Bev, with solo songs, were in top voice. Highlights included on the album entitled *The Christmas Evangel* were plentiful. Included were several King James Version Bible readings plus some great poems by Cliff. Bev's Christmas offerings were outstanding. They included "Ring the Bells," "O Little Town of Bethlehem," "The Virgin Mary Had a Baby," "Silent Night," "Thou Didst Leave Thy Throne" and many more.

Thou didst leave Thy throne and Thy kingly crown, When Thou camest
to earth for me;

But in Bethlehem's home there was found no room For Thy holy nativity:
O come to my heart, Lord Jesus! There is room in my heart for Thee.

Heaven's arches rang when the angels sang, Proclaiming Thy royal degree;
But of lowly birth cam'st Thou, Lord, on earth, And in great humility,
O come to my heart, Lord Jesus! There is room in my heart for Thee.

The foxes found rest, and the birds had their nest, In the shade of the cedar tree;
But Thy couch was the sod, O Thou Son of God, In the deserts of Galilee.
O come to my heart, Lord Jesus! There is room in my heart for Thee.

Thou camest, O Lord, with the living word That should set Thy children free;
But with mocking scorn, and with crown of thorn, They bore Thee to Calvary.
O come to my heart, Lord Jesus! Thy cross is my only plea.

When heaven's arches shall ring, and her choirs shall sing, At Thy coming to victory,
Let Thy voice call me home, saying, 'Yet there is room, There is room at My side for thee.'
And my heart shall rejoice, Lord Jesus, When Thou comest and callest for me.
—Emily E. Elliott (1836-1897)

"Thou Didst Leave Thy Throne" was a favorite that mainly addressed the Christmas story but it really bridged the themes of the First and Second Advents of Christ, too. The Gaithers' song "The King Is Coming," sung by Bev, unmistakably addressed the blessed hope of the Second Coming. By the end of the twentieth century, the duo was being heralded among the greatest hymn-writers of history because of songs like "The King Is Coming," "Because He Lives," "There Is Something About That Name," and "He Touched Me." Bev considers that these friends made an indelible mark on modern-day hymnology. He believes that there are no more two important figures in modern sacred music than this humble husband and wife couple. Many of their heartwarming songs are already found in church hymn books around the world—an incredible achievement for living songwriters.

Born on March 28, 1936, Bill grew up in Alexandria, a rural area of Indiana. Coming from such a down-to-earth farming family, he learned to take pleasure in everyday essential farm jobs like milking the cows. "I think this helped me to develop a sensitivity to life and for the caring of the newborn. When someone speaks about simple, everyday things I know what they're talking about!"

Jokingly, Bill tells everybody that he never planned to take up farming as a career because as he says, "I have always had a bad case of hay fever! That's always been a problem to me even as a child working outside!"

That may be true but Bill always loved music and wanted to make it a career. Yet he gave up the idea of making it a professional career after high school because he thought he was not good enough to do it full time. "In those days," Bill said," there were not that many opportunities for a young person interested in full-time music. So what I did was to go to college and major in English. Later I taught English in public high school for seven or eight years, planning to do that for the rest of my life. That's where I met my wife Gloria. She was also teaching school at the same place."

They duly fell in love and started partnering each other in their song-writing. Then the duo musically hit the road as part of a trio that included Bill's late brother, Danny. The big factor that interrupted Bill and Gloria's teaching careers in the early sixties was when they started writing original hit songs.

HOMECOMING

Forty years later in 2000, Bill phoned Bev. "Hello, Bev! I'm glad to tell you that at last us Gaithers and our Homecoming friends plus our assorted brigade of audio, video and lighting technicians are traveling to The Cove in North Carolina to record a video. We'd like to include you, Cliff and others in the Graham connection. We'll be recording several days of music by artists who have worked with the Billy Graham crusades through the years. We're all coming together to sing the gospel and share our personal testimonies and some of your incredible stories on video. Can you come, Brother?"

Nevertheless, in his typical jovial way, Bev thought that he'd give his friend Bill a hard time. "Oh, I don't know Bill. You know, I'm on old psalm singer that's not too used to raising his hands and getting too emotional."

The line went dead for a few seconds. Bill started to wonder whether his friend Bev was really giving him a no. Then there was a deep chuckle from the Shea side as the Canadian broke the silence. They joined in mutual amusement. "You had me worried for a few seconds, Bev. I can't wait to hear you sing 'How Great Thou Art' on a *Homecoming Friends* video. I've delayed using the song until you are available!"

Such a celebrated event had been in planning for a year or two, but dates never seemed to fit. When all was set, Bill suffered a heart illness and all was canceled even though some artists already traveled to The Cove. When the event was rescheduled, unfortunately, Dr. Graham was too frail to attend. Nevertheless before the camera, Bev, Cliff Barrows, Ruth Graham and Franklin Graham shared some unforgettable anecdotes about the long history of their Billy Graham Evangelistic Association ministry. Bill and Gloria Gaither, Michael

W. Smith, CeCe Winans, Andrae Crouch, Avalon, the Goodmans, The Martins, Evie Karlsson, James Blackwood, Larry Ford, Hovie Lister, Wesley Pritchard, Ivan Parker, Joy Gardener, Ricky Skaggs, Avalon and many others led the group in emotional spiritual songs and testimonies of God's faithfulness. It was time for fun and fellowship, too. Bev recounted to comedian Mark Lowery how he still enjoyed boating and was given a new one for vacation times. Mark said that he was knocked out by Bev's youthful enthusiasm.

Better than all the fun, fellowship and banter on the day was the heartfelt worship and testimony of God's goodness. Bev and Cliff were visibly moved as they wiped tears from their eyes. The larger audience at The Cove was made up of old friends and a host of new ones. The loving manner in which they embraced the corporate praise songs and accepted the humble song offerings proffered by each other, demonstrated beyond the slightest shadow of a doubt that there was an invisible tie that binds their hearts in Christian love.

TRADITIONALIST

Like the old hymns, Bev strongly attested to the reality of scripture, grateful for his Christian heritage that he says set him on the right course in life. Asked about old age, longevity and success, he smiled sweetly and gently dismissed self-gratification by quoting scripture.

He agrees that each descendant of Adam's race, whoever he is, is the sum total of his or her own personal environment and very individual influences. That said, it follows that he is, musically speaking, the sum of all the influences of Canadian colonial Methodist hymnology, spirituals, folk and Southern gospel finely blended together. Each musical genre left its special mark on him. What became his unique style must have evolved from those influential trends and sounds that he grew up with and was exposed to throughout the twentieth century.

Bev always believed that it was important to sustain good hymnal traditions, keeping to the straight and narrow. He said, "Things get so complex nowadays that believers often forget that there is a tried and tested way!"

He believed that there was always the need to hear more quality gospel songs that said something of value. When anointed lyrics are hitched to suitable melodies and attractive arrangements, whatever the style, they touch people's hearts. He was concerned that the focus of modern radio was narrowing down to only hot pop sounds. He said, "Christian young people cannot sing the secular pop tunes of the day and have created their own entertainment and praise songs, helping to bring many unbelievers into the fold."

Team Harmony

Deep down in his inner being, Bev always sought for truth in whatever he chose to sing, a discriminating attitude that kept him ultimately always scripturally-based. His positive aim as a musical evangelist was to initiate personal repentance and faith in his listeners leading them into a deeper, satisfying walk with Christ. This one consummate basic message, he musically always shared, without theatrics, with millions across the globe. He was never keen on experimentation, at the expense of bringing people to the deep certainties of faith and reality. He only ever wanted to move out in the depths of divine revelation and encourage others to swim, too. "I never felt like I've reached anywhere near perfection in my own life. I just live each day and pray as the song says, 'Little is much when God is in it. We labor not for wealth or for fame. There's a crown and you can win it when you go in Jesus' name.'"

Bev was a loyal member of the Billy Graham team since 1947 but have all the team members always seen eye to eye? "I believe so, yes. I have yet to have an argument with Mr. Graham, Cliff Barrows, Tedd Smith, John Innes and the others. Of course, we do have some teasing on occasion that helps to put a point across. But it has been remarkable! We always look forward to seeing each other again in every new mission situation. It's been a marvelous relationship. Our wives, too, have known each other and always appreciated each other. I've heard so many people comment on the long standing teamwork that is unique. I know it is God. No crusade meeting is commonplace. It's new and wonderful when people come forward or later when they've gone home to surrender to the Saviour."

INDUSTRY OR MINISTRY?

In 2001, artist John H. Sanden, a Presbyterian layman was nearing the grand completion of his painted portrait of Bev. His subject was posing at the age of ninety-two. In some good-hearted irritated jest, John lightly commented, "Mr. Shea is in wonderful health but something of a fidget!"

Unfortunately, the setting for the Shea portrait by the talented artist was in the living room with the grand piano. It was like a magnet to the old psalm singer. John reported, "While painstakingly painting at my color-splashed easel, Bev would think of a song, bounce up and go to the piano to play and sing!"

John Sanden had no choice but to laughingly conclude that his elderly model was still a great enthusiast: "To say that George Beverly Shea genuinely loves his music is no exaggeration—of that there is no doubt!"

Shy but gregarious in nature, Bev was still a physically strong man in his nineties with a soft heart of deeply-felt sympathies. Friends and acquaintances said that he would listen endlessly to the troubles of others but dismiss his own with a word and a smile. Despite his great sense of humor, he was noted for the earnestness, sincerity and simplicity of his faith and testimony. To him, to compromise would be a serious sin and, therefore, unthinkable. All his life and works were aimed at telling people about Christ.

In 2001, although awaiting eye surgery to remove cataracts, he was grateful that he was in remarkably good heath. "I have had a final going over with all the physical tests on the modern machines and am encouraged with the results. But the family doctor did make the quiet suggestion that I should hold down those all too frequent trips."

Predictably, Bev was genuinely and eternally grateful for the huge influence and inspiration of gospel songs and hymns in his life. Culturally in childhood, they blended into his inner soul and personality. His beloved hobby uniquely mixed Christian values into his life's future outlook and lifestyle. Clearly, Christian songs made an enormous contribution to his emotional development since he first heard them as a young bright-eyed child growing up in Winchester. Ever since the earliest Sunday school songs he heard, he grew to love the grand old gospel songs of the church. As years passed, that love never faded. He and Karlene still cherished relaxation with sweet uplifting and inspiring hymnal sounds. Notwithstanding the ups and downs of life that all are liable to, Bev and his dear wife Karlene are auspicious role models to many. Evidently in all matters of family values, the couple enjoyed a most successful marriage partnership. "I'm so grateful for Karlene, my dear spouse and also for my late wife, Erma, who went to be with the Lord many years ago. I'm thankful, too for my children and grandchildren."

Early sincere Christian commitment meant that Bev seldom battled with commercialism. Mercenary attitudes sometimes haunt professional gospel singers. Most continuously struggle to successfully retain a delicate, sensitive balance between commercial interests and ministry. From the early days, Bev fortuitously chose to always bend towards ministry rather than commercial interests thus remaining—as he saw it—true to the Master's Great Commission.

Saved by Grace

In all the many years of his life and ministry, Bev never gave ammunition to the trouble-making, narrow-minded religionists keen to magnify human imperfections, question motives, and generally seek to find fault. He surprisingly seldom upset such people from that camp. He chose not to fly high in career terms. Rather he served quietly, conservatively and humbly. He concluded that he does not pretend to be perfect, "I'm a sinner saved by grace."

Only the Divine Master Himself is without flaw. No matter how devout, committed, or genuine any human servants may be, all fall hugely short when it comes to the test of ultimate perfection. Perfection is only to be found in Christ! "I look back at my life and wonder why I have been given the privilege to be with Mr. Graham and his team. At the beginning and all through these years, I have felt so inadequate. Perhaps it is okay to feel that way. There are people who can sing so much better than I. God is gracious in giving me this privilege to sing a quiet gospel song before a man of such stature lifts up the Lord Jesus to great crowds and in such a precious and faithful way."

Interestingly, Bev never praised God for success in his singing career because success was not something he contemplated or aspired to. But he did praise God for the enormous longevity of his serving career. It has been much longer than a showbiz career could anticipate and it afforded him, he said, the privilege of service. "The recording ministry has been a marvelous experience, too for me. I have never had an agent, even though they say one is supposed to. Some of the personnel of RCA, Word and EMI have often asked how it was possible to do so many albums. I always say, It has always been a privilege to lift up the Lord Jesus in songs this way!"

Factors that normally contribute to the demise of a normal showbiz career are many and varied. The biggest factor of all is the fickleness of public taste and demand. Winds of change blow constantly through all departments of life especially fashion, culture, art and, not least, musical taste. Experience tells Bev that attitudes, fashions, fads and taste in art will always inevitably change with the passage of time. He should know, having lived through so many changing scenes of life. Commonly, no matter how innovative one's professionalism may be in the music industry, it will never ultimately survive the ravages of circumstance and time whether your name be Crosby, Sinatra or Presley. However, as Bev strongly points out, he has never considered that his career was ever in the music industry but rather in the 'music ministry'! Between the two is a vast gulf. Earthly success comes and goes with every season but the solid, underlying Christian message of God's truth endures forever. That's where his treasure was always to be truly found. As the Apostle Peter told the early church in Jerusalem, 'For all flesh is as grass, and all the glory of man as the flower of grass. The grass withereth, and the flower thereof falleth away: But the word of the Lord endureth for ever. And this is the word which by the gospel is preached unto you!' (1 Peter 1:24-25).

NEWCOMERS

The twenty-first century's new church generation is constantly looking for fresh, innovative musical performers to join the ranks of the great Christian music artists of the past. Since Bev first moved into the music ministry, thousands of Christian radio and television stations seeded themselves around the globe. He is delighted to have witnessed their growth, believing many Christian stations present the gospel with distinction and discernment. Although he deeply loves his conservatively-held traditional heritage, he also recognizes that the Christian music ministry is like a choir or orchestra that continually needs sprightly new recruits to fill its ranks! Unless a stream receives quickening supplies, its waters soon turn stagnant. As we entered a new millennium in gospel music, styles and methods have changed, of that Bev has no doubt. The church has seen a media revolution in Christian music via the stage, records, radio, television and videos. Today's Christian music inheritance is a bountifully diverse tapestry of art, color and sound that encircle past, present and future generations. All styles can be relevant, authentic and bona fide in their own way. Speaking of himself, he is certainly a traditionalist who grew up in conservatism but happily embraces some contemporary tempos, remaining at peace with God about it.

An unlikely partner for Bev was the successful twenty-first century Christian rocker Michael Tait of dc Talk. Together, they documented what must be the most unusual duet version ever of Bill and Gloria Gaither's "Because He Lives." Bev's summing up commentary about the duet was that although music can oft times separate generations, it can also bring them together!

Does Bev have to sing contemporary Christian or rock gospel music to be legitimate in the Christian music of today? He does not think so! Today's gospel music shows up in manifold manifestations. Quality sacred songs survive, still transferred down from one generation to another. In latter life, he recognized that because of the mass media, gospel music secured a very prominent position in the world's musical arena. Many professional artists from various traditions adopt inspirational music into their personal musical repertoire. In the past, Christian music remained homegrown or church-grown. In his lifetime, the commercially acceptable form of the music evolved and today captures the devotion of millions in all walks of life. Inevitably, the forced fusion of entertainment and evangelism and ministry and business causes ongoing debate, tension, and occasional controversy.

GOD'S LOVE AND FORGIVENESS

In mid October 2001, the four-day Central Valley Billy Graham Crusade in Fresno, California ended. It was held in one of the most culturally diverse and agriculturally plentiful regions of the

US. The evangelistic meetings reaped a record spiritual harvest amidst the questioning and searching experienced by individuals throughout the country in the wake of the September 11th terrorist attacks in New York City, Washington DC and Pennsylvania. Held at the Bulldog Stadium, everyone was delighted to see crowds averaging more than 46,000 in the 42,000-seat stadium each night. Furthermore, an average of more than 3,310 came forward to make commitments to Christ. The Saturday evening crowd of 62,000 shattered the stadium attendance record.

Billy addressed the hushed audience and his team with fire, wisdom and authority. Bev listened to his insightful words and pondered them carefully. "We are living in a different world. The changes after the September 11th terrorist attacks will be felt in every area of our society for years to come. We are in troubled and difficult times. We're going to have to rethink our lives. But in the midst of all that, there is one hope, that Jesus Christ said that He is coming again! Without hope, our nation will not go on! Something about what happened on September 11th caused people to think about spiritual things for maybe the first time in years. The greatest need in the world is the transformation of human nature. A radical change is needed by everyone to find complete fulfillment in this life and to be acceptable to God in the future life!"

Despite breaking his foot in three places two days before the crusade in Fresno began, Billy preached while standing, focusing on every man's need to experience God's love and forgiveness in the modern world. The message had never changed. It was the same one preached by Bev's dear old father in Canada, considered that this tired, beaten old world was no longer the simple place it was when Bev was born or when he first started to sing his heartwarming gospel songs. Indeed, as he truthfully attested, everywhere he looked, things are not what they used to be. Indeed, they never were to be the same again. But mankind still had its hope in Christ! He foresaw in future generations millions more ordinary people, whether they regularly attended church or not, still turning to Christ around the world. Millions more still enjoyed singing or listening to the message of the gospel in music. Just as his ancestors sang, his generation of believers, he said, still liked to find genuine inspiration and peaceful consolation in the music of the gospel! Christians still enjoyed sentimental music that tugged at the heart, moistened the eyes, set feet tapping, and voices humming in praise!

SERVANTHOOD

Bev has sung to more people than anyone else in history, according to the Guinness Book of World Records. Yet, he remains so humble! His whole attitude and persona spoke of servanthood. He was a true disciple of the Christ that he served, an example to us all! Indeed, the same could be said of the Billy Graham team as a whole.

September 11, 2001 was a decisive date in history for all Americans and others in the free world as they witnessed live on TV the suicide attacks on the Twin Towers in New York and the Pentagon in Washington.

A few days later, on September 14, a still stunned Bev was booked to sing for Reverend Ralph Bell in meetings in Conover, North Carolina. Due to flight disruptions, Ralph could not catch his plane and Congressman Robin Hayes agreed to be his preaching replacement. Fifteen hundred were in attendance. Bev's song that evening "Is There No Comfort For Sorrow?" met the mood of the moment as it affirmed the promise of the Second Advent.

Renowned Anglican minister of All Souls Church in West London, Richard Bewes recalled his meeting with Bev in the American capital just weeks after the terrorist attacks. Indeed, it was just before Christmas 2001 and the war was raging in Afghanistan. Meanwhile in Washington DC, there was an especially auspicious event taking place. It was the conferring of an honorary Knighthood on Billy, by the British Ambassador, Sir Christopher Meyer on behalf of the Queen Elizabeth II. "It was a black tie dinner occasion, and Bev and his wife Karlene were both there. The next morning I had breakfast with Cliff Barrows. As I left the Marriott Hotel breakfast room, I encountered Bev and Karlene coming in. 'Come and have breakfast with us, Richard!' they invited. It was an invitation I couldn't resist so I sat down for a second breakfast with the Sheas, and we spent the next hour and a half reminiscing about the wonderful years we had witnessed. I mentioned Billy's comment that he had sung to more people face-to-face in the whole of history. 'Well, that was only because of being with Billy!' he smiled. We also touched on the many songs that he had sung. I told him, 'Bev, that song of yours—'I'd Rather Have Jesus'—I've often sung it to people on their hospital beds, sometimes when they're dying; it's been such a blessing.' I think he was rather touched."

Billy's witty but sincere and humble response to the ambassador's speech tickled Bev's funny bone that day. Speaking of the team's many UK experiences since 1946, Billy broached the subject of accents. "We often had difficulty with accents especially when we were in Scotland or Yorkshire. George Beverly Shea was in

London for our meetings in 1954, and he was singing—'It took a miracle to put the stars in space.' But one person, a member of the press, misheard the word and wrote that it seemed awfully arrogant that an American would say, 'It took America to put the stars in space!'"

GOD-HONORING TESTIMONY

Relatively speaking, the audio recorded works of all mankind's music belong to recent history—mostly from the last century. Although much of what is produced may commendably serve its own fickle generation, the majority may not deserve to stand the test of time.

As we start the third millennium, many feel that Bev's musical expressions of faith will durably remain more ongoing, tangible reminders of God-honoring testimonies. His recordings will continue to inspire those who follow in subsequent generations, yet unborn. These descendants will still continue to find genuine inspiration and peaceful consolation in his gospel music of the twentieth century! Despite the flagrantly permissive attitudes and actions of society around us, Christian communities will remain musically still generally, down to earth, unpretentious, conservative and happy to wear religion on the sleeve. Surely all agree with the great founder of the Salvation Army General William Booth when he said, "Music is for the soul what wind is for the ship, blowing her onwards in the direction in which she is steered!"

Many testify how they loved to hear Bev sing because they felt spiritually uplifted. In later life, tributes to Bev became plentiful. In Europe, Word Records' souvenir tribute CD album entitled *George Beverly Shea: Golden Jubilee* was brimful of celebrated commendations to him from a multitude of celebrities including Billy Graham, Cliff Barrows, Sir Cliff Richard, Pat Boone, Bill Gaither, George Hamilton IV, Sheila Walsh, Wes Davis, Wanda Jackson, Kurt Kaiser, Arthur Smith, Bud Tutmarc, Paul Wheater and many others. The album also uniquely featured Bev in duet with Amy Grant, Bill Gaither Trio, Cliff Barrows, Evie, Sandi Patty, and many others. The twenty-two favorite songs ranged from the pens of Graham Kendrick to Bill Gaither to Bev Shea himself plus others.

Bev remained in the saddle, a perpetual enthusiast for evangelism even in the sunset of his years. Throughout his century, his rich baritone voice epitomized the sermon in song. Indeed, as Bill Gaither said, the legendary George Beverly Shea was "the epitome of what a gospel singer should be!" Like a powerful preacher, Bev faithfully ministered the gospel of the Kingdom. His communication of the gospel via music succeeded in melting cold hearts to repentance and faith, even when sermons initially failed. When discussing the Johnny Cash song about Christ's Second Coming entitled "When He Comes!" Billy Graham said, "preaching will no longer be needed in heaven but music and singing will be enjoyed in heaven throughout eternity!"

When Bev does arrive on that heavenly strand, it will be interesting to see how many of that vast gathering will thankfully praise God for his steadfast musical witness, grateful to him for his integrity, consistency, godly example and brotherly love. When asked what he would want to be remembered for, he predictably avoided self praise with a light-hearted but deep reply. "I want to be remembered for staying on key and when I ever go off key—tell me, Paul 'cause I'll quit then!"

How Music has Changed Over the Years

When asked how crusade music had changed over the years, Bev said, "The crusades have had more and more of the youth expression in music but Mr. Graham loves the old gospel songs and so we've kept those. I've never attempted to do contemporary because I wouldn't do it well."

The broad appeal of George Beverly Shea's music is not puzzling or complex to understand. He sings in the universal language of inspiration. Simply, he sings with spiritual ardor and heartfelt lucidity. He prays as much about his part in the meeting as does the preacher about his sermon. His career of ministry has included countless crusades, international radio and television dates, and about 70 albums. Every performance, he said was "a testimony to God's love and the saving power of Jesus Christ" and are statements attesting to his ongoing faith in Him.

As part of the documentary record of this biography, Bev was most earnest about credit being given to his lifelong musical partner, Cliff Barrows. Cliff was always his wise, soft-spoken confidant exuding a cheerful refreshing charm. Yet he was also characteristically serious when required. Like Shea, a veteran of musical evangelism, Cliff is one of Christian music's most respected dignitaries mirroring his productive legacy. Wise in perceptiveness, he discerningly exercised his leadership role in the BGEA as a sacred trust.

When choosing songs in the crusade ministry, like Bev, Cliff looked for arrows that were sharp and specifically designed to address spiritual issues within the human heart. His motive was to find their target so that—by God's enabling—each message accomplished its intended purpose.

Multitudes of Bev's admirers, including hundreds of Christian singers and musicians that he has inspired to follow their calling, would echo the words of the Apostle Paul. "I thank my God upon every remembrance of you for your fellowship in the gospel from the first day until now! Being confident of this very thing, that He which hath begun a good work in you will perform it until the day of Jesus Christ!"

Singer, Paul Wheater, founder and organizer of the Whitby Gospel Music Festival in Yorkshire, England, speaks highly of the lasting value of Bev's audio legacy listed in this impressive discography that follows. "George Beverly Shea has given a lifetime of service singing for the Lord. Millions have heard him perform live with the Billy Graham team and even greater numbers have been touched by his voice on radio and through the recordings that he has made down through the years. Songs that he has brought to the attention of other singers are not only his own compositions like 'I'd Rather Have Jesus' but also some of the beautiful old gospel songs that would otherwise be almost forgotten. My favorite is 'Lead Me Gently Home, Father' because I'm sure that the voice of George Beverly Shea has already led and will continue to lead large numbers of pilgrims—including me—on their way home to glory!"

Pass the Baton

On Saturday, May 29, 2004, thousands of Christians from all of the UK attended a reunion meeting entitled *Passing The Baton* at London's Royal Albert Hall. The meeting nostalgically paid tribute to the fifty years of Graham ministry in the UK. The plan of the evening was to feature Noel Tredinnick and the All

Souls Orchestra plus guests invited from the US introduced by British evangelist, Steve Chalke.

Billy Graham was unable to travel but invited were Franklin Graham, Cliff Barrows and Bev Shea. Unfortunately, a few days before the event, just after his rendezvous for the Atlantic flight with Cliff in North Carolina, 95-year-old Bev suffered a mild heart attack and was hospitalized for several days thus disappointedly missing the Royal Albert Hall event. Coincidently, Bev spent seven days in the same hospital where Billy Graham was being treated for a fractured pelvis and they wrote encouraging notes to each other.

Bev was advised for the time being by the doctors that he should sit on his back porch rocking chair rather than rushing around appearing on crusade platforms. The physician's grounding marked the first time since 1947. "It's the doctor's decision," Bev said, "but I asked Mr. Graham if he takes the doctor's advice? He said, 'Yes, I do.'"

Thus Bev impatiently, but obediently, awaited the forthcoming consultations with his doctor saying, "I had some ticker trouble and the heart people say it takes a good six months for a football player to get over something like that so I'm hopeful about participating in the crusades in Los Angeles and New York. I trust I can!"

Just before the Christmas holidays of 2004, Maurice Rowlandson, the faithful, long serving head of the Billy Graham UK office told me that that "Bev Shea has been continually improving since the time of his heart incident last May. In fact, he was well enough to go to the Billy Graham Crusade in Los Angeles in November, and actually sang a song from the platform—although, from a seated position! At his age it is quite remarkable. I suppose so long as Mr. Graham keeps going, Bev has little choice but to do the same. What a pity we all get older!!!!"

Los Angeles

More than 1,400 churches made preparation for the Greater Los Angeles Crusade and 45,000 filled the Rose Bowl in Pasadena on Thursday, November 18 for the initial night that marked the 55th anniversary of historic Billy Graham Big Tent Meetings in Los Angeles in 1949. Over 1,700 responded to the message of God's love. On the next evening, another crisp winter night, 77, 500 were in attendance. Among those in the stadium to hear Mr. Graham speak were members of the entertainment industry including Jim Caviezel, star of Mel Gibson's film *The Passion of the Christ*. He sat on the platform, with his wife, Kerri near Bev.

The Graham team and the spectators were delighted at Bev's return to the crusade platform. Bev was particularly delighted as he was unable to attend the previous month's Heart of America Crusade in Kansas City, the first domestic crusade he had missed in more than 60 years of evangelistic ministry with Billy Graham.

During the Pasadena meetings, Bev appeared on the platform one night to sing from his chair. He said, "That night, I was between Cliff and Billy. There were 77,000 people there as I sang a verse of 'The Love of God.' Rick Warren was close by and gave me a pat on the back as did Dr. Lloyd John Ogilvie and Pat Boone."

On Saturday, November 20th, 2004 the third day of the Greater Los Angeles Billy Graham Crusade began with a special KidzNet program, featuring Jump 5, rapper Lil iROCC, Wheels of Freestyle, Bibleman, and a 4,000 voice children's choir. Overall attendance for Saturday morning was 18,000—and 1,419 boys and girls committed their lives to Jesus Christ. Bev was delighted with the news and could not help but recount to himself how although the message was unchanged the packaging was ever changing to engage each new generation.

In the afternoon, Feasts of Faith took place in disadvantaged communities around Los Angeles, as part of the *Love in Action* activities. Participants were offered bus transportation to and from the Rose Bowl in order to attend the World's Largest Tailgate Party and the evening's Crusade program. Held on the Jackie Robinson Memorial Field, just outside the Rose Bowl, the party served fresh-cooked hamburgers to more than 6,000 underprivileged and homeless persons. The recipients were then honored by a Rose Bowl VIP ticket for that evening. Musical groups Kutless, The Tait Band, and Third Day warmed up the crowd at the evening's *Concert for Our Generation*, and many teens in front of the platform jumped and swayed to the music. With silver locks blowing in the air, Billy Graham then spoke on the rich young man of Mark's Gospel to the 90,000 in attendance. More than 3,800—most between the ages of 10 and 18—prayed to commit their lives to Jesus Christ.

New Year

To herald the new year of 2005, I received a warm handwritten letter of warm greetings from Bev from his home in the Blue Ridge town of Montreat. It said, "Our friendship carries on! It never ceased! With the years adding up here, I'm about 96 years of age, coming up soon. I'm finding that keeping in touch is more than can be handled."

Despite understandably feeling the strain of the fast advancing years, Bev nevertheless continued to anticipate the future of another year. Notably, he then added the prayerfully poetic lyrics of Frances Ridley Havergal. Her poem was initially penned in 1874 for a new year's card.

Another year is dawning, dear Father, let it be
In working or in waiting, another year with Thee.
Another year of progress, another year of praise,
Another year of proving Thy presence all the days.

Another year of mercies, of faithfulness and grace,
Another year of gladness in the shining of Thy face;
Another year of leaning upon Thy loving breast;
Another year of trusting, of quiet, happy rest.

Another year of service, of witness for Thy love,
Another year of training for holier work above.
Another year is dawning, dear Father, let it be
On earth, or else in heaven, another year for Thee.
—Frances Ridley Havergal (1836-1879)

By then, Billy was suffering from fluid on the brain, prostate cancer and Parkinson's disease. He was using a walker due to the pelvic fracture and was largely confined to his home in Montreat, North Carolina.

THE LAST CRUSADE

Shortly after 9/11, many of New York's Christian leaders invited Billy Graham to respond to the spiritual hunger that remained after that tragic day. June 24-26, 2005 was chosen for the Greater New York Billy Graham Crusade. New York was special to Billy and his team for many reasons, most dramatically, because of how God moved during the 1957 Billy Graham Crusade when a six-week crusade turned into sixteen weeks.

Thus for many months of 2004-2005, New York pastors were busy preparing for a new spiritual awakening in Madison Square Garden. During the May 5th National Day of Prayer, 25 concerts of prayer took place throughout Greater New York. Just prior to the crusade, Billy Graham appeared on the Larry King's CNN show talking about his last crusade in New York City. A newspaper reporter wrote how he had seen several presidents, many senators, a few titans of industry and a whole bunch of athletes from a close proximity and was impressed. "But then their luster faded into a vapor that disappeared. Not so, with Billy Graham."

For many older New Yorkers, the voices of Billy and Bev were burned into memory. Many loved Bev's singing, purchasing his songs from iTunes and played them on computers. The message was still clear, simple and strong and pure gospel.

Bev Shea's son, Ronald worked in the preparations for the New York Crusade and one of his interesting assignments was to have some of the 9/11 firemen and policemen give their Christian testimonies. Before the crusade, Bev reminisced, "When I was in my twenties, I worked in the medical department of the Mutual Life in New York down near Wall Street and to have my son there now is quite a thrill. He is having a taste of New York."

The Graham team looked out at the more than 60,000 who gathered Friday night at Flushing Meadows Corona Park. The service was simultaneously translated into 20 languages. President Clinton praised Billy's fidelity over an epochal career as the preacher was greeted with an enthusiasm that could only be called rapturous.

As well as the sermons, the weekend included costume drama for kids, Christian rock music for young adults, gospel tunes sung by Bev and hymns from the 285-voice Brooklyn Tabernacle Choir. Saturday evening's concert featured Christian rockers Tree 63 and Jars of Clay, as well as hip hop dancers under Nicole C. Mullen. Many were pleased to see the heavy emphasis on finding ways to communicate with youth and were almost moved to tears as each meeting came to the final moment of dedication to Christ.

On most people's minds was the question that was often posed to the preacher. Was this the final Graham mission? But Billy seemed to toy with the press over the question, saying he hoped "to come back again someday." Previously, he told journalists who asked if this was the last Graham crusade, "never say never." Others knew better.

Bev knew that Billy was considering requests to attend the Royal Albert Hall rally in November in London, but thought that chances were slim that he would accept. Eventually, Billy's son, the Rev. Franklin Graham, stated that his father did not like to be away from his wife, Ruth, who was also in serious ill health. Revival draws a diverse crowd, and Billy, of course, drew a large post 9/11 throng in New York. Many didn't want to believe it was the end and came to see him preach one last time. It was an historic moment.

The stage—shaded by a massive canopy—had a pulpit with a movable seat hidden from view, so Billy could sit down if he felt unsteady. The total turnout for the three New York meetings was 230,000, and BGEA staff estimated 5,582 registered Christian commitments on the first two nights.

The program was hosted by Cliff Barrows, now 82-years-old, and mixed contemporary Christian bands with a nostalgic "How

Great Thou Art" sung by Bev, now 96. The duo were given a round of applause at Billy's request remarking how grateful he was that "they put up with me for the sixty years we've been together."

In the crowd, English preacher Richard Bewes remarked that he was emotionally moved to see his white-haired, grey-suited friend Bev receive his well deserved standing ovation at Corona Park. Richard declared, "After sixty years of singing for Billy, as his song says 'The Wonder Of It All' is that Bev is still moved by the sacredness of the moment." Like Billy, Bev had witnessed to more than 220 million people in about 185 countries. When asked about his achievements, Bev shyly replied, "That is simply explained as Billy's congregations worldwide, but those people didn't come to hear me; they came to hear Billy."

A Celebration Marking a Century

On February 1, 2009, George Beverly Shea marked one century of life. More than 250 of his closest friends and family members came to The Cove in Asheville, North Carolina to celebrate his 100th birthday. Each face in the crowd represented memories, milestones and moments in Shea's life: among them Ricky Skaggs, Bill and Gloria Gaither, Arthur Smith and of course, Rev. Billy Graham who was seated by his side.

Among the night's highlights was the presentation of North Carolina's highest honor, the Order of the Long Leaf Pine, awarded to Bev by his old friend and Evangelistic Association board member Graeme Keith.

Even though it was Bev's birthday party, the friends and family members that had gathered were given a gift themselves—when the 100-year-old recited one of his favorite hymns, "The Shadow of a Cross," a song he's been singing for many years, on many stages, in many continents.

Tired of a life without meaning,

Always in a crowd yet alone.

Not knowing what I was needing,

I walked down a long dusty road.

As the sunshine beamed brightly I saw not.

Not a cloud, nor a tree where I walked;

Yet I looked and I saw there before me the shadow of a cross.

"It is I!" said a voice – It was Jesus,

And a hand was outstretched to me;

And my soul came alive in the shadow of the cross of Calvary.
—Arthur Smith

Bev, too, received a gift that night, a Rodgers organ adorned with a large red bow. The gift is his for as long as he lives, Franklin Graham explained. Then it will be donated to the Angola State Penitentiary where it will be used in the chapel there. According to the BGEA, they donated funds to build the chapel following a Franklin Graham Prison Festival at Angola in 2006. The chapel was dedicated in April 2008.

"Men who have blood on their hands, but who have been redeemed by the blood of the Lamb will get to play this," Franklin said.

Friends helped Bev across the room so he could get a closer look at the newest addition to his collection of organs. Anxious to try out his generous gift, Bev began to play, but stopped after just a moment. "I'll have to practice on it a little," Bev joked to the audience.

Many friends stepped up to the microphone that night to wish Bev a happy birthday and to thank him for his years of ministry. Franklin Graham spoke simply and powerfully of Bev's contribution. Franklin said, "All these years, daddy always said that a crusade really began when Uncle Bev walked up to the mic and began to sing."

Too weak to hold the microphone on his own, a frail and ailing Billy Graham shared very few words, but still managed to communicate eloquently his gratitude and compassion for Bev. Leaning forward he spoke slowly, "I couldn't have had a ministry without him. Thank you and God be with you. I love you."

As the birthday celebration came to an end, Bev remained humbled by the event. "I was overwhelmed that so many people were here tonight," he said. "And I never dreamed I would get a gift like this." But it's the world that's been given a gift, in the music, the ministry and the man of George Beverly Shea. It's a gift many will treasure through the recordings he's produced, the songs he's written and the example he's provided of a life well-lived with Christ.

'Make a joyful noise unto the LORD, all ye lands. Serve the LORD with gladness: come before his presence with singing. Know ye that the LORD he is God: it is he that hath made us, and not we ourselves; we are his people, and the sheep of his pasture. Enter into his gates with thanksgiving, and into his courts with praise: be thankful unto him, and bless his name. For the LORD is good; his mercy is everlasting; and his truth endureth to all generations!'

(Psalm 100)

Discography

"It would be impossible to count the number of times that George Beverly Shea has sung 'I'd Rather Have Jesus.' But the line in the song that speaks to my heart says, 'I'd rather have Jesus than men's applause.' As an entertainer who has found my salvation in the Lord Jesus Christ, these words in the song express exactly how I feel. How can the world and its acclaim adequately be compared to the untold riches in Christ? I'm so grateful to Bev for sharing and co-writing this classic sacred song. It seems to have been written for people like me. His song has become my heartfelt testimony!"
—Wanda Jackson, Oklahoma City, Oklahoma

RECORDS

1953
SINGING I GO
REDEMPTION RLP-102

1953
JESUS WHISPERS PEACE
REDEMPTION RLP.112

1953
EVENING VESPERS
HMV DLP1119

1953
INSPIRATIONAL SONGS
RCA VICTOR LSP-1187

1954
SACRED SONGS OF GEORGE BEVERLY SHEA
RCA VICTOR LPM 1235

1954
BEAUTIFUL GARDEN OF PRAYER
HMV DLP1075 / RCA VICTOR LPM 3078

1957
AN EVENING PRAYER
RCA LPM 1349

1957
A BILLY GRAHAM CRUSADE IN SONG
RCA VICTOR LPM 1406 / RCA
RS-50005

1958
GEORGE BEVERLY SHEA
RCA LPM 1564

1958
THROUGH THE YEARS
RCA VICTOR LPM 1642

1959
THE LOVE OF GOD
RCA VICTOR LPM 1949

1959
BLESSED ASSURANCE
RCA VICTOR LPM 1967 / RCA RS-50005

1959
CHRISTMAS HYMNS
RCA VICTOR 2064

1960
GEORGE BEVERLY SHEA
RCA CAMDEN CAS 568 (RCRS-5069)

1960
THE HOLY LAND
RCA VICTOR LPM 2189

1961
CROSSROADS OF LIFE
RCA VICTOR LPM 2252

1961
TENDERLY HE WATCHES
RCA CAMDEN CAL-653

1961
HYMNS THAT HAVE LIVED 100 YEARS
RCA VICTOR LPM 2348 / RS50009

1962
IN TIMES LIKE THESE
RCA VICTOR LPM 2503

1962
A MAN NAMED MOSES
RCA VICTOR LPM 2586

1962
THE LORD IS MY SHEPHERD
RCA CAMDEN CAL/CAS-718

1963
GEORGE BEVERLY SHEA'S
FAVORITE SONGS AND SPIRITUALS
RCA VICTOR LPM 2651/RS-50012

1963
THE EARTH IS THE LORD'S
RCA VICTOR LPM 2753 / RCA RS-500013

1964
HYMNS OF SUNRISE AND SUNSET
RCA VICTOR LSP 2839 / RS-50016

1964
THE BEST OF GEORGE BEVERLY
SHEA
RCA VICTOR LSP-2932

1964
HARK! THE HERALD ANGELS
RCA VICTOR LSP 2937

1965
GEORGE BEVERLY SHEA SINGS
BILLY GRAHAM'S FAVOURITES
RCA VICTOR LPM 3346 / RCA NL 89265

1966
SOUTHLAND FAVOURITES
RCA VICTOR LPM 3440 / RS 50018

1966
SINGS FIRESIDE HYMNS
RCA VICTOR LPM 3522 / RCA RS-50021

1966
SOUTHLAND SONGS THAT LIFT
THE HEART
RCA LPM 3634

1967
SINGING I GO
PILGRIM KLP 18

1967
TAKE MY HAND
RCA VICTOR LSP 3760

1967
SURELY GOODNESS AND MERCY
(With the Blackwood Brothers Quartet)
RCA VICTOR LPM 3864

1967
THE BEST OF GOERGE BEVERLY
SHEA VOL.2
RCA VICTOR LSP-3904

1968
BE STILL MY SOUL
RCA VICTOR LSP 3945

1968
WHISPERING HOPE
RCA VICTOR LSP 4042

1969
HOW GREAT THOU ART
RCA VICTOR LSP 4120

1969
I BELIEVE
RCA VICTOR LSP 4208

1970
THESE ARE THE THINGS THAT
MATTER
RCA VICTOR LSP-4308

1970
THERE IS MORE TO LIFE
RCA VICTOR LSP-4402

1971
AMAZING GRACE
RCA VICTOR LSP-4512

1971
I'D RATHER HAVE JESUS
RCA VICTOR LSP-4597

1972
EVERY TIME I FEEL THE SPIRIT
RCA VICTOR LSP-4687

1972
SILENT NIGHT
RCA CAMDEN CXS 9026

1972
THE KING IS COMING
RCA VICTOR LSP-4782

1973
HALLELUJAH
RCA VICTOR APL1-0160-A

1973
TEN FAVORITES FROM GEORGE
BEVERLY SHEA
RCA VICTOR APL1-0358

1974
CLOSE TO THEE
RCA VICTOR APL1-0471

1975
THE LONGER I SERVE HIM
WORD WST 8671

1975
EVENING PRAYER
RCA CAMDEN CAS-2349

1976
ANGELS SHALL KEEP THEE
WORD WST 9564

1976
SINGS 20 BEST LOVED HYMNS
SHARON SRN 310

1978
THE OLD RUGGED CROSS
WORD WST 9589

1980
EARLY IN THE MORNING
WORD WST 9594

1983
I'D RATHER HAVE JESUS
PILGRIM PLM 518

1984
MY FAVORITE SONGS
WORD WRD 3007

1986
GEORGE BEVERLY SHEA AND
FRIENDS
WORD WSTR 9679

CD'S

1993
PRECIOUS MEMORIES
READER'S DIGEST RCD 116/CD1

1994
SONGS FROM MY HEART
RCA/BMG DIRECT DMC2-1167

1996
OUR RE COLLECTIONS
WORD 70113530360

1995
CLIFF BARROWS AND GEORGE
BEVERLY SHEA - THE CHRISTMAS
EVANGEL
WORD TIME DO10

1995
FULLY PERSUADED
WORD TIME002

1996
MOMENTS VOLUME 1
STAR SONG 7243 82010128

1997
GOD OUR HELP IN AGES PAST
VICTORY VOICES AND
ORCHESTRA (GUEST
SOLOIST:GEORGE BEVERLY SHEA)
WORD PWCD010

1997
*CLIFF BARROWS AND GEORGE
BEVERLY SHEA - GREEN
COUNTRY PASTURES*
WORD TIME DO24

1997
ECHOES OF MY SOUL
STAR SONG CGD 0700

1997
*ARTHUR SMITH & GEORGE
BEVERLY SHEA OUT IN THE
COUNTRY*
HOMELAND HD9712

1998
THE BLESSED LIGHTS OF HOME
WORD TIME19

1998
*GEORGE BEVERLY SHEA &
FRIENDS GOLDEN JUBILEE*
WORD TRIBD001

1999
IF THAT ISN'T LOVE
EMI STRAIGHTWAY SWD 0216

2004
HOW SWEET THE NAME
J & B MEDIA 50141 82135523

BOOKS

1968
THEN SINGS MY SOUL
An autobiography (with Fred Bauer).
Fleming Revell Company

1972
*SONGS THAT LIFT THE HEART
(WITH FRED BAUER),*
Bev tells about his favorite songs.
Fleming Revell Company.

2004
HOW SWEET THE SOUND
Stories and reflections on beloved
hymns and gospel songs

FILMS/VIDEOS

THEN SINGS MY SOUL'
Film Musical/Documentary hosted by
Ralph Carmichael and Joan Winmill
Brown. World Wide Pictures

THE WONDER OF IT ALL
TV show production of his life story.
Hosted by George Hamilton IV, Bev
was supported on the show by Cliff
Barrows, Paul Overstreet, Radney
Foster, the Moody Brothers and others.
North Carolina Public Television.

ONE NATION UNDER GOD
A musical short on the theme of 'God
and Country', World Wide Pictures.

TO GOD BE THE GLORY
A musical short on the theme of the
Gospel, World Wide Pictures.

WHERE JESUS WALKED
A musical short on the theme of the
Holy Land, World Wide Pictures.

SONG MUSIC FOLIOS

1955
GEORGE BEVERLY SHEA'S ALBUM
OF SACRED SONGS
Lillenas Publishing, Kansas City, Missouri

1957
GEORGE BEVERLY SHEA SINGS
HIS FAVORITES
Rodeheaver, Hall-Mack Company,
Winona Lake, Indiana

1962
GEORGE BEVERLY SHEA'S
HYMNAL TREASURES
Hope Publishing, Chicago, Illinois

1963
THE CRUSADE SOLOIST
Lillenas Publishing, Kansas City, Missouri

Photography Section

The welcome sign for Bev's birthplace. Winchester held a dedication ceremony for him in 2002.

A Christmas gathering around the piano with friends Cliff and Billie Barrows, Clayton Bell, Billy and Ruth Graham, George Beverly Shea and Tedd Smith at the piano.

Christmas time in North Carolina with Johnny Cash, June Carter Cash and friends.

Bev singing "Rock of Ages" with Cliff Barrows and George Hamilton IV in 1984. This rock near Cheddar Gorge in England inspired Augustus Toplady to write the famous hymn.

Bev and longtime ministry partner Cliff Barrows
singing a duet in 1988.

Bev joins with singer-songwriter Michael W. Smith for a
Christmas performance in 1990.

The Shea family—Bev, wife Karlene and Bev's son Ron at the
New York Crusade in 2005.

Bev, Cliff Barrows and Billy Graham bowing their heads in
prayer at a 2005 press conference at Rockefeller Center during
the New York Crusade.

Bev and his wife Karlene surrounded by members of the
Tommy Coomes Band.

Singing "This Little Light of Mine" with Billy Graham's
grandson Will and Cliff Barrows.

On stage at the Franklin Graham Festival in Mobile, Alabama
in 2006. Bev is singing with the Tommy Coomes Band while
Ted Cornell plays the piano.

Bev singing while John Innes is at the piano on stage in
Calgary, British Columbia.

Cliff and Bev singing a duet at the Billy Graham Library
dedication in 2007 in Charlotte, North Carolina. Enjoying the
performance are Rev. Graham and three former US Presidents:
George HW Bush, Jimmy Carter and Bill Clinton.

Bev and Karlene relaxing on the porch of their
North Carolina home.

Bev at his home in North Carolina.